CELTIC UNITED

CELTIC UNITED

GLASGOW and MANCHESTER
Two Football Clubs, One Passion

Frank Worrall

MAINSTREAM
PUBLISHING

EDINBURGH AND LONDON

This book is dedicated to Angela . . .
and Frankie and Jude, my boy wonders.

Copyright © Frank Worrall, 2007
All rights reserved
The moral right of the author has been asserted

First published in Great Britain in 2007 by
MAINSTREAM PUBLISHING COMPANY
(EDINBURGH) LTD
7 Albany Street
Edinburgh EH1 3UG

ISBN 9781845962760

A catalogue record for this book is available
from the British Library

Typeset in Caslon and Headline

Printed in Great Britain by
William Clowes Ltd, Beccles, Suffolk

ACKNOWLEDGEMENTS

MY SINCERE thanks to: Rod Stewart; Jim Divers of the Celtic Supporters Association; the Independent Manchester United Supporters Association (IMUSA); both Manchester United FC and Celtic FC; Gordon Strachan, Sir Alex Ferguson, Martin O'Neill, Neil Lennon, Roy Keane, Henrik Larsson, Lou Macari, Paddy Crerand, Brian McClair, Sir Bobby Charlton, Sir Bobby Robson, Denis Law, Tommy Docherty, Wayne Rooney and Cristiano Ronaldo; the Jungle Bhoys and the K Stand Boys; Bill and Sharon Campbell, Graeme Blaikie, Ailsa Bathgate, Paul Murphy and all at Mainstream; Declan Heeney; Lee Clayton, sports editor at the *Daily Mail*; Alex Butler, sports editor at the *Sunday Times*; Hugh Sleight, editor at *FourFourTwo*; David W. Potter; Andy Bucklow, Martin Creasy and Stevie Murray; Dominic Turnbull, deputy news editor at the *Mail on Sunday*, and also Tim Smith, Derek Whitfield, Nic Petkovic, Adrian Baker and Pravina Patel at the *Mail on Sunday*; the following people at *The Sun*: Nick Chapman and Alan Feltham (sport), Sam Wostear, Natasha Harding and Paul Collett (features), and Dave Morgan (news); Tom Shields; Eamon Dunphy; Graham McColl and George Sheridan; Archie Macpherson; Roy and Pat Stone; Lee Hassall; Emma Lloyd; Tom Henderson-Smith; my brothers Bob and Stephen; Frank snr and Barbara . . . and, last but never least, Roz Hoskinson.

CONTENTS

1

THE SPECIAL RELATIONSHIP

I've lived in Manchester since I was 13. Most of the
United fans I know also support Celtic. I was just
wondering why.
> *– United fan on BBC 606 website, 2007*

There is an affinity between the two clubs.
> *– Jim Divers, secretary of the Celtic Supporters Association*

FOR ME, the Celtic United love-in began on the Stretford End
in 1975. My team had been relegated to the Second Division
the previous year and the summer of '74 had been miserable
and dark. But by Christmas, things had much improved:
Manchester United, under the new-broom regime of the caustic
yet wonderful Tommy Docherty, were flying again. United were
running away with the title and we were all having a great time
along the way, seeing a bit of the country and visiting places
we would never have passed through, such as Blackpool and
Oxford, unless, of course, the FA Cup drew us together.

The club's directors had kept faith in the Doc after the trauma
of relegation from the top flight – and he had rewarded them
with the second-tier championship and a brand new team to

blow away the cobwebs of the post-Busby eras of Wilf McGuinness and Frank O'Farrell. Out went the old 'beyond their sell-by date' guards and in came the vibrant skills of Gordon Hill, Steve Coppell, Jim Holton and Stuart Pearson.

It was a wonderful time to be a young United fan. It was also a wonderful time to acknowledge allegiance to a no-less-colourful second team . . . Celtic, up in Scotland.

It felt OK to support another club from a different country, and one as legendary as United . . . and everyone else on the Stretford End seemed to support them as their 'Scottish team'. It being the advent of the era of the Doc, everything Scottish, like the man himself, was in vogue at Old Trafford. His early signings were predominantly Scottish, as he tried to establish a braveheart Celtic spine in a team that had previously been flimsy and timid. Everyone wore tartan jackets, had tartan scarves hanging from their arms and was trying to look like Rod Stewart with that mullet cut.

It was childish but enjoyable; tribal but an identity we young kids were eager to embrace. Even the visiting supporters would join in the chants: we would shout 'Celtic', they would answer immediately with 'Rangers'.

Then Rod made it all official. In the year when the Doc would be unceremoniously kicked out of Old Trafford for 'falling in love', Mr Stewart sang about his feeling for the woman – Britt Ekland – from whom he himself had just split and how, despite it all, she had been so dear to him that she was like Celtic, United. Ah . . .

Rod was born in north London to a Scottish father and an English mother. His dad, Robert, was from Edinburgh and his mother, Elsie, from Upper Holloway. Rod's older brothers, Don and Bob, and his sisters, Mary and Peggy, were born in Scotland, but by the time young Rod came along the family was living above the newsagent's shop they ran on Archway Road in Highgate. The former Brentford trainee, who played on the wing for England schoolboys, admits he loves both clubs equally – although at international level he now supports Scotland.

Jimmy 'Jinky' Johnstone was the catalyst for Rod's affection for one of the two biggest clubs in Britain. He knew Jinky personally and admitted, 'He was the reason I became a Celtic fan in 1971. We were doing some concerts in Scotland and he dragged me along to a game.'

Then, in 1973, Rod met United superstar Denis Law – and the Red Devils became his English team. At the time, Stewart recounted the occasion for his curious bandmates, his awestruck tones conveying the way he viewed both Law and United.

Was he happy with the meeting? Absolutely. 'I saw Denis Law's cock in the locker room!' he said.

Two years later, as the new United started to take shape in Division Two, Rod also paid homage to the brash manager of United, saying, 'I would like Tommy Docherty made Prime Minister!'

His devotion to watching the clubs – Celtic especially – is legendary. In 2004, he made sure his US tour ended a week before the date of the Scottish Cup final, so he would have enough time to return to see the Hoops play Dunfermline. In November 2006, he broke off from working in London to fly to Lisbon to see Celtic in their Champions League fixture against Benfica – which they lost 3–0. 'I flew all the way to f***ing Portugal to see my team get beat,' Rod said. 'Everything was absolutely marvellous until the game started. Then, as we say, it all went pear-shaped. And I'm Celtic's most famous supporter, so when the other team scored their first goal, the whole stadium looked at me like I'm responsible. It was horrible. I put far too much energy into football.'

It is hardly surprising that Celtic and United and their fans have a great affinity. Each is the undoubted glamour outfit in their respective countries; each has the biggest support, and the biggest and best ground; each has the most memorable players and history, and is intensely disliked by fans of certain other teams; and each assumed legendary status, becoming the first two British teams to win the European Cup.

A spokesman for Celtic FC agrees. 'There is a special relationship between the clubs. It has lasted over the years, probably starting up in the late '50s and '60s, when it became clear United and Celtic were by far the biggest clubs in Britain. The European triumphs of '67 and '68 cemented the ties and the uniqueness of the two clubs. Celtic and United fans hold a special affection for each other.'

This was clear recently at Roy Keane's testimonial and the two Champions League matches in 2006, according to an official at Manchester United FC. 'They were great occasions and showed the affection both clubs have for each other,' he commented. 'It was also good to see the way the fans embraced in all three games, with no trouble (I recall there were even a few Celtic fans in the Stretford End during the matches). It was heart-warming. We at United continue to see Celtic as our great friends.'

Each club was also formed with altruistic intent: Celtic were founded by a Marist monk, Brother Walfrid, with the aim of raising funds to feed the poor children of the east end of Glasgow, while United founding father Louis Rocca encouraged the Catholic priests of Manchester to help talented youths out of the poverty trap by sending them to him for trials.

As a consequence of their origins and their mass support among the Irish, both also formed a bond by becoming known as the Catholic clubs of England and Scotland. Inevitably, as the decades rolled by and they proved they were non-sectarian by signing Protestants and welcoming fans of all creeds, this would become less of an issue – not that I can ever remember it being one at Old Trafford. At Celtic, however, it is a different story. Hoops legend Billy McNeill says even though the rivalry between City and United is as intense as that between Celtic and Rangers, 'there is none of the religious baggage that overshadows the Old Firm and at times causes such grief'.

Having said that, the club has done sterling work lately to break down the barricades of any alleged bigotry. As chief executive Peter Lawwell says, 'No club does as much as Celtic in seeking to eliminate bigotry from football . . . Celtic supporters have, uniquely, received awards from both FIFA and UEFA in recent years, recognising and applauding their good behaviour.' I think most Hoops fans would rather their club be associated with its success on the football pitch than the battles for religious supremacy off it.

In the early days, United and Celtic were both reliant on the goodwill of inspirational businessmen to secure them financially: Celtic owe an eternal debt to the endeavours of John Glass in backing Walfrid's vision, while United's survival in different eras depended upon the drive of John H. Davies and James Gibson.

Both clubs were likewise linked by the determination of their managers. In an article in the *Daily Telegraph*, Robert Philip compares the football philosophies of Jock Stein and Matt Busby and their roots in the harsh Lanarkshire coal-mining communities where they were born. Robert writes, 'It could never be enough for Celtic and Manchester United simply to win, they had to win in a manner that brought a smile to the faces of the common man who parted with a chunk of his wages to throng the terraces of Parkhead and Old Trafford.' The journalist also points out their similarly forward-thinking attitudes in terms of the European game. They saw domestic football, Robert writes, as 'merely a passport to the European Cup, in which the true greatness of teams could be most accurately judged'.

Busby was Celtic mad. A supporter from an early age, his one unrealised ambition was to play for the Bhoys – the invitation never came.

When he joined United as manager in 1945, Matt set about turning the club upside down as he tried to breathe life into a sleeping giant; one of the ways he did this was to bring in some players he knew well – from Scotland – including the great Jimmy Delaney. The newspapermen of the day would quickly dub Busby's new United 'Celtic in exile'.

Busby was great friends with Jock Stein and that also helped the special relationship thrive. The two men from similar backgrounds found they had much in common when they chatted after the Coronation Cup semi-final of 1953.

Celtic Supporters Association secretary Jim Divers believes that the relationship between the two men is important in assessing why Celtic and United have been such staunch allies over the years. 'There is an affinity between the two clubs that probably goes back to the days of Busby and Stein, and started around the time of the Coronation Cup,' he explains. 'Matt and Jock had a lot in common, a lot upon which to build a friendship. Both were from Lanarkshire and I think Busby was a Celtic fan.' Indeed, he was, Jim: in fact, like Stein, he was Celtic crazy.

Long-time Celtic fan Stevie Murray, from Ayrshire, adds, 'I have always supported Celtic, but United are my number two team. They are the only other team I would consider cheering for. They are the Celtic of England – everyone else envies them because of their success and support, just like Celtic in Scotland. The clubs are very alike in their history, their star players and their highs and lows, what they've been through over the years – and how they always both come back when people think they're finished. Of course you will get some people who will say there is no link, who will try to stir up trouble between United and Celtic, but you get such people in all areas of society. They are not real fans – they are on the periphery of our two great clubs.'

David Scott, of the Celtic Internet fanzine site cybertims.com, also believes the clubs and their fans have a shared bond. 'Celtic fans view United fans as friends. Both teams come from the same industrial-type cities and both teams have a strong Irish support. When we went to Old Trafford for Roy Keane's testimonial, a great time was had by all and the fans had a great time mixing together.'

During months of exhaustive research into the two clubs, I found the work of author and Celtic historian David W. Potter to be among the most rewarding and illuminating. He has views on the special relationship too – how and why it exists. He also believes they are the two best-supported clubs in the world but argues Celtic have slightly more worldwide fans because of the effect of the Irish and Scottish diasporas. As an example of their joint popularity, he points to Dublin, explaining that a visit down O'Connell Street proves how big the clubs are. The football tops being worn by the locals are not those of Shamrock Rovers, Shelbourne or St Patrick's, but of Celtic and Manchester United.

In his book *Jimmy Delaney: The Stuff of Legend*, Potter sums up the bond between the clubs as follows, also pointing out how they both thrive on the diverse emotions of love and hate among football fans in their respective countries:

> Both teams have huge support and tend to be associated with brilliant players and glorious triumphs. There tends to be a huge dichotomy about them; they are either loved or hated. In the same way that Celtic fans often feel the supporters of Motherwell, Hearts, Kilmarnock and others will side with Rangers when the chips are down, so too there is a tendency for any defeat of Manchester United to be received with greater joy among the average fan than reserved for anyone else.

On the United fans' side of the fence, acclaimed writers Andy Bucklow and Martin Creasy are also convinced there is 'a magical link' between the two footballing citadels of Glasgow and Manchester. Long-time United fan Creasy is one of many who looks out for Celtic's results north of the border. A United nut – what you would call a 'superfan' – he has followed the club since the 1960s and has been a season-ticket holder since he was a youngster. 'I don't remember how it started really,' he says. 'It was just a sort of unspoken thing. I was so young when I chose United as my team that I didn't even know where Manchester was! I think I liked the fact they played in red and I loved the sound of the name.

'I could only have been about five years old. But at some point after that I must have picked up that if you were a United fan, then Celtic must be your Scottish team. I was told that United and Celtic were both "Catholic clubs" and the bonding was largely because of this. I couldn't see what religion had to do with football. As far as I was concerned, the only religion that mattered was supporting your team. I cared about United and if Celtic were their friends on the other side of the wall, that was good enough for me.'

Englishman Creasy is embarrassed to recall that he briefly rooted for Scotland over England because of his allegiance to Tommy Docherty at United. 'When the Doc was running United, there were eight or nine Scottish players in the team, so I decided to support Scotland instead. Massive egg on the face when England beat them 5–1 in a Home International at Wembley. There was I, an Englishman, being jeered by my English mates because England had just beaten Scotland 5–1. Crazy days!'

Creasy says that another thing that links United and Celtic fans is their love of flair and style rather than ruthless efficiency. Back in the 1960s, there were obvious comparisons between George Best and Celtic's own diminutive but inspirational winger Jimmy Johnstone. 'Bestie could only ever belong at United,' says Creasy. 'His unique gift would have been wasted anywhere else. Only the finest stage could do justice to his magic, weaved dazzlingly in front of the loudest and most passionate fans in the country every week. He may not have found every club so indulgent. Would the ruthless machines of Leeds or Liverpool have welcomed such a precocious yet unpredictable talent within their ranks? Would frustrated teammates have ended up berating him for not passing, getting tackled (just occasionally), not chasing back or piling into the tackles? I bet they would.

'Even Bestie's United mates recorded their own occasional impatience with him, but, us fans, we loved him. He represented everything the club stood for. Magic. Genius. Pure inspirational brilliance. Skill and technique that you couldn't learn from a manual. A gift that he was born with. Celtic fans, of course, felt the same way about their own wing wizard. United fans appreciated Johnstone's talent, too. What Georgie was doing south of the border, Jimmy was emulating north of it. The swagger of the hips, the half-smile as yet another lumbering defender was dumped unceremoniously on his backside. Of course, Bestie and Jimmy shared the "Celtic" impudence too, and every now and again the temper.

'Visions instantly recalled of them making as if to take off their shirts to give to the defender if they really wanted it that much. Or the occasional tantrum – aiming a quick kick or handbags-style lunge at an opponent who had dared to provoke the genius just a little too much. Georgie and Jimmy represented the game in its purest form. The sports business truly was the entertainment business. Style, flair and magic – even if it didn't pay off every time. Take on the opponent and risk losing possession rather than play safe, stand on the ball and then roll it five yards for a sideways pass. United fans instinctively knew that Celtic supporters shared their sense of football style.'

Creasy believes that one of United's most significant signings from the 1960s was a Celtic player. 'The young generation of

United fans know Paddy Crerand as the one-eyed rose-tinted-glasses expert on MUTV,' he says. 'Supporters of my age also know him as one of the most important United players of the past 50 years. The thing about the press in the 1960s is that they always wrote about Sir Matt's holy trinity of Best, Law and Charlton, and that's understandable. These were three players who were world class and would have been in any era. What younger fans may not know is that Paddy was every bit as important in that United side.

'It sounds ridiculous to talk of him being an unsung hero or underrated because everybody knew how good he was. It's just that history naturally throws its biggest light on the special three. But for those who don't realise what a big favour Celtic did United when he signed for us in 1963, let me attempt to explain. Pat was the hard man and creative genius rolled into one. He could roll up the sleeves and jump into battle when it was needed, and after he had piled in and won the ball he could then elegantly play it Scholesy style, inch perfect to the feet of Besty, Law or Charlton. Think of a player you'd like in the trenches with you. Think of a player with sublime touch and vision who can pick out a pass that other players couldn't see. Roll the two players into one and you have Paddy. There's no doubt in my mind that he was just as important a part of the United jigsaw as those famous household names.'

Andy Bucklow, a senior journalist on the *Mail on Sunday*, has followed United's fortunes for 40 years. He is also proud of the long association between Celtic and United. 'My first proper season as a rookie United fan coincided with Celtic winning the European Cup – and as a nine year old watching from afar as the Reds won what was to be their last league title for twenty-six years. My second team, for a reason I was then too young to understand, let alone care about, was Celtic.

'There was something mystical about the green-and-white

Hoops in glorious black and white as Jock Stein's Bhoys prepared for their now legendary European Cup final on live TV against Inter Milan in 1967. Even at that age, for me, instinct kicked in. I was due to attend my weekly early evening piano lesson, which would all but rule out watching most of that final, but an imaginary stomach bug, coupled with a rolling-around act that Didier Drogba would have been proud of, got me a prized sickie from my parents.

'Even then, it was easy to differentiate between the stifling *catenaccio* tactics of the Inter defensive juggernaut and the flair and never-say-die spirit of Stein's Lisbon Lions. Good guys don't always win, but they did that night, which straddled my earliest football memories: the '66 World Cup and, for United fans, the even more important 1968 Wembley triumph. That now legendary Celtic comeback was part two of my initiation into watching legends making history. Part three was to be just a year away.

'My support for the two clubs continued even during the dark days of the '70s. While United sank slowly into the Division Two abyss, via four years of mediocrity, I sought comfort from my "other" team and sat gripped in front of a fuzzy black-and-white TV supporting Celtic as they beat the choking Leeds "Invincibles" in the 1970 European Cup semi. I was living in the Midlands and had no Scottish, Glasgow or Catholic connections whatsoever.

'But while United were by then always my team, even under the stewardship of McGuinness or O'Farrell, Celtic provided the ballast during those barren Old Trafford years. Docherty arrived and so did the preponderance of tartan scarves at the Stretford End, which was a reflection of the Scots he called on to bail him out of the first relegation dogfight – Alex Forsyth, Stewart Houston, Jim Holton and the man who more than anyone epitomised the spirit of the Reds at that time, ex-Celt

Lou Macari. And Bobby Charlton wasn't daft when he chose Celtic as the opponents for his 60,000 sell-out testimonial at Old Trafford in 1972 – a trend that was to be followed by the likes of Bryan Robson, Mark Hughes, Denis Irwin and, of course, Roy Keane.

'The testimonial link was not all one-way traffic either, as Celtic legends Jimmy Johnstone and Bobby Lennox invited Docherty's United to Celtic Park for their joint testimonial in 1976.'

The great Paddy Crerand earns a special mention by Bucklow as well. 'For me, the template for all the Celtic stars to make the successful transition from green to red has to be Crerand – thankfully not the last Gorbals boy to make a bit of an impact at Old Trafford.

'After six years at Celtic, Crerand arrived in 1963 as part of Busby's post-Munich rebuild. As an integral part of that glorious free-flowing side of the mid- to late '60s, Crerand made his mark as the next best player outside of the holy trinity. In his own way, he was perhaps even more influential.

'Crerand started a sporadic north–south trend of top Scottish players moving between Glasgow and Manchester which continued up to Brian McClair's transfer for £850,000 in 1987. The only significant player to go the other way was, of course, Roy Keane.'

One thing that caused friction between some United and Celtic fans at Roy's testimonial in May 2006 needs clearing up right now: the truth about the Celtic anthem, 'You'll Never Walk Alone'. At that match, many United fans booed and hissed when the thousands of visiting supporters starting to sing it, flags aloft – because of course United associate it with their arch rivals, Liverpool. Many United fans believe it shows a special Celtic link with the Kop. I dug deep and found this is not the case – the Stretford End can rest easy!

The truth of it is that Celtic supporters believe they have as much right to sing it as those on the Kop. Far from showing respect to the Kop, it is sung because they think they were the first to adopt it. Celtic supporter Stevie Murray says, 'Yes, I never even knew United fans thought we were pals with Liverpool over the song. We thought "You'll Never Walk Alone" was our song – I thought Liverpool had pinched it off us!'

Bobby Casey, a Celtic old-timer, notes, 'I can recall one Celtic fan telling me years ago that they had "You'll Never Walk Alone" as part of their repertoire on the terraces for the 1957 Scottish League Cup final, as a tribute to the years of failure they had endured. And given Liverpool's penchant for nicking things from Celtic – Dalglish, the huddle and "The Fields of Athenry" – it wouldn't be any great surprise if they also pinched "You'll Never Walk Alone"!'

Originally from the 1945 musical *Carousel*, it was a hit for Liverpool's Gerry and the Pacemakers in the '60s – hence the city's connection. However, Fulham also claim they were the first to adopt it, before the Kop and Celtic, after the musical was performed in London.

To spice up the debate a bit more, I tracked down a source who said that none of the above clubs were the rightful terrace owners of the song – that in actual fact it belongs to . . . Manchester United! Grandmother Jane Hardwick claims that Liverpool fans stole the anthem from United supporters. A lifelong Red Devils supporter, she claims it was originally sung by her and thousands of fans at Old Trafford long before it became associated with Liverpool.

Jane was a teenage opera singer when many of her footballing heroes were killed in the Munich air crash. As her own special tribute to the Busby Babes, a heartbroken Jane persuaded her friends from New Mills Operatic Society in Derbyshire to join her in a rendition of the song at one of the games following the tragedy.

They were singing the song as part of a *Carousel* performance they were rehearsing at the time. Jane says that thousands joined them when they started singing it at Old Trafford in 1958 – at least five years before it was first heard on the Kop.

'It has annoyed me so much that people think the song was first sung by the Liverpool fans,' Jane said. 'The Munich crash was so horrible and everyone was feeling down and despondent and it just seemed an appropriate song to sing.

'The whole ground was singing it and many people, including me, were in tears. I never dreamed it would become the anthem of our old rivals, but I wanted to put the record straight about where the song originated from on the terraces.'

Returning to the Keane testimonial, it still amazes me that apart from the multitude of similar benefits over the years, the Champions League encounters at Old Trafford and Celtic Park in 2006 were the first competitive matches between the clubs since they met in the semi-final of the Coronation Cup in 1953 at Hampden. Back then, Celtic, captained by Stein, beat Busby's United 2–1.

Of course, Stein would go on to lead the Bhoys as manager to the European Cup in 1967, while Busby's United became the first English victors at Wembley in 1968.

Journalist Robert Philip sums it up: 'Stein's Lisbon Lions were assembled around the genius of Jimmy Johnstone, the guile of Bobby Murdoch, the grit of Bertie Auld and the goalscoring of Bobby Lennox; the United side Busby rebuilt around the genius of George Best, the guile of Bobby Charlton, the grit of Nobby Stiles and the goalscoring of Denis Law.'

The clubs epitomise a dream union made in footballing heaven: from the unusual bond and uncanny similarities in their developments dating back to the start of the twentieth century and the altruistic natures of the club's founding fathers, the initial glory days and subsequent struggles in the '20s and '30s, the tragedies and the periods of sustained triumphs under Stein and Busby, to the wonder of Jimmy Delaney in the late '30s and early '40s and the days of Best and Jinky in the '70s. There are also the fans who have no equals – the boys from the Jungle and the Stretford End – and the men who are confidently taking Celtic and United forward to new heights.

This book is for them all, as Celtic end 2007 celebrating the 40th anniversary of winning the European Cup and United enter 2008 with the memory of their 1968 triumph at Wembley – and the tragedy at Munich in 1958 – very much in mind.

Let's begin our journey by turning the clock back to the late nineteenth century, to humble beginnings in the poverty-stricken east end of Glasgow and a deprived area of Manchester and the emergence of the two most legendary football clubs in the world . . .

2

....

BROTHER WALFRID: PARADISE FOUND

A wonderful, organising power . . . of lovable nature
. . . [a man who] only had to knock and it was
opened.

      – Former Celtic player Tom Maley on Brother Walfrid

AS ANDREW Kerins was walking despairingly around the
grimy tenement blocks of Glasgow one particular autumn night
in 1887, he stopped abruptly. It was as if the Good Lord himself
had spoken. The man who was also known as Brother Walfrid, of
the Marist order of monks, in that moment determined exactly
what his ordained role was to be in this world. In that moment
of enlightenment, he knew his very *raison d'être*.

He surveyed the scenes before him and felt a stab of deep
compassion in his heart. Malnourished infants were kicking
cans around in the street, this entertainment offering a brief
escape from the horrors of the damp, dirty rooms in the rundown tenements they called home. The Irish immigrants around
him were dressed in ripped clothes unfit to be termed rags, with
holes in their shoes, their faces black and emaciated from the
smog and the ravages of a poor diet.

Fifty years earlier and four hundred miles away in London,
Charles Dickens had written about the disgraceful scenes in

the workhouses, where similarly dispossessed youngsters were ill treated; however, compared to Glasgow's forgotten Irish children, they were relatively well cared for, receiving at least regular meals and exercise.

As he surveyed the pitiful images before his very eyes, he questioned how he could help provide the basics of food, clothing and exercise. It was at this point the answer came to him: the birth of a mission to which he would devote himself for the rest of his life. He would set up a football club to raise funds for them, along the lines of Edinburgh club Hibernian – the Roman word for 'Ireland' – formed in 1875 by Canon Edward Hannan.

The club had won the Scottish Cup the very year Brother Walfrid found himself amidst the grimy tenements and Hibs had held their celebrations in the east end of Glasgow. Walfrid had been invited to the joyous victory bash. The idea of his own club in his own city had germinated at that point. It is believed to have taken further shape when he asked Hibernian to play in a charity match against Renton in Glasgow. The game took place on Clyde's Barrowland ground and drew a crowd of 12,000, as the Scottish Cup holders were held 1–1. The money raised from the match astounded Walfrid and convinced him that Glasgow should have its own version of the Edinburgh club.

So was formed Celtic Football Club of Glasgow's east end – a true God's football club, in every sense.

Andrew Kerins was born in 1840 in the village of Ballymote, County Sligo, to parents John Kerins and Elizabeth Flynn. He took the religious name Brother Walfrid in 1864 when he joined the Marists, a Catholic order founded in France in 1817 at La Valla, near Lyon, by Saint Marcellin Champagnat, a young French priest of the Society of Mary (Marist Fathers). He named himself after a wealthy eighth-century citizen of Pisa, Galfrido della Gherardesca, who was called to religious life and later canonised as St Walfrid. The Marists were devoted to educational work throughout the world and, in 1858, they arrived in Glasgow and founded St Mungo's Academy, which would play a vital role in the education of poor Catholic children in the east end of the city. It was originally located at 96 Garngad Hill but moved first to St Mungo Street and then in 1883 to Parson Street.

Kerins, an educational missionary for the Marists, arrived in Glasgow in the early 1870s and taught at St Mary's School in Abercromby Street before becoming headmaster of the Sacred Heart School in Bridgeton. There he saw the anguish of slum life at first hand, his pupils comprising the needy, the starving and the suffering.

But poverty was nothing new to him; back in the west of Ireland, he had been privy to the horrors of the Great Famine. His family were poor crofters and had suffered, as did many, Sligo being one of the worst affected areas. Kerins was six when the blight hit and would escape with many of the rural Irish population to Scotland along a well-trodden route, hoping for a better life.

As Brother Walfrid, Kerins had taken vows to cut all ties with 'life in the world', but the images of suffering in Ireland continued to haunt him in Scotland. They would be his lifetime link with the real world.

Far from finding nirvana in Glasgow, the Irish immigrants had simply swapped one hell for another: suffering and starving in the countryside for suffering and starving in a city devoid of food. Awaiting them in the most densely populated city in Europe at the time was poorly paid menial, unskilled work, disease and deprivation. Housing for the working classes in Glasgow was appalling. According to the 1861 census, at least 64 per cent of families lived in one- or two-bedroomed accommodation; 1 per cent of these homes were even without windows.

The Scottish infant mortality rate between 1855 and 1859

stood at 118 in every 1,000 live births and the infant death rate was four to five times higher in the east end than in more affluent areas such as Kelvinside. Of the 11,675 registered deaths in Glasgow in 1888, 4,750 were children under five years of age.

Ethnic, linguistic and religious barriers made integration into Scottish society almost impossible for the Irish immigrants and they remained isolated in their own little communities. They were also not welcomed by some locals, who feared the influx would affect their chances in the job market and put a further strain on amenities and facilities. This was the desperate situation as Brother Walfrid walked through the tenements that October evening.

Walfrid had set up Penny Dinners for the youngsters of his parish in the early 1880s in an attempt to ensure they all received a nourishing, warm meal each day for a penny. 'Should parents prefer, they could send the bread and the children could get a large bowl of broth or soup for a halfpenny,' Walfrid announced, 'and those who are not able to pay get a substantial meal free. This has been a very great blessing for the poor children.' Indeed, it was. For some, it was a lifesaver. But Walfrid had realised it was not enough. This remarkable, compassionate, altruistic man saw that there remained widespread suffering among the young. The solution, he decided, lay with the formation of a football club.

On 6 November 1887 in St Mary's Parish Hall on East Rose Street (now Forbes Street) in the Calton district of Glasgow, Brother Walfrid met with local businessmen to thrash out a way of setting up the Celtic Football and Athletic Club.

A number of names were suggested for the new club at the meeting – including Glasgow Hibernian, Emerald, and Emerald Harp – but Walfrid insisted on using the name Celtic (or 'Keltic', as was Walfrid's preferred pronunciation). For Walfrid, the name was as much an embodiment of Ireland as it was of Scotland and it represented his new side's values perfectly.

Dr Joe Bradley, an expert on football, communities and cultural and religious identity, notes there was another angle to Walfrid's founding of the club alongside the fundraising: it was to give a sense of self-esteem to the Irish population in the city:

> People haven't forgotten what Walfrid and Celtic did at that particular time. That's why the descendants are still part and parcel of the club and form the essential community that revolved around the club.
>
> He organised football matches between other clubs and it culminated with the founding of Celtic in 1887 and 1888. In terms of the Irish Catholic community, business people directed their success into it. When they came together with Walfrid, there was a magic that took place and that was the basis of the success.

Paddy Doherty, of the Sligo Brother Walfrid Committee, said, 'There would have been no Celtic without Brother Walfrid. Certainly some of his identity and roots may have been lost, but the connection with Ireland will never be lost.'

In January 1888, the club issued a mission statement outlining its aims and hopes. It read:

> Celtic Football and Athletic Club, Celtic Park, Parkhead (Corner of Dalmarnock and Janefield Streets). Patrons His Grace the Archbishop of Glasgow and the Clergy of St Mary's, Sacred Heart and St Michael's Missions, and the principal Catholic laymen of the East End.
>
> The above Club was formed in November 1887, by a number of Catholics of the East End of the City. The main object is to supply the East End conferences of the St Vincent de Paul Society with funds for the maintenance of the 'Dinner Tables' of our needy children in the Missions of St Mary's, Sacred Heart and St Michael's. Many cases of sheer poverty are left unaided through lack of means. It is therefore with

this principal object that we have set afloat the 'Celtic' and we invite you as one of our ever-ready friends to assist in putting our new Park in proper working order for the coming football season.

We have already several of the leading Catholic football players of the West of Scotland on our membership list. They have most thoughtfully offered to assist in the good work. We are fully aware that the 'elite' of football players belong to this City and suburbs, and we know that from there we can select a team which will be able to do credit to the Catholics of the West of Scotland as the Hibernians have been doing in the East.

Again there is also the desire to have a large recreation ground where our Catholic young men will be able to enjoy the various sports which will build them up physically, and we feel sure we will have many supporters with us in this laudable object.

Under Walfrid's guidance, the newly established club would develop quickly. They played their first-ever game, what was described as a 'friendly encounter', on 28 May 1888, beating Glasgow Rangers, a club fifteen years older than Celtic, 5–2 in front of 2,000 fans, with Neil McCallum scoring the first goal for the club after just ten minutes. Celtic appeared in white shirts with a green collar and a red Celtic cross on the breast.

The match took place at the first Celtic Park, a vacant lot next to St Mary's Church near to the club's current ground. The patch of land on Janefield Street was rented at a cost of £50 a year and the local community had worked for free to transform it into a football pitch. There was a level grassy playing field measuring 110 x 66 yards, terracing around three sides of the stadium and an open-air stand for 1,000 spectators, which also contained a referee's room, an office, dressing-rooms and washing and toilet facilities. The gate receipts from that first match yielded £400, which was, as planned, used to feed the hungry in the city's east end.

Within four years, the club had to move when the landlord increased the rent from £50 per annum to £450. Celtic upped sticks across the Janefield Street Cemetery to what would become known as 'Paradise', their current home. Again with the help of a volunteer workforce, the second Celtic Park was built in time for the start of the 1892–93 season.

In 1893, Brother Walfrid was sent by his religious order to the east end of London. There, he continued his good work, organising football matches for the barefoot children in the districts of Bethnal Green and Bow. He is said to have considered setting up a 'London Celtic' but decided against it because he felt that London's Irish population was too scattered across the capital.

In 1911, Walfrid met the Celtic team in Scotland after they had returned from a European tour and he was moved at the reception he received from club officials at a celebration dinner. Tom Maley, who had been a Celtic player 23 years earlier and was now working as a reporter for the *Scottish Observer*, was one of the guests at the dinner and quoted Walfrid as saying, 'Well, well, time has brought changes and, outside of ourselves, there are few left of the old brigade. I know none of these present players, but they are under the old colours and quartered in the dear old quarters and that suffices.'

Five years later, in 1916, Tom Maley would add his own personal tribute to the role played by Brother Walfrid in inspiring others, as well as remaining fully committed himself. Writing in the *Weekly Mail and Record*, Tom noted:

> Through the organising genius, the wonderful persuasive powers and the personality of Brother Walfrid, the Celtic club was established. His men carried out his every wish and idea. They knew and

trusted their leader, and in the knowledge that he, like them, wanted the club for the most laudable objects – charity, and as a recreation for his loved East Enders – they persevered.

Brother Walfrid died on 17 April 1915 and was buried in a Marist graveyard in Dumfries in Scotland. Some critics harshly claim that Walfrid's legacy is a tarnished one, that he set up a club that would inevitably be eternally immersed in controversy because of its Catholic origins. Even in 2006 there was fiery debate about the subject.

Tommy Docherty in his autobiography, *The Doc: Hallowed Be Thy Game*, would point out that 'for many years Celtic had a turnstile reserved for the use of Catholic priests only'.

In much the same way, Louis Rocca, one of the two key pioneers at Manchester United, would have a close relationship with that city's Catholic priesthood, asking them to keep their eyes peeled for any promising young footballers among their congregations.

Yet Brother Walfrid had never conceived of Celtic as being purely a Catholic club. As Dr Bradley wrote:

> Celtic, from the first days, was a Catholic club and Irish but never in an exclusive sense. It would have gone against the ethos of the members who started the club, and certainly Brother Walfrid, in terms of his Christianity.

Walfrid's true legacy, and the measure of the deep love and gratitude in which he is held in the east end of Glasgow, was highlighted on 5 November 2005. Thousands of people turned up at Celtic Park for the unveiling of a bronze memorial by sculptor Kate Robinson in honour of the memory of the monk. It shows Walfrid in contemplative mood, reading his Bible. The cost of the statue, which amounted to £67,000, was solely met by Celtic supporters. It was blessed by Archbishop Mario

Conti of Glasgow, who also presented the club with a specially commissioned Celtic cross, incorporating materials from the now demolished St Mary's church hall where the club was founded.

Archbishop Conti said on the day, 'While I was always aware of the part Celtic played in the history and culture of the Catholic community in Glasgow over the past 100 years and more, I have, since coming to the city as Archbishop, learned more about that history and have grown to appreciate how much we should value it.'

Hoops chairman Brian Quinn added his own tribute to the part Walfrid had played in the club's history. 'We are a movement founded on principles established by a quiet, determined man who set out to bring out the best in people and promote a generosity of spirit that endures today.

'He also saw this as a means of bringing together the Scottish as well as the Irish strands of Glasgow's disadvantaged population. From the very outset, Celtic Football Club commanded the passionate support of communities it was intended to represent. This was something with which, in their deprived conditions, they could identify and from which they could draw inspiration, a sense of self-worth and some kind of positive response to those that did not make them welcome. These are powerful sentiments and they drove the club and its supporters forward.'

A Celtic FC spokesman said at the time: 'Brother Walfrid is recognised as the most important figure in the club's illustrious 117-year history and one who embodies the positive Irish connection which Celtic has become so famous for across the globe. The unveiling event is a wonderful occasion and a fitting tribute to someone who made such an important contribution to the club.'

Eddie Toner, the chair of the Brother Walfrid Memorial Committee, said the statue was 'a lasting memorial to a great humanitarian'. He said, 'Walfrid gave us a vision – one that was Christian, charitable, inclusive and about never forgetting our roots. He gave us a symbol for the community, a sense of identity and something to be proud of.'

Billy McNeill, who lifted the European Cup as Celtic skipper in 1967, paid tribute to Walfrid's remarkable and far-reaching achievement. 'For a Marist brother to start a football club in the East End of Glasgow which now has a reputation across the world is amazing.' McNeill also stressed the idea of Walfrid establishing a club for all-comers as being an all-inclusive concept: 'Celtic set out to be non-sectarian right from the outset. Even the name was carefully chosen because it reflected the Scottish and Irish roots.'

A further sculpture of Brother Walfrid, commemorating his links with his home town of Ballymote, was unveiled in the public park there in 2005.

Previously Walfrid's contribution to the club had only been recognised in the naming of a hospitality suite after him at the stadium – a rather ironic tribute for a man who had raised money for food for the poor, given that the suite was renowned for its lavish five-course meals for the wealthy.

A Celtic fan in Glasgow had this to say on the matter: 'Want a fitting tribute to Brother Walfrid? Don't name a f***ing restaurant after him, for a start! Such crass insensitivity you would expect from Ye Olde Board, but still. Fund an initiative that will directly help the thousands of Glasgow's poor, that's more like it.'

And there is, of course, an argument that the cost of the statue now outside Celtic Park should not have been met solely by the fans and that the club should have readily funded the memorial, as Manchester United did with the bronze statue of Sir Matt Busby that graces the forecourt at Old Trafford.

Gareth Savage, a Celtic fan, put it this way: 'We have to collect for a Brother Walfrid statue. A f***ing disgrace! Did Man Utd or Liverpool fans have to collect for Busby's or Shankly's? There should be seven-foot statues outside Celtic Park of both Brother Walfrid and Jock Stein paid for by the board, but are there? No chance.'

While the argument over the funding of the statue raged, a Hoops fan commented, 'I think that for once Celtic should try and do something right and commission someone to do this on behalf of the supporters. It is the least that they can do. Or some of the players should donate a wee bit of their wages as a gesture to the fans. While they are at it, they should start getting one ready for the Lions as well!'

Similarly, after the initial euphoria at the club, there ensued argument and ill feeling. Not everyone viewed the advent of Celtic Football Club in warm terms. Hibernian, in particular, became disillusioned with it within a year of its formation. The Edinburgh club had gone out of its way to help set up its Glasgwegian 'double' but felt their ultimate reward was to be ripped off. Stuart Crowther, the Hibernian historian, explained the roots of this discontent as being down to Celtic's misuse of Hibs' generosity – particularly in terms of players. He points out that in Celtic's first match, the 5–2 win over Rangers, they 'leaned heavily on their friends from Edinburgh and seven of the players in their side that day had connections with Hibs'. Worse was to follow. Crowther believes the Edinburgh club was too trusting of its Glaswegian friends and paid a heavy price when, in August 1888, the best players from Hibs defected to Celtic with the promise of rich rewards. He believes Celtic quickly renounced their charitable beliefs as hard-nosed businessmen propelled the club forwards and is particularly critical of John Glass, credited by Walfrid as being a key player in the establishment of Celtic. While Walfrid was the patron saint, the instigator, Glass was the businessman-cum-politician whose nous and financial drive helped the dream become a reality.

A joiner by trade, also a local politician, Glass was a charmer who persuaded well-known players to sign up for the fledgling Celtic. He was later described by the club's first manager, Willie Maley, as the man 'to whom the club owes its existence'. At Celtic Park, he is spoken of with affection and reverence, as a respected leader of the Irish Catholic community of the day and as Walfrid's right-hand man. Not so at Easter Road.

Crowther sums up the resentment like this: 'John Glass had recognised the massive financial rewards that would ensue from professional football. The game had gone professional in England sometime before and Scotland was about to follow; all the same, the way he set about using the loyalties of the Irish immigrant population left a sour taste in many a mouth. Celtic were seeking to have the best of both worlds, they would sign any players they wished while still retaining an appeal to the Irish community. Business had, not for the first time, trampled over idealism; money had spoken.'

Celtic's first competitive match came in September 1888 with a Scottish Cup tie against Shettleston – the team included several top-notch players who had left Hibernian. John Glass had also secured the services of James Kelly, an excellent centre-half from Renton.

In a remarkable end to their debut season, Celtic reached the final of the competition, losing 3–0 to Third Lanark at Hampden Park in front of 18,000 spectators. This match was played in February 1889 in a blizzard and because of the adverse weather conditions the Scottish Football Association decreed that it should be replayed. A week later, battle was done once more, Third Lanark again emerging as winners, this time by a 2–1 scoreline. Yet it was still a feat, given the club had only been in existence for a mere nine months.

The club did actually win its first trophy that season, the North-Eastern Cup (a local competition) – beating Cowlairs

6–1 in the final – and it presented £421 to east end charities after a successful campaign.

Willie Maley would look back on that debut year with fondness and not a little admiration for the success achieved. 'An extraordinary fact in connection with the start of Celtic is that not a man among the founders knew anything about the practical side of football,' he said. 'None had ever played the game. Some, perhaps, had never seen a match. Yet in the first year of the club's life, Celts were within an ace of winning the Scottish Cup.'

The club quickly became a major force, drawing record crowds in Scotland, including 26,000 against Queen's Park in the 1889 Scottish Cup first round, and was a major influence on the evolution of football in Scotland.

The English Football League, the first in the world, was formed in 1888, with 12 clubs based around the north of England and the Midlands. An exiled Scot, one William McGregor, came up with the idea of a 'league' competition to replace the ongoing diet of friendlies which were only interrupted by the occasional FA Cup tie. McGregor's plan was that the clubs would play each other twice in a season, on a home-and-away basis, with two points being awarded for a win and one for a draw. The team with the highest number of points when all fixtures had been played would be declared the champion.

Two years later the Scottish Football League followed, thanks largely to the efforts of Celtic, who swiftly realised they also needed more than local friendlies and cup-competition fixtures to thrive as the English clubs now appeared to be doing. Indeed, the motion for the new league was proposed by Hoops committee member John McLaughlin.

Opposition was strong and bitter. The *Scottish Sport* newspaper objected on the grounds that football was better off remaining an amateur sport. The paper thundered, 'Our first and last objection to the League is that they exist. The entire rules stink of finance, money making and money grabbing.' One club in particular, Queen's Park, felt so strongly about the advent of professionalism that it wanted to play no part in the establishment of the Scottish League and boycotted the inaugural season of 1890–91.

Thankfully, they and other tunnel-visioned objectors of the era were overruled and McLaughlin's motion was adopted. An official spokesman said, 'The prime reason, however, why a Scottish League was formed was not initially to form a professional set-up [although that would soon follow] but was to provide clubs with a regular diet of competitive football.'

Celtic, not for the first or last time, were the trailblazers. In that first season, 11 clubs formed the Scottish Football League: Abercorn, Cambuslang, Celtic, Cowlairs, Dumbarton, Heart of Midlothian, Rangers, Renton, St Mirren, Third Lanark and Vale of Leven. The Bhoys kicked off with a match at Celtic Park against Renton, a fixture that attracted a crowd of 10,000, most of whom were deflated as the Hoops crashed 4–1.

The following week, Celtic won their first-ever Scottish League fixture when they triumphed 5–0 at Hearts. The Hoops would finish third in that first league season.

The club won its first national trophy in 1892, beating Queen's Park 5–1 on 9 April at Ibrox in the Scottish Cup final. Johnny Campbell and Sandy McMahon each grabbed a brace. That season they finished runners-up in the league to Dumbarton. But a year later, they finally cracked the big one: they became Scottish League champions for the first time – less than five years after their first competitive match – and they would retain the crown the following season, winning it again in 1896 and 1898.

Celtic, now wearing green and white stripes, also registered their record triumph during their 1895–96 league-winning season with an 11–0 thrashing of Dundee at Celtic Park.

In 1897, the advent of the professional era was sealed for Celtic at Parkhead when the club's members agreed to it becoming a limited company. The dreams of Brother Walfrid and his initial altruistic zeal had been overcome by a drive for profits and success. It was inevitable and those involved would have been naive not to expect the change. After the formation of the Scottish Football League in 1890, Celtic had been forced to move with the times or be left behind. In another sense, it was sad that Walfrid's ideals were being swept under the carpet. But the club was in an unenviable sink-or-swim predicament – and realism dictated they survive by becoming businesslike.

That same year, in line with the club's new professional ethos and limited company status, Willie Maley was appointed Celtic's first secretary-manager. His achievements and importance to the evolution of the club are discussed in chapter four, but, suffice it to say, he certainly earned his status as a Celtic legend from the beginning, taking a trophy back to Celtic Park in his first three seasons.

As an interesting aside, it is worth pointing out that Maley would come to power at the tender age of just 29 at the time of one of the biggest ever shocks in Celtic – and the Scottish Cup's – history when the Scottish league champions lost 4–2 away to non-leaguers Arthurlie. As that doyen of Scottish football writers Bob Crampsey says, 'Willie Maley, who had never sat easily with defeat, was furious.' Crampsey also points out that in Maley's book, *The Story of Celtic*, published in 1939, the manager writes, 'It is no exaggeration to say this was probably the greatest sensation ever known in Scottish football.'

He had witnessed how Celtic had surrendered to Arthurlie without their key players: big-name bought-in stars who had refused to play because of a dispute over wages. Now, he would bring about a radical policy change at Celtic Park, focusing upon the development of a production line of home-grown talent for which the club would become renowned during the twentieth century. Celtic's days of relying on star players from other teams were numbered.

A year later, the club built a glass-fronted grandstand – final proof, if needed, that its central mission was changing. Its members were now establishing Celtic at the forefront of corporate hospitality – as far back as 1898.

By the turn of the century, the club was certainly well run and professionally solvent with a massive support. It had come a long way since Brother Walfrid had the idea to use it to provide basic sustenance for those suffering in Glasgow's east end. Celtic now had the base to one day become something even such a remarkable man could hardly have imagined – champions of Europe and one of the biggest, and most loved, football clubs in the world. But there would be other battles to be won before then . . .

3

....

THE HEATHENS COME

AS CELTIC owed their existence to the altruistic mission of a monk, so Manchester United prospered after the compassionate intervention of two men, Louis Rocca and John H. (Henry) Davies. Rocca was the man who came up with the name Manchester United in 1902; at one stage, the club could have ended up being called Manchester Celtic . . . now there's a thought. The son of an Italian immigrant and, like the pioneers of Celtic, a devout Catholic, Rocca would also ask the city's Catholic priests to keep an eye open for any boys who might make the grade at United. In this way, he was the instigator of a youth policy that would influence the club's rich tapestry over the next decade. He is also the man who would bring Matt Busby to the club.

Just as Celtic are indebted to the redoubtable efforts of businessman John Glass, so United would be forever grateful for the interest shown in the club by John H. Davies, the chairman of a Manchester Brewery. The story of how Davies became the club's saviour for the love of a dog is now part of United folklore and is certainly worth relaying here.

Newton Heath, United's previous incarnation, were on the verge of going bust in 1902. The club's creditors had foreclosed and the cost of the contractors working on alterations to the

Clayton ground would bankrupt it. However the FA had offered them a way out by agreeing to the reformation of the club: all that was needed was some businessmen to clear the debt of £2,670 and Heath could re-emerge in a new guise. Three businessmen each put in £500, but it was Davies who was the real knight in shining armour. He offered a similar amount, plus he took over the club, providing a further £3,000 for players, and rubber-stamped Rocca's suggested name change of Manchester United.

Davies' involvement was down to the quick thinking of the Heath skipper at the time, Harry Stafford. The captain knew Davies through the brewery trade – Stafford planned to become a publican when he hung up his boots and, as boss of the brewery Walker & Homfray, Davies was one of the men he had obviously got in touch with for a job. While quizzing Davies about employment opportunities, Stafford had mentioned the club's plight and made it clear that with investment it could be turned around and make him money. The story goes that Stafford eventually talked the businessman around to his way of thinking when they bumped into one another while Davies was walking with his daughter, Elsie, and the captain with his St Bernard, Major. It has been claimed that Davies was drawn to the pet after it came running to him, but my research suggests that it was actually Elsie who was so taken with the animal that she pleaded with her father to buy it for her. Stafford subsequently sold the dog to Davies on the condition that he took over the club.

Davies, who became club president, invested heavily in the development of Old Trafford. After it was completed in 1910, it became one of the best stadiums in England. He will forever be remembered with fondness by United fans, as it was he who secured the club's future at a time of uncertainty. During Davies' reign, the club became known as 'Moneybags United', though it was also censured by the league and FA for misleading financial statements.

Davies died in 1927, aged just sixty-three, after enduring three years of poor health. Just four years later, the club was back in financial trouble.

* * *

At this stage, let's backtrack a little and take a look at United in embryonic form as Newton Heath – after all, they played under that name for 24 years.

Newton Heath (L&YR) FC were formed in 1878 as the works team of the Lancashire and Yorkshire Railway depot on the north-east side of Manchester. The name Newton Heath has its origins in Old English and means 'the new town on the heath'. This particular heath originally stretched from Miles Platting to Failsworth and was bordered on all four sides by brooks and rivers: the River Medlock, Moston Brook, Newton Brook and Shooters Brook.

The year Heath were formed was also key in the development of association football. The game had previously been played under local rules, which meant the teams involved could decide on the format ahead of kick-off – some would allow handball, while others would not enforce the offside rules – but by 1878 a common set of laws, the basic predecessor of today's rules, had been established by the FA. Two other notable developments at this time were the formation of the Lancashire FA with 28 clubs and the following year the Lancashire Cup, which was contested by 40 teams. The attire of the players was also changing. Those who had been turning up for action in their work clothes and nailed boots were now appearing in shorts and football boots. The Heath team would soon be seen in gold-and-green half-shirts – their first kit.

I am indebted to the terrific efforts of Alan Shury and Brian Landamore, experts on all things Heath, as exemplified in their wonderful book *The Definitive Newton Heath FC*. They explain how the club was initially based on a piece of unused ground leased to the railway on the edge of a former clay pit known as North Road: 'There were no changing rooms at the ground; players walked half a mile to the local public house in the Oldham Road.'

There is no record of the first games played by the club. The first match report was in the *Bolton Daily Chronicle* on 25 January 1881:

> Bolton Wanderers (a Team) v Newton Heath, Lancashire and Yorkshire Railway. The return match of the above clubs was played on the ground of the latter on Saturday last, and, as in the previous game, ended in victory for the former by six goals to nil . . . a very pleasant and agreeable game ending in victory for the Wanderers.

Heath's first recorded players were Minchley and John Cramphorn, who scored the goals in a 2–0 victory over Bootle reserves in February 1881. Football at this amateur level was still very much a haphazard affair for teams like Heath, as Shury and Landamore point out:

> All the Newton Heath team members of this period were employed in the wagon and carriage works. They would have needed time off work to play football, so we may assume games took place in the evening or on Saturday afternoons; the Saturday half holiday was in general observance in England from the 1860s onwards.

By 1882, the club was playing in eight fixtures a season against local opposition and in 1882–83 would offer supporters their first season tickets. A year later, they entered the Lancashire Cup for the first time, though crashed out 7–2 in the first round against Blackburn Olympic at North Road. It was a crushing result, but no real disgrace, as at the time Olympic were one of the best teams around, positively outshining their town rivals

Blackburn Rovers. Indeed they became the first northern team to lift the FA Cup in 1883, when they beat Old Etonians 2–1 at the Kennington Oval.

Full-back Sam Black and centre-forward Jack Doughty were the first stars of the Newton Heath team: Black had represented the Manchester and District team against its Liverpudlian counterparts in March 1884 and Doughty had played for the Welsh national team.

In 1885, Newton Heath made their first appearance in the Lancashire Association Cup, beating Haydock Temperance 4–0 in the first round before losing 4–1 in the next to Baxenden. A year later, they were runners-up in the final to Hurst. Heath became a renowned cup team of the time, lifting their first trophy, the Manchester and District Cup, in 1886, beating Manchester 2–1 in the final at Whalley Range in front of 6,000 spectators.

The team seemed to love competing in that particular competition, reaching the final for the first time in 1885 (though losing 3–0 to Hurst) and after the 1886 triumph appearing in another five consecutive finals. They lost 2–1 to West Manchester in 1887, then regained the cup the following year with a 7–1 thrashing of Denton. Heath retained the trophy with another big victory, this time a 7–0 battering of Hooley Hill, and in 1890 kept their hands on it with a 5–2 win over Royton. In 1891, they lost 1–0 to Ardwick in the final.

Newton Heath made their debut in the FA Cup in 1886. They drew 2–2 with Fleetwood Rangers away but were thrown out of the competition after refusing to play extra-time. They next took part in the event in 1889–90, when they were thumped 6–1 by league champions Preston North End in the first round.

As Celtic evolved at a rapid rate in Scotland and Newton Heath were propelled towards their date with destiny and their transformation to Manchester United, so English football was moving forwards at pace. Professionalism was legalised in

England in 1885; the Football League was founded in 1888; goal nets and the penalty kick were introduced in 1891, while promotion and relegation were brought in two years before the turn of the century.

Newton Heath were not slow to prosper from the evolution. The club turned professional in 1885 and introduced a number of new faces in the team, many of them Welshmen who were employed in the wagon works. In 1889, the club left the Combination League and joined the Football Alliance, the Football League's second division, finishing eighth out of 12 clubs. They opened their campaign with a 4–1 home win over Sunderland.

An interesting aside to the 1890–91 season is that the final of the Manchester and District Cup took place between Heath and Ardwick. Yes, this was Manchester United against Manchester City in embryonic form! Ardwick won with the only goal of the game in front of 10,000 fans at the West Manchester ground.

A new grandstand opened at Heath's North Road home the following season, which could hold up to 1,000 spectators. It was full when Heath again took on Ardwick for an FA Cup first qualifying-round match in October 1891. More than 11,000 fans packed into the ground for a match in which Heath gained revenge for their defeat by Ardwick the previous season, recording a thrilling 5–1 triumph.

In 1891–92, the club finished as Alliance runners-up and, with the expansion of the Football League, Newton Heath were elected to the league for the following season. This meant they would need better players – with increased wages. This demanded an improved business outlook at the club and a harder edge to their development. It was decided that it would become a limited company with the loss of 'Lancashire and Yorkshire' from their name. As *Athletic News* rather solemnly declared: 'Newton Heath L&YR is no more, the latter part of the name being chopped off.'

Their first match was away at Blackburn Rovers' Ewood Park on 3 September 1892 – a fixture they lost 4–3. It was a heroic showing, as Rovers were a major force. They had won the FA Cup five times and fielded a team of internationals. Blackburn went 3–0 up but, just before half-time, the Heathens hit back with goals from Fred Donaldson and James Coupar. The goal by Donaldson was the first ever scored in the league for the team that would become Manchester United. Donaldson went on to score 16 goals in that inaugural season, including a hat-trick in the record 10–1 league win against Wolves. Again, the rather haphazard nature of their progress through the leagues to this fairly exalted stage is summed up in the Laurel and Hardy-like way in which they finally made it onto the pitch at Blackburn. *Athletic News* reported it like this:

> There was not an opening game sort of crowd on the Rovers' ground to see how the Heathens shaped in their first league match, and no wonder, for at half-past three, when the match should have started, the rain came down in torrents and continued to do so until play began, when it began clearing up. Owing to the Salford Station fire, the Newton Heath team had to journey round by Bury, which delayed the start half an hour.

Heath finished bottom of the 16 clubs in Division One in that first season with just 18 points, conceding 85 goals. The team were drawing crowds on average of around 2,500–3,000.

There was a colourful incident at the club in October 1892 when Donaldson was hit by a flying hammer. Heath had just drawn 0–0 away at West Bromwich Albion and were training midweek for a rematch with the Baggies when poor Fred was knocked cold. The *Courier* reported the incident in this rather strait-laced fashion:

> An accident of a somewhat serious nature, and which was nearly attended with fatal results, occurred yesterday at the Newton Heath football ground. While the players were undergoing a course of training, Stewart, the centre halfback, was in the act of throwing a hammer, when by some means or other it slipped from his hands, and it struck Donaldson, the centre-forward who was standing close by, on the side of his face, just below the temple, the force of the blow causing the unfortunate player to fall down insensible.

The *Courier* went on to speculate how long the hapless Donaldson would be absent from the Heath front line – yet he was back a few days later in the home fixture against West Brom and even scored Heath's opener in the 4–2 loss.

The record 10–1 win against Wolves and a 7–1 victory over Derby were the only real highlights of a tough debut campaign. Their dismal finish meant they went into a play-off against Division Two champions Small Heath, which Newton won 5–2 in a replay to secure their status in Division One.

Small Heath had lost only three matches all season to top the second division and were hot favourites to defeat the Heathens. The match was played at Stoke in front of 4,000 fans and ended in a 1–1 draw. The Football League had not worked out what would happen if it ended all-square and it was only after much deliberation that they decided the teams should replay at Sheffield the following week – a match that the Heathens strolled 5–2, thus ensuring Division One football for Manchester.

But these top-flight matches would no longer take place at North Road. Another milestone was chalked up in 1892–93, with the final home league game ever at that ground on 30 April 1893, a 3–3 draw with Accrington in front of 3,000 spectators.

North Road had initially been owned by the railways but then passed on to the Deans and Canons of Manchester. They did not agree with Newton Heath charging admission prices to games and so the club was forced out. Not that many people would miss North Road – certainly not the opposing players, who complained constantly after visiting about the swampish state of the pitch.

Heath upped sticks and moved across Manchester to a new ground on Bank Street in Clayton. It was larger, with an increased capacity, but was still far from ideal, as it was next to a chemical works that often emitted toxic fumes – another bone of contention for visiting teams. The ground had one stand running the full length of the pitch, divided into several paddocks, with a further stand behind one of the goals and a bank of terracing behind the other.

The first match at Bank Street on 2 September 1893 was against Burnley, to which an encouraging crowd of 10,000 turned out to see the Heathens triumph 3–2. But their first season there would end much the same as the last at North Road. Newton Heath once again finished bottom of Division One and faced another play-off – or test match, as they were dubbed at the time – to secure their status. They had amassed just fourteen points, with just six wins in thirty games, and their last match of the season – a 3–1 loss to Preston – saw just 4,000 spectators make the trip to Bank Street, 6,000 fewer than on that opening match with Burnley.

This time there would be no play-off reprieve. Heath were up against Liverpool, who had been formed just two years earlier and had not lost a single game in their march to the Division Two title. In the winner-takes-all fixture, held at Ewood Park in front of 6,000 fans, the Merseysiders duly took all with a 2–0 triumph, elevating themselves to the top league and condemning Heath to a return to Division Two.

There was one consolation the following season: a return to the Manchester derby matches. Heath would now take on

Manchester City. Financial troubles the previous season had led to a reorganisation of the club, with the result that Ardwick were reformed as Manchester City FC. Heath drew a then record crowd of 10,000 to Hyde Road, home of City, on 3 November 1894, with Heath running out 5–2 winners. The following January, Heath hammered them again, 4–1, in front of 12,000 spectators at Bank Street.

Scotsman John Clarkin grabbed two goals in the win at Hyde Road and another at Bank Street. They were certainly the most important, and most welcome for the fans, in his short stay at the club. The striker, who had been signed from Glasgow Thistle in July 1893, scored a total of 12 goals in 56 appearances for Newton Heath before transferring to Blackpool in 1896.

A year later, having finished third in Division Two, Newton Heath failed to return to the top flight after losing the vital play-off against Stoke at Burslem 3–0.

The 1895–96 campaign began with a five-match unbeaten run, but again hopes were dashed as results trailed off in the new year, Heath ending up fourth in Division Two.

There were further disappointments. Ground improvements had continued at Bank Street, as the club installed a new 2,000-capacity stand from Broughton Rugby Club and built new embankments. The directors believed the new set-up could host a crowd of 30,000 and were hoping for that figure when First Division Derby County arrived for an FA Cup second-round match in February 1896. They thus felt somewhat let down when a crowd numbering fewer than 10,000 actually materialised to witness Heath grind out a 1–1 draw and were positively gutted when the team crashed 5–1 in the replay.

The following season saw the Heathens soar to second place in the second division, but it would not be enough to propel them back into the big time, though a looming, brash Welshman by the colourful name of Caesar Jenkyns would make club history that season, becoming the first known player to be sent off for the Heathens/Manchester United.

The Builth-born defender, who weighed in at 14 st 4 lb, was in his first and only season with the club when he was dismissed for a series of fouls on Notts County players during Heath's 3–0 defeat at Trent Bridge on 19 December 1896. He won eight caps for Wales in his career, including one while at Newton Heath. He had joined Heath from Woolwich Arsenal, where he made his mark in their history books by becoming the club's first-ever international player. After his season at Bank Street, Jenkyns moved on to Walsall.

Heath, despite finishing runners-up in 1897, would suffer again in the play-off fixture. By now, it had been decided it should be a three-way battle, so the Heathens lined up against Division One outfits Sunderland and Burnley for a return to the top flight. Although Heath were on a £10-a-man win bonus they could not do enough to make it back to Division One, losing the deciding game 2–0 at Sunderland.

A small consolation was that they lifted the Manchester Charity Cup by beating Manchester City 5–2, with Scotsman Joe Cassidy grabbing a brace against the club he would join three years later. Cassidy is a name worth noting in the context of Manchester United and Celtic – he was the first man to leave United for Celtic and then later return. Cassidy was born in 1872 in Dalziel, Lanarkshire, and first joined Newton Heath from Blythe for the play-off against Small Heath in March 1893.

After just two months, he returned to Scotland, making twenty-eight appearances and scoring ten goals for Celtic during 1893–94 before returning to the Heathens in March 1895. He was Heath's leading scorer for four seasons before joining Manchester City in April 1900 for a fee of £100. In seven seasons with the Heathens, Joe played a total of 152 league games and scored 91 goals. He was not Heath's all-time top scorer – that accolade goes to Bob Donaldson, who totalled 122 in 252 games.

There was another big name lining up for Heath's 5–2 victory over City that day – Billy Meredith, who grabbed City's opener. He would go on to play for United and is widely recognised as Welsh football's first soccer superstar. The man known as 'the Welsh Wizard' was born at Chirk in Denbighshire in 1874. The son of a miner, he started work himself at the Black Park Colliery as a pony driver at the age of 12.

By the 1890s, he was starring for Chirk's successful first team and won his first Welsh Cup medal in 1894. Following a brief period as a semi-professional at Wrexham, then as a professional with Northwich Victoria in the second division, Meredith arrived in Manchester, signing for City in late 1894. He continued work at the colliery, however, until 1896, when City told him he had to give it up and concentrate solely on football.

From 1896 until his retirement in 1924, he remained a full-time professional, playing for both City and Manchester United. He would make over 650 league appearances, play in 53 FA Cup ties, appear for Wales 48 times and score almost 200 goals in his career. He had a successful career with City for more than ten years, winning the Second Division title twice (1899 and 1903) and captaining the team to an FA Cup final victory, until he was caught up in a scandal – in 1905, Meredith was accused of bribing an Aston Villa player to lose a match. He denied the charge, but the FA banned him for a year.

In 1907, two years after he was voted Footballer of the Year by the readers of a national newspaper, he stunned the football world by signing for City's rapidly emerging city rivals, Manchester United. His career with the Reds would last from 1907 to 1921 (including the war years). The dazzling winger – some would say a Ryan Giggs prototype – would ironically enough make his debut for United against Villa on New Year's Day and would lift the Division One championship, along with the FA Cup, while serving the club under the glory days of Ernest Mangnall.

But back in 1897 he had to make do with a runners-up medal for City in that demoralising 5–2 Manchester Charity Cup crushing by United incarnates Newton Heath. A year later, the Heathens were still unable to make it back to the top flight, this time finishing fourth in Division Two, though there was more good news in the cup competitions. Heath won the Lancashire Cup for the first time in 1898, beating Blackburn 2–1 at Goodison Park in front of a crowd of 5,000. James Collinson put Heath in front early on and secured the trophy with a second-half winner.

The *Athletic News*, in the typical stoical, stiff-upper-lip style of the era, proclaimed:

> For the first time in the history of Manchester football, Newton Heath last month won the Lancashire Cup ... Last night in order to celebrate the event, a dinner was held at the Spread Eagle Hotel, in the city, at which about 100 persons were present ... After the feast, the eleven players who took part in the final tie were presented with their gold medals awarded by the Lancashire Football Association. A smoking concert followed.

Did it indeed ... it is difficult to envisage a smoking concert following a cup final victory nowadays, given the strict continental approach employed in terms of players' health and fitness.

Defender Fred Erentz had played a sterling role in the victory, helping keep Rovers at bay, and he carved his own niche in the club's history that season by becoming the first player to earn a benefit match for loyal service. The Dundee-born footballer had joined the Heathens in June 1892 as a half-back but quickly switched to left-back. He scored nine goals in 280 appearances – a Newton Heath club record – before retiring in 1902.

Two other stalwarts of the Heath team of the late 1890s made the history books for rather more infamous antics. Henry Boyd and John Cunningham were suspended by the club after it was learned they had been knocking back too much of the hard stuff – and were in no fit state for training some days. 'If men who are paid good wages don't think it worth their while to keep themselves in condition, they are better off out of the team,' thundered the *Athletic News*. Boyd was a reliable goalscorer signed from Woolwich Arsenal, for whom he had hit 32 goals in 41 games. He signed for Heath in 1897, but his disciplinary problems led to his departure for Falkirk two years later.

John Cunningham is worth mentioning also because he had a couple of stints at Celtic. He had a trial with them in 1889 before moving on to Burnley, then signed for the Hoops full time a year later, staying for two years. He joined Heath in 1898 but, like Boyd, was shipped out the next year because of disciplinary problems.

The 1898–99 and 1899–1900 seasons saw Newton Heath again finish fourth in Division Two, with the added indignation of seeing their great rivals, Manchester City, promoted to Division One.

Financial problems were also mounting at Bank Street due to salary commitments for the best players. The need to raise cash helps explain the sale of the legendary Joe Cassidy to Manchester City in April 1900. The club organised numerous other bazaars to try to bring in further funds. It was a desperate situation to which the only solution was a takeover and a major injection of cash. Cue John H. Davies ...

Worse was to follow, however, before Davies could come to the rescue.

In 1900–01, Newton Heath finished tenth in Division Two and from an average gate of 10,000, which they had come to expect, the turnout for the final home game that season – a 1–0 win over Chesterfield – had fallen to just 1,000.

The club were caught in that vicious cycle of the footballing world: they had experienced a drop in income as attendances fell and so were unable to bring in new players to improve their performances.

The warning signs of bankruptcy, which had been gently flashing, were now blinking non-stop. The creditors were circling like vultures above Newton Heath as a first major financial crisis hit the club. On 23 January 1902, a winding-up order was issued at Ashton-under-Lyne magistrates' court and on 15 February a meeting of creditors was held at the Official Receiver's office in Manchester. The list of those owed monies included some of the club's players.

It was only on 11 April, after more twists and turns, that Harry Stafford and his four business saviours, including Davies, were able to announce that the football club would survive, much to the relief of its worried core of supporters.

That season ticked slowly away, with Heath finishing 15th but securing their final trophy, the Manchester Senior Cup, in a 2–1 victory over Manchester City in the final at City's Hyde Road ground on 26 April 1902. It would prove to be the final act but one for Newton Heath Football Club. On 28 May 1902, the last act was played out when the minutes of the Lancashire FA confirmed their approval of a name change at Bank Street, the one that had been decided by Louis Rocca a month earlier. It was the end for Newton Heath, but the beginning for Manchester United.

Yet just as Celtic began the new millennium struggling to maintain their reputation as top dogs in Scotland, so Manchester United were taking tentative steps to be the undisputed kings of English football. It would be 1908 before United won their first league championship and 1905 before Celtic regained their Scottish title crown – a gap of seven years after the 1898 triumph.

The emergence of United and the re-emergence of Celtic was down to the drive and energies of two men at the heads of the two clubs: Ernest Mangnall, the first real manager at United, from 1903 to 1912, and Willie Maley, the manager who inspired Celtic to the remarkable six-in-a-row titles from 1905 after that spell in the wilderness.

Let's now take a look at the influence and achievements of the two men – again, uncannily, recorded at similar times in the history of the clubs. First up, to Celtic Park in 1903 as Maley set about re-establishing his club as the dominant force in Scottish football.

4

WILLIE MALEY: SIX OF THE BEST

Oh, Willie Maley was his name,
He brought some great names to the game,
When he was the boss at Celtic Park.
He taught them how to play football,
He made the greatest of them all . . .

– 'The Willie Maley Song'

Willie Maley must of necessity top the poll as the
most illustrious of Scotland's sons. Is he not the maker
of the world's finest football machine – the super-
splendid, unstoppable Celtic?

– From the Glasgow Observer, *1914*

IN 1903, Celtic finally switched design from stripes to the hoops
that still grace the players' shirts today. Revolution was sweeping
through the club as the new century began. The altruistic fervour
with which Brother Walfrid had set about establishing the club
had been replaced by a new mindset: if Celtic were to not only
survive but prosper, they would need to become a powerful
business enterprise off the field as well as a success on it.

The latter was in doubt at the dawn of the twentieth century.
After their initial flurry of glory, Celtic appeared to be treading

water. Cup success was still a possibility, but the league title seemed to have drifted away from their grasp. A new saviour, however, was about to put that right. And he was already serving at the club.

William Patrick Maley would live to within 23 days of the ripe old age of 90. Without his efforts, Celtic would not be the global icon it is today. He was the first manager of the club and one of the most successful in Scottish football history, leading Celtic to 30 major trophies in 43 years.

Maley was born on 25 April 1868 in Newry Barracks, Ireland, where his father was a soldier with the British Army, but he moved to Scotland with his family while still a youngster. Willie was the third son of Thomas Maley, a sergeant in the Royal North British Fusiliers.

Willie favoured athletics, particularly running, over football in his youth, but, by 1886, he had played a few games for Cathcart Hazelbank Juniors and turned out for Third Lanark reserves later that same year. Education-wise, he was no great scholar, leaving school at the age of 13, but he was not stupid; indeed, he would train as an accountant before devoting his life to Celtic.

His moment of destiny came towards Christmas 1897, when Brother Walfrid and John Glass visited his family home. They had come to ask Willie's brother, Tom, if he would like to sign for their fledgling football team. They explained the club had not yet played a game but that they thought Tom might be interested as the team would essentially consist of Irishmen. As Tom had previously played for Edinburgh Hibernian, they hoped he would take up their offer.

Young Tom agreed, admitting that what he had not liked about Hibernian was their insistence that only Catholics could play for their club. There was no such religious bias on offer with Walfrid and Glass – the thought of helping others less fortunate also played a part in his decision.

As he was on his way out of the house, Brother Walfrid saw Willie and felt he looked left out and so invited him along too, as an afterthought. Call it compassion or a God-given instinct, whatever: it would lead to Celtic's three key men – Walfrid, Glass and Maley – being on board from the start of what would become a most remarkable, awe-inspiring adventure.

In 1888, Willie Maley was signed by Celtic as a midfielder, or right-half as his position was then known, and became one of the club's first players. He made his debut in Celtic's debut, on Monday, 28 May, at the first Celtic Park, in the match against Rangers. His accountancy skills also led him to become the first secretary-treasurer of the new club, although his initial aim was to show he could hack it as a player. He was certainly committed and keen enough to make the grade. He would say of himself: 'I was young, strong, with plenty of speed and had a happy knack of quickly absorbing advice and tuition.'

That ability to learn paid off – and quickly. Along with brother Tom, Willie played in the Scottish Cup final in the club's first year of existence, although they would end up gallant losers to Third Lanark. Willie would gain revenge and win his first major trophy as a Celtic player in the Glasgow Cup final on 14 February 1891, when they thumped Third Lanark 4–0.

A year later, he won three more medals as Celtic retained the Glasgow Cup, lifted the Glasgow Charity Cup and, most prestigious of all, the Scottish Cup, when they walloped Queen's Park 5–1. Maley and Celtic won the league championship for the first time in 1893, overcoming by one point a battling challenge by arch rivals Rangers. They retained the title a year later but lost out to Rangers in the Scottish Cup final – Maley's consolation being that he scored the Hoops' goal in their 3–1 defeat.

Willie played in Celtic's 11–1 record win over Dundee on 26 October 1895, but by this stage he was waning as a top-class player. He was at the crossroads of his career and his life, and it is said that he would have preferred to retire and concentrate on his administrative duties at the club. However, in February 1896, he made a remarkable, unusually rash decision for a man who was usually measured in his choices: he moved to England to join Manchester City on a month's trial.

Willie was like a man shuffling around in the dark, unsure about where he was going or what he should do to find the light. Inevitably, the light proved to be the pull of home: Glasgow and Celtic Football Club. He left City after playing in just one match and returned to Paradise.

He would not stay long as a player; his destiny would be to steer the club to greatness as its manager. In a decade, he had won the Scottish Cup, three league titles and two Scottish caps.

In 1897, the board of Celtic directors appointed Willie as secretary-manager of Celtic. He won the league championship for the club in his first full season in this role, one for which he earned the princely sum of £150 a year. He was also instrumental in helping put the club on a business footing, encouraging it to move forwards and prosper.

He believed the club should be run as a company, with paid officials and a board of directors, rather than at the mercy of a few volunteers. With the introduction of the Scottish Football League in 1890 and the onset of professionalism three years later, Maley had been perceptive enough to see that football was outgrowing its amateur origins – and that Celtic had to move with the times or get left behind.

On 4 March 1897, Celtic became a limited liability company and its ability to now raise capital was illustrated at the end of the year when the club bought the site of Celtic Park from its landlord for £10,000, thus becoming the first club in Scotland to own its own ground. In their excellent work on the history of the club, *Dreams, And Songs to Sing*, Tom Campbell and Pat

Woods succinctly explain the change in the club's fortunes like this:

> Opponents of the new set-up could feel more than justified in questioning the real motives of its advocates when they noted the distribution of funds in the first year of its operation. An income of £16,267 (a new record amount for Britain) resulted in a 20 per cent dividend for the shareholders and directors – but for charity, nothing. The original impulse was truly dead.

If Brother Walfrid was the founding father of the embryonic Celtic FC, then Willie Maley was the man who took the club onwards and upwards to greatness – although at the cost of some of its original ideals. But he was as much an innovator and visionary off the pitch as he was on it.

He wanted to change direction so that Celtic would rely on home-grown players rather than continue to be a buying club. In this way, he also became its pioneer of youth development; he actively encouraged a youth policy so that the club would not be forced to splash out crippling amounts on players who were more interested in money than playing for Celtic FC. Maley decided to rely almost entirely on recruiting youngsters fresh from junior football.

He ran the club like an autocrat, his influence powerful from the top to the bottom of the organisation. He demanded the respect of his young players, yet made sure he had time for them if they needed to talk through problems. Maley was not one for taking training; he watched games from the directors' box and never indulged in team talks or spoke to his players at half-time or post-match. He would not even announce the team: players learned if they were in or out by reading the line-up in the newspapers. Yet at other times, if his boys needed a reassuring arm around the shoulders, he would act as if a compassionate father. Indeed, you could argue that the way he ran the football club, as if it was his own personal fiefdom, marked him out as a prototype of the likes of Stein, Busby and Ferguson. And just as they prospered, so Maley's methods paid massive dividends for Celtic FC as the twentieth century got under way: put simply, at the time he had no equal in world football at getting the best out of his players.

His dream of a young, talented team would take shape and as the players grew together, they won together, claiming the first-ever Scottish League and Scottish Cup double. They would become arguably the best club side in the world – and the six-in-a-row record would remain unbroken until the 1970s. The stars of the team included some Celtic immortals: right-back Alec McNair, inside-right Jimmy McMenemy and legendary centre-forward Jimmy Quinn.

When they grew old, Maley would build anew, creating a Celtic that would lift four titles in succession between 1914 and 1917 and set what is still the UK record for an unbeaten run in professional football: 62 games (49 won, 13 drawn), from 13 November 1915 until 21 April 1917.

The *Glasgow Observer* summed up Maley's managerial skills – and how well he performed the balancing act of being both boss and supporter of the young men in his charge – stating:

> He is at once a chum and a guide to the young player; he is 'Mr Maley' and 'Willie' at the same time. He has the happy knack of gaining the confidence and respect of every man on the wage-list, and knows full well how to draw the line between undue familiarity and rigid aloofness. It is this feeling of comradeship between players and manager that has enabled the club to stand where it does and, so long as this spirit remains, success will follow.

In 1899 Maley had led his team to the Scottish Cup, a trophy they retained the following year. But there would follow a four-year drought as Maley reconstructed his team: a period of transition and disappointment for the expectant hordes at Celtic Park.

The wilderness years came to an end in 1904. In the decade up to 1903, both Glasgow giants had won four league championships, with two Scottish Cups going to Celtic Park and four to Ibrox. The battleground between the two clubs that would dominate Scottish football to the present day was being drawn. The phrase 'the Old Firm' originates in that 1904 cup final from a cartoon in the pages of the sports paper, *The Scottish Referee*. It showed a man wearing a sandwich board bearing the now immortal slogan: 'Patronise the Old Firm – Rangers, Celtic Ltd.'

That year, Celtic came out on top in a thrilling match at Hampden Park, the first cup final to be played at the enlarged venue, with a team that had changed dramatically; the youthful side contained only 30-year-old Willie Orr from the Hoops teams of the previous century.

The match would mark the true beginning of the story of the legendary Jimmy Quinn, the man who won the cup for the Bhoys that brave day. Aged 25, and by no means a regular in the side, he came, he saw and he conquered – with a magnificent hat-trick that ripped the heart out of a talented Rangers outfit. The Ibrox men had soared into a 2–0 lead only for Quinn to net twice and take Celtic in level at the interval. With just ten minutes remaining in the second half, he dribbled past three men and slotted home the winner. It was the first hat-trick ever in a Scottish Cup final and brought his club its first trophy of those four depressing, barren years. When describing his winning goal and the effect it would have on the club, Quinn recalled: '. . . a dash right through the Rangers defence . . . finishing with a real trimmer which brought us our first Scottish badges and the confidence which made our team for the next six years'.

Authors Campbell and Woods brilliantly sum up the start of the great man's iconic stint at Parkhead:

The legend of Jimmy Quinn had begun. His courage, his physical commitment and pace, his shooting power: combined, these attributes would make him the most feared centre in British football. Destined to be the most prominent figure in a glorious epoch for the club, his likeness would be painted in bright colours on five-foot-square cloth banners, embroidered with cord of golden thread and displayed with pride by brake clubs en route to matches.

Ironically, Rangers had paved the way for the record-breaking Quinn's big entrance on the major stage. Alec Bennett was the usual number 9, but, as the Gers had been trying desperately to sign him, Maley left him out of the final thinking his head might not be right. Again Maley had proved a master with his managerial skills – both with his confidence in throwing Quinn in at the deep end and in the way he stood by his belief in youth. His young team had cost just £200 – paid to junior clubs – to put together.

Maley had a vision of the team he wanted to build and how they would function, and he was a man who would not take no for an answer; Quinn is an example of how the manager would get what he wanted against the odds. The big man had been playing for Smithston Albion and was initially not interested in playing for the Hoops when he was approached. He felt the life of a professional footballer was a precarious one financially and, being a small-town boy, he did not fancy living in Glasgow. Maley kept up his persuasion tactics, continuing to watch Quinn play and nagging him, and was eventually rewarded for his perseverance when the player signed pro forms in 1901.

It was Maley, in a move that pre-empted Arsène Wenger's redeployment of Thierry Henry from peripheral winger to striking superstar almost a century later, who decided that Quinn should be transformed from a left-winger into a centre-forward, giving him shape and dynamic power.

Maley signed another talented young man by the name of David Hamilton to serve him in the Ryan Giggs role and also drafted in James McMenemy. McMenemy would be one of Maley's best signings; he has certainly gone down in history as a Hoops great. He made his debut for Celtic in a 3–0 victory over Port Glasgow on 22 November 1902, scoring in that match. Between then and 1919, he made 515 appearances and scored 168 goals. He played his part in the 1904 Scottish Cup triumph and would be a vital component of Maley's fine team.

Slightly built but difficult to dislodge once he had the ball, he had great vision and was a master strategist, nicknamed 'Napoleon' by grateful fans and teammates. McMenemy would win eleven league championship titles and six Scottish Cup medals before the First World War intervened. He left the club in 1920 but would return in 1934, when, for six years, he was the trainer/coach at Celtic Park. He also played for Partick Thistle between 1920 and 1922 and won the Scottish Cup with them in 1921. McMenemy, the great uncle of Lawrie McMenemy, who managed Southampton and was at one time No. 2 to England manager Graham Taylor, also played twelve times for Scotland, scoring five goals.

If the 1904 cup win had given Maley hope he was on the right track with his babes, the following year and the next five after that would prove it without any doubt, as his brilliant team won the league championship six times on the trot. The first came in 1905 and was their first title since 1898. In that 1904–05 season, Celtic had finished level on points with arch rivals Rangers at the end of the 26-game campaign. Rangers' goal difference was far superior, but that was not taken into account at the time. It was decided a play-off match would be the most suitable solution, so on 6 May 1905 Celtic beat the Gers 2–1 in a hard-fought battle at Hampden to secure the crown, with goals from Hamilton and McMenemy.

Rangers had taken the spoils in a controversial Scottish Cup semi-final at Celtic Park two months earlier, one in which Quinn was again a central figure. It was a match that would go down in history with the unenviable tag of being the first at which there was known crowd trouble. Quinn was sent off by referee Tom Robertson after just eight minutes for allegedly kicking out at Rangers' Alec Craig and his dismissal led to fans twice invading the pitch. The second time, Robertson abandoned the match – and Celtic, down by two goals, would later concede the tie.

It left a bitter taste in the mouth for the Hoops, but resentment would soon give way to unqualified joy, as the team went on to even greater glory – with inspiring skipper Jimmy Hay leading his men to the title in 1906 and then to Scotland's first-ever double in 1907.

Hay would also become a Scotland great, captaining the national side, but with Celtic he won six league titles and three Scottish Cups. As a left-half, he had it all and won it all. In 1911, he moved to Newcastle for £1,250, spending eight fine years there before joining Ayr United.

Hay and his teammates completed that first double with an emphatic 3–0 win over holders Hearts in the Scottish Cup final. This time Quinn was not the man who stole the glory, the goals instead coming from a Willie Orr penalty and a brace from Peter Somers.

The following season, Celtic notched up a second successive double, this time crushing hapless St Mirren 5–1 in the cup final. A week after the final, Celtic clinched their fourth successive league crown by beating Rangers 1–0, with Alec Bennett scoring the decisive goal. That 1907–08 season would go down in history as one of the best – certainly one of the most successful – in the club's garlanded history. It would be almost 60 years before the club lifted every trophy put before them again.

Celtic won the Glasgow Cup in October 1907, beating

Rangers after three attempts, and their quadruple was finally achieved on 30 May, when Celtic walked over Queen's Park 3–0 in the cup final. Maley had guaranteed his place in the club's history books and a spot forever in the hearts of the fans, thanks to the exploits of his thrilling, all-conquering team of babes and more experienced old hands.

Celtic also fared well when they played English and continental teams and, with some justification, Maley would in the summer of 1908 claim he was the manager of the best club side in the world.

By then, one member of that outstanding team had already left Celtic Park: the talented Alec Bennett, who had been left out of the 1904 Scottish Cup final. Bennett joined Rangers after four years of intrigue and angst on both sides of Glasgow; it was a dream move for Bennett, a Rangers fan, and Maley would not stand in his way – he had blocked his path four years previously but was a proud man who believed players should want to play for Celtic Football Club and not need persuading over and over again.

The following year brought a fifth league title in a row, but also controversy and disappointment in the Scottish Cup. There was to be another Old Firm confrontation on 10 April that year, ending 2–2. The Bhoys had been 2–1 down with just ten minutes left when Bennett's short-term replacement, Dan Munro, crossed and Gers keeper, Henry Rennie, fumbled the ball over his own line. His blunder took the tie to a replay, which also finished all-square at 1–1, Quinn scoring his third goal of the final for Celtic. The crowd had grown restless and angry when the expected period of extra-time did not materialise; there were cries of 'fix', the implication being that the Old Firm clubs had stage-managed another draw, wanting to cash in with a lucrative third tie (the first two matches had been watched by crowds of 70,000 and 60,000). Spectators surged onto the pitch to voice their discontent. Violence ensued, as the police charged with batons drawn, assisted by mounted officers.

The rioters uprooted the goals, cut up the turf and set fire to the pay-boxes and other buildings. Barricades were torn down and a bonfire was started, with whisky being used to keep the blaze going. At least 100 people, mostly police and firemen, were injured. A correspondent wrote in the *Glasgow Evening Times*, 'I would suggest the withdrawal of all policemen from football matches, and substitute a regiment of soldiers with fixed bayonets.'

The London-based *Pall Mall Gazette* suggested that military training rather than military intervention was the solution:

> Saturday's display of savagery shows what a mockery it is to drag the word sportsmanship into such an atmosphere. The football craze is one of the most active deleterious influences to which the character of the masses is now subjected, and we cannot too soon set about counteracting it with the wholesome discipline of military training.

The cup and medals were withheld after both clubs petitioned the Scottish FA to abandon the tie. There were no winners in the Scottish Cup that year – and for Celtic the disappointment was particularly heavy: if they had won the cup, it would have marked their third consecutive double. They, like Rangers, also had to pay £150 to Queen's Park for the damage to Hampden.

Celtic did at least have the consolation of a fifth league crown in a row. Because of fixture congestion, they had played eight league games in twelve days and went on to pip Dundee for the title by a point. Those matches included a final three away from home, on three successive days, at the end of April. They won the first, beating Queen's Park 5–1 at Cathkin (the damage at Hampden had meant an alternative venue had to be found), then lost the second 1–0 at Hibernian, but finally won the vital third 2–1 at Hamilton Academical. McMenemy and Hamilton scored the goals that won the league, ensuring the Hoops finished on 51 points.

The club's sixth consecutive crown was won in 1910, when Celtic finished two points ahead of runners-up Falkirk. It was the end of a glorious era – as Graham McColl and George Sheridan sum up in their excellent *The Essential History of Celtic*:

> It proved to be the end of the most glorious run of championships that British football had yet seen and in 1911 Celtic were presented with a special shield from their fellow First Division clubs to commemorate their winning six titles in a row.

David W. Potter, author of the revelatory *Willie Maley: The Man Who Made Celtic*, makes the telling point that the end of Celtic's six-year domination also mirrored the conclusion of an historical epoch, with the death of the British King: 'Somehow, it was fitting that the monarch, Edward VII, should die on 6 May 1910, a matter of days after Celtic won the Championship. Maley's great team have been called the "Edwardian Celts" and it seemed to personify that era.'

The six-in-a-row record would last for 60 years – and it would take another magnificent team to grab it. Maley had no time to bask in the glory he had brought to the club, however; no, once again he was forced to show his skills as a manager as a period of relative decline – in terms of title wins, at least – set in at Celtic Park.

Key players followed Alec Bennett out of the Celtic Park exit door, including Peter Somers, who was allowed to leave to join Hamilton in 1910. But the biggest loss was skipper Jimmy Hay. He had cost Celtic only £50 when he had joined from Glossop nine years earlier and left the Hoops with a £1,200 transfer profit when he moved to St James' Park, though the club also had to deal with the loss of his inspirational skills and captaincy.

Celtic lost their grip on the league crown in 1910–11 and 1911–

12, although there would be consolation with two successive Scottish Cup triumphs. In 1911, they beat Hamilton 2–0 in a replayed final and the following year overcame Clyde, again with a scoreline of 2–0. These victories were merely papering over the cracks, though, and by 1913 the decline was obvious: for the first time in a decade, Celtic ended the season trophy-less. Maley at least had the consolation of being awarded the sum of 300 guineas as an honorarium for his contribution to the development of Celtic FC, it being the club's silver jubilee year. Maley made a thank-you speech, saying, 'Working for Celtic is a labour of love . . . the club is part of my existence . . .'

But Maley knew the era of his first great team was over and quickly set about rebuilding – again, on a shoestring. Young Patsy Gallacher had made his first-team debut against St Mirren at Parkhead in November 1911 and within two years had become a key performer for the club. A magical inside-right, he would provide the skill and spark to light up Celtic's play over the next decade. He was their creative fulcrum and a fine marksman.

The likeable Irishman was born in the Donegal town of Ramelton, where he started to play football from the age of eight. As a schoolboy, his first team was that of Holy Redeemer Primary School. Patsy had to organise the team, acting as captain and secretary, because every teacher in the school was female and showed little interest in the sport. He then joined Benvue, a team in the Clean Speech League, moving on to the juvenile side Renfrew St James, then Clydebank Juniors. The scouts could see he had talent but were worried he may not have the physical strength to make it as a pro. Those doubts were eliminated when, during his trial period with the Hoops, he scored twice in a 6–1 defeat of Dumfries and three times in a 5–0 win against an Army XI.

Full proof of his talent would come in that 1912 cup final, when he scored the second goal in the 2–0 win over Clyde. Patsy had come home for good; he would become a Celtic legend, starring for 15 years, from 1911 to 1926, and featuring in 569 games in all competitions. In 464 games in major competitions, Patsy scored 192 goals. He ranks as Celtic's sixth-highest goalscorer behind Jimmy McGrory, Bobby Lennox, Henrik Larsson, Stevie Chalmers and Jimmy Quinn.

Patsy Gallacher was one of the men who would breathe new fire into Maley's fading great team, which had slipped to fifth place in the league in 1910–11. At Celtic, he would go on to win seven league championships, four Scottish Cups, four Glasgow Cups and eleven Glasgow Charity Cups.

Maley would build from the back as he set about assembling his second great side around the dazzling skills of Gallacher. In May 1913, he brought in goalkeeper Charlie Shaw from Queen's Park. Only 5 ft 6 in. tall, to some critics he appeared a gamble, but he was confident in goal and would serve the club for 12 seasons. Shaw would form a solid defensive shield with his two full-backs, Alec McNair and Joe Dodds. Maley, looking back on the triangular partnership for the *Weekly News* in 1936, paid tribute in this way: 'Shaw, McNair and Dodds understood one another so well that they developed the back-pass into a scientific move of which there have been many imitators but none equal to the originators.'

James Young took over from the departed Hay as skipper and within a year of winning nothing in 1913 the Bhoys were back in the glory business. The backline conceded just 14 goals in 38 league matches in the 1913–14 season: they were the bedrock upon which the club's third double success was achieved. Celtic finished the campaign six points ahead of nearest rivals Rangers and hammered Hibernian 4–1 in a replayed Scottish Cup final. And, yes, Maley did finally find a replacement for the seemingly irreplaceable Jimmy Quinn, who was coming to the end of his career.

Maley had hoped that Londoner Ebenezer Owers could be the man, but he ruled himself out of the running by missing a stack of easy chances in the drawn Scottish Cup final against Hibs at Ibrox in 1914. In the replay, Maley dropped Owers and gambled on the pint-sized Jimmy McColl to deliver the goals. The Glaswegian-born striker, who had signed from the city's junior side, St Anthony's, did not let him down, scoring two goals in the opening ten minutes to put the Hoops in control of the match. The man who became known as 'The Sniper', due to his penchant for squeezing the goals trigger whenever he was in the box, would become the club's first-choice centre-forward as they romped to four more league titles.

The turnaround from transitional hopefuls – no league title since 1910, no trophy at all in 1913, and with it the fear of further decline – to a second great team in 1914 is testament to the brilliance of Willie Maley, the manager. The 1913–14 season was wrapped up with the winning of the Glasgow Charity Cup, as Celtic thrashed Third Lanark 6–0.

It seemed nothing could stop Maley and his brilliant new team from dominating Scottish football for years to come – but the dark days of the First World War would inevitably cloud their successes over the next four years, during which they won the Glasgow Cup (1915 and 1916) and the Charity Cup (1915–18).

Maley volunteered to serve in the war but was turned down – much to his chagrin – because he was too old. Author Tom Campbell succinctly sums up Maley's and Celtic's status as war broke out:

> Maley, in his mid-40s during the war years, was at the height of his powers as a manager, although chafing at being rejected for military service. He had served the club for more than a quarter of a century as player, secretary and manager . . . Celtic's domination of the Scottish game spilled over into wartime.

Players were drafted in to the war effort after hostilities broke out late in 1914 and as a result the Scottish Cup was suspended. League football continued, however, and Maley's men took four titles in succession, from 1914 to 1917 – with a record-winning margin in Scottish football of 11 points clear of runners-up Rangers in 1915–16. But it was hard to celebrate with men serving and dying in the armed forces.

Seven players associated with Celtic FC perished: Patrick Slavin, Leigh Roose, Donnie McLeod, Archie McMillan, Robert Craig, John McLaughlin and Peter Johnstone. Johnstone, who played 223 times for the club, died at the Battle of Arras on Wednesday, 16 May 1917. Aged 28, Peter had joined the 6th Battalion of the Seaforth Highlanders as a private to get into the action quicker. He was involved in very heavy fighting while his battalion attempted to capture a chemical works. His name is inscribed on the Arras Memorial to the missing, his body never having been recovered.

Robert Craig was the last Celt of the seven to die in the conflict; he passed away on Friday, 19 April 1918. His Celtic career spanned 1906–9, during which he appeared 13 times as full-back. Robert was a private in the 5th Battalion of the South Wales Borderers (SWB) and was wounded on 11 April as the Germans recaptured the Belgian town of Messines. He died in hospital eight days later.

Two players, Joe Dodds and Jimmy McMenemy, would each lose a brother in the Battle of Loos in 1915. Another player, Willie Angus, who signed for the club in 1911 and played for the team during seasons 1912–13 and 1913–14, became the first-ever Scottish Territorial soldier to win the Victoria Cross. Then aged 27 and a lance corporal with The Highland Light Infantry, he won his VC on 12 June 1915 at Givenchy for an act of true heroism. Willie lost an eye, damaged a foot and was wounded 40 times as he successfully rescued Lt James Martin, a fellow native of his home town of Carluke, who was lying injured a couple of feet from the German front lines.

Other Celtic staff played their part in the war effort. Gallacher worked in the shipyards, Dodds in munitions, and director John Shaughnessy was colonel of the Glasgow Citizen Training Force. Maley himself would suffer from depression and melancholy as the war dragged on. He was devastated by the death of Peter Johnstone and by the news that his own son, Charlie, had been hospitalised in London with war wounds from front-line action in France. His grief deepened when his eldest brother, also called Charlie, and a priest, died of a heart attack in Ayr in 1917, at just 58 years old.

By the end of the First World War, Celtic were still the team to beat. But soon Maley would face a more stringent challenge from city rivals Rangers as the Old Firm duelled for supremacy in the 1920s. It was a gauntlet that Maley would, of course, pick up and accept with relish. A new era that he would, as always, try to adapt to with his customary zeal and attention to detail. He was still Mr Celtic as the '20s loomed – just as ten years earlier and two hundred miles to the south Ernest Mangnall was ready and willing to take on the mantle of Mr Manchester United. Like Maley at Celtic, he would build United's first great football team.

5

ERNEST MANGNALL: THE FIRST GREAT RED

WHILE WILLIE Maley was producing his six-in-a-row title team in the first decade of the twentieth century, so excitement was brewing at the newly formed Manchester United. Within eight years of the new century, from the depths of despair and the no-man's land of Newton Heath, United would rise to glory, winning their first top-flight championship. It was essentially down to the backroom efforts of three men, the already mentioned John H. Davies and Louis Rocca and the man upon whom we will now shine the spotlight, Ernie Mangnall.

Like Maley at Celtic, he was the first real manager of his club and, again like Maley, he was also the first *great* manager of the club. Both Celtic and United were progressing at a rate and would quickly mirror the other's success on a road that would lead them to become major footballing forces – and legends – within their respective countries.

In 1903, as we have noted, Celtic changed their strip from stripes to the now world-famous hoops; similarly, the previous year Davies had decided that the old green and gold colours should be abandoned for the red and white that United are now universally associated with. On 30 September 1903, Mangnall arrived at Bank Street – which, with the aid of a Davies cash injection of £4,000, had been dramatically improved with a new covered stand, providing accommodation for 8,000 fans. He was a man who was going places – and in Davies, Rocca and Manchester United, he found kindred spirits.

He was the third man to lead the club, but the first to be classed as manager of the football team. A.H. Albut had been the first full-time secretary of Newton Heath in 1892 and had remained in that position until James West took over in 1900. West was the man who had overseen the collapse of Newton Heath and its rebirth as Manchester United FC on 28 April 1902.

Mangnall was appointed by United after the president, Davies, had noted the work he had done at Burnley FC. It was there that he had nurtured his reputation as a man who could turn a football club around. Like Maley at Celtic, Mangnall had done a fine job unearthing young talent with the Clarets. This certainly appealed to Davies and Rocca, who were keen that United develop their own youngsters in the future. Mangnall had joined Burnley in 1899 after previously working at Bolton Wanderers as a director and then secretary. He had helped Burnley through one of the biggest financial crises in their history; at one point, he was the only member of staff not being paid. He even had to mow the pitch in an effort to cut back on expenses.

Mangnall was born in Belmont, near Bolton, in 1866, the son of Joseph and Anne, and he was a keen fan of the Wanderers while growing up. Ernie was educated at Bolton Grammar School and played inside-right for the school football team, then for the Old Boys. A versatile footballer, he also played in goal for the Lancashire county team. Mangnall's main hobby was cycling; in later life, he would often regale United players and fans with the story of how in his youth he cycled from Land's End to John O'Groats. Some days he would even ride to Bank Street, and then to Old Trafford, on his beloved cycle.

Mangnall would take United to promotion and in 1906 back to the promised land of the First Division. He would preside over six glorious years, during which they would win two league titles (1908 and 1911) and the FA Cup (1909). Then in 1912, in a move that would shake the Red Devils to the core, Mangnall would desert ship to join local rivals Manchester City, where he would stay for the next 12 years before becoming a director with his first love, Bolton. The league crown of 1911 would be United's last for 41 years – until the magic of Matt Busby started to work new wonders.

Soon after his appointment at Bank Street in the autumn of 1903, Mangnall swiftly busied himself with constructing a team of which United could be proud. Like Maley, he was a deep thinker and a man keen on building from the back. Within a year, he had brought in goalkeeper Harry Moger and fashioned a brilliant half-back line-up of 'Captain Marvel' Charlie Roberts, Dick Duckworth and Alex Bell.

United finished third in the Second Division that season, Mangnall's first, and again in 1904–05. The following season would go down as a vital turning point in the early life of Manchester United: the year when they finally made it back to the big time. The half-back line played a major part in the achievement, as United reached the quarter-finals of the FA Cup – in the process notching up a magnificent victory over a then mighty Aston Villa. Villa had won the league championship in 1894, 1896, 1897, 1899 and 1900, and the FA Cup in 1887, 1895, 1897 and 1905. They were hot favourites to beat Second Division United, but in front of a record crowd at Bank Street of 40,000 (gate receipts were £1,460) United thumped them 5–1. The Red Devils then crashed out 3–2 to Woolwich Arsenal, but this result would pale into insignificance when United finished runners-up in the Second Division by beating Leeds City 3–1 and Burton United 6–0. Twelve years after being relegated to the Second Division as Newton Heath, United had reclaimed their place in the top flight. The team had scored ninety goals and lost just four in thirty-eight matches in a momentous campaign.

Mangnall was rewarded with a salary rise of £1 per week. To celebrate his good fortune, Mangnall signed Billy Meredith from rivals Manchester City on 1 January 1907. As we have seen already, 'the Welsh Wizard' had been implicated in a bribery scandal at City and was due to be auctioned, along with 17 other players. Mangnall made his move early and acquired Meredith's signature before the bidding began. Canny Mangnall took another three stars from City: forwards Jimmy Bannister and Alex 'Sandy' Turnbull, and England defender Herbert Burgess.

It would prove to be an inspired piece of business by the United boss. Burgess stiffened an already impressive defence, as United finished eighth in their first season back in the big time, and Meredith set up goals galore for Sandy Turnbull in 1907–08, when United won the league title for the first time in their history. Meredith and Charlie Roberts were United's key men; at the time, many people considered the duo to be the most talented players in Britain.

United had begun their championship-winning campaign in style, with a 4–1 win over Aston Villa and a 4–0 triumph against Liverpool, and by the end of it were finally on the footballing map. Another important change occurred in 1907, this time a backroom one, involving Louis Rocca's role at the club. He was United's man of many talents during a lifetime association, his stretch at United beginning in 1898, when he was signed as a junior player with the Heathens. He never made the first team but appeared in some friendlies. He would remain a registered player with the club as a part-time pro until his retirement in 1907 for a scouting role. The legendary Rocca also worked as a teaboy from 1898 until 1907 and had been there at the very start of the new club with Davies. As we know, he came up with the name Manchester United.

It was as a scout that he truly excelled, from 1907 bringing some fine young talents to Old Trafford for bargain prices. In 1945, he created a further legacy at the club when he encouraged Matt Busby to leave Liverpool and become manager of United.

After lifting their first-ever league crown, United played in the inaugural Charity Shield in 1908, also lifting that trophy, as they overwhelmed FA Cup winners QPR 4–0. The emerging team had toured central and eastern Europe a month earlier, playing in front of the biggest-ever crowd in Hungary, when they defeated Ferencváros 7–0 in Budapest.

Mangnall took United to their third trophy under his stewardship in 1908–09: their first FA Cup, as they beat Bristol City 1–0 in the final at Crystal Palace, thanks to Sandy Turnbull's winner.

It had been a long road to the Palace, starting with a 1–0 home win against Southern League Brighton 1–0. The draw favoured them again in the second round, with another home tie. This time they saw off the challenge of Everton, again by a 1–0 scoreline. Then Blackburn were hammered 6–1 at Bank Street. In the quarter-finals, they looked as if they were going out in a tough tie at Burnley, but fortune favoured Mangnall's braves – a snow storm halted the match with United one goal down. In the replay, they won 3–2. They were drawn against Newcastle United in the next round, a solitary goal settling the Manchester team's first FA Cup semi-final appearance – from prolific marksman Harold Halse – and United were through to the final. Newcastle were a fine team at the time and it was a great victory for Mangnall, although the Toon would still gain revenge by taking the league title from the Red Devils.

The United team arrived at Manchester's central station the following day and were stunned to be welcomed home by 300,000 fans. The victory procession continued to the club's ground in Bank Street, where another 30,000 fans had been awaiting their arrival for four hours. The legend that would become England's greatest football club had truly started to take shape.

There was, however, a little controversy over the trophy itself. United had a duplicate of it made, but the FA said they had acted without their consent and so a newly designed cup was made. Even greater controversy loomed.

Four months after lifting the FA Cup, the United team was suspended by the FA for refusing to renounce the trade union they had helped form. Every professional player in the country had initially joined the union, but, after pressure from the FA, all had dropped out, with just the United team left. The players were dubbed 'Outcasts FC' for their stance – but then players from other teams rejoined the union, admitting their admiration for the stance of the United boys. This led to an eventual climbdown by the FA: the Manchester players' stubbornness ensured the survival of the union that thrives in modern-day English football. Charlie Roberts had played a significant role in the rebellion and is today recognised as one of the founders of the Players' Union; indeed, he was its chairman until September 1921. The pressures of taking on the FA certainly hit United's hopes of winning the league again – that year, they finished 13th.

By 1910, United were becoming major players both on and off the pitch. Davies' money helped pay for a new stadium for the club, in Trafford Park, in the Stretford area of Manchester. The United president had decided that his club's Bank Street ground was too hemmed in to satisfy his and the club's ambitions. United played their last game at Clayton on 10 January 1910, defeating Spurs 5–0. The Bank Street stadium was sold to Manchester Corporation for £5,000.

The new ground, named Old Trafford, had an 80,000 capacity and excellent facilities for both players and spectators. *The Sporting Chronicle* paid tribute on its opening day, 19 February 1910:

> The most handsomest, the most spacious and the most remarkable arena I have ever seen. As a football ground it is unrivalled in the world, it is an honour to Manchester and the home of a team who can do wonders when they are so disposed.

The first game to be played at Old Trafford that February day was against Liverpool, though the script did not run to plan, United losing 4–3 after being 3–1 ahead at one stage – but they would not lose again at the new ground for another 20 months. Two days previous to the Liverpool opener, the old wooden stand at Bank Street had been blown down by strong winds – a providential sign to some that United had got out just in time and that Davies was vindicated in the big-money move.

The stadium had taken a year to build and had cost £60,000 – a massive sum at the time. It had terraces on three sides, costing fans sixpence a time to stand, with a seated main south stand undercover, which would set you back up to five shillings per seat. The original Old Trafford owed its design to the famed Scottish architect Archibald Leitch, who had also designed stands at Hampden Park, Ibrox and White Hart Lane.

The 1939 FA Cup semi-final between Wolves and Grimsby would draw a record attendance of 76,962 (a record which stands to the present day) at what would one day become known as 'the Theatre of Dreams', a phrase coined by Sir Bobby Charlton.

United finished fifth the season they moved into Old Trafford but marked their first full season in their new home by lifting another league title in 1911. This was to be their last major honour for many years. Some pundits believe Mangnall's final success was achieved with a side arguably as talented as the great Celtic team of the day, built in the same era by Willie Maley. They lifted the title, finishing one point ahead of Aston Villa, losing eight and drawing eight of their thirty-eight matches, at the same time scoring seventy-two goals.

Yet what should have been the start of a glittering era of success for the Red Devils ended in disaster. By August 1912, Mangnall had gone to Manchester City and a period of decline had set in. The manager's decision to quit appears to have been off-the-cuff – only days before leaving, he had turned down a £1,500 bid from City for his United captain Charlie Roberts. Surely, if he had known for certain he was going, he would have been glad of Roberts to lead an advance party? After an emergency meeting of the board at Old Trafford, it was decided that Mangnall's mind could not be changed and he left with their blessings.

Eighteen months after Mangnall walked out of Old Trafford, City were top of Division One while United were struggling at the bottom. Later, some pundits would argue that Mangnall's desertion was karmic retribution – after United had nipped in and pinched four of City's best players while they were suffering from the fallout of the bribery scandal in 1906–07. Whichever way you see it, it is certainly a measure of Mangnall's talent and influence on the club that it was not until Matt Busby took over that Manchester United began to re-emerge as a force in English football.

No one could have guessed at such an outcome as United lined up against Swindon Town for the traditional Charity Shield season opener in August 1911. As newly crowned champions, United were full of optimism; and it seemed well founded, as they demolished the Southern League winners 8–4 at Stamford Bridge. Harold Halse, the man whose goal sent United into the FA Cup final of 1909, was again their hero, scoring six of United's eight goals. The Londoner had joined United in 1908 in a £350 transfer from Southend. He had scored a remarkable two hundred goals for Southend in just two seasons and would earn FA Cup-winner's medals with United and Aston Villa and a runners-up medal with Chelsea in the same competition. Small and slight, Halse was capped once by England.

After Mangnall's departure, United suffered a crisis of confidence: that 1911–12 season saw them finish 13th in the league, with more defeats (14) than wins (13). The following campaign – under new manager John Bentley – would finish with United in a respectable fourth.

But at the end of that season, a year to the day almost after Mangnall had quit for City, United were again shaken by an outgoing transfer. This time it was inspirational skipper Charlie Roberts, who was allowed to leave in August 1913 to join Oldham Athletic for a fee of £1,750. It was indicative of the new era at United: the manager and skipper had gone and the team was breaking up. The sacrifice of the captain was part of a cost-cutting exercise; even Davies' pockets had limits and he was still lumbered with a huge debt for the development of the new stadium.

Roberts' departure left the fans distraught. He was one of the first heroes of the terraces: an early version of Roy Keane, a rebel without a pause who would do anything for Manchester United. Also like Keane, he did it his way or no way. He wore his shorts short at a time when the FA had ruled all shorts must cover the knee, and he was unstoppable when he got running. He was sturdily built and extremely fast; it was claimed Roberts could run 100 yards in 11 seconds. The centre-half had given the Red Devils magnificent service for nine seasons and his authority at the back and within the team would be greatly missed. His departure certainly contributed to their imminent decline.

He had appeared in 302 senior games for the club, scoring 23 goals. He was capped only three times by England; some critics argued he deserved many more caps but paid the price for his pivotal role in the Outcasts FC crisis. It was undoubtedly England's loss: Vittorio Pozzo, who became the Italian national team coach, was a huge fan of Roberts and later in his life publicly admitted he had built his team in the image of the Roberts he had witnessed play while on a fact-finding mission to England in the early 1900s. Pozzo knew what he was talking about – he has the distinction of being the only coach to win the World Cup twice, taking Italy to glory at home in 1934 and defending the title in France four years later.

Further proof of Roberts' worth, and United's folly in letting him go, came swiftly once he had been edged out of Old Trafford: he led Oldham to their highest-ever league position, Division One runners-up to Everton in the 1914–15 season. That same season, United, without Roberts, were battling relegation.

Roberts would go on to manage the Latics from January 1921 to December 1922 and then earn a crust as a tobacconist until his death in 1939, famously creating a cigar called the Ducrobel, in honour of the brilliant half-back line of Duckworth, Roberts and Bell.

New manager John Bentley could hardly be blamed for the exit of Roberts; his hands were tied, to an extent, as Davies tried to bring in some urgently needed cash. Indeed, Bentley's first season offered promise, with that fourth-position finish. Though it would not last and he would be gone by December 1914, as United lurched unsteadily onwards, like a floundering ship heading for the rocks.

Bentley had lost out to Mangnall for the City job, but his disappointment had been eased in replacing Ernie at Old Trafford, though he knew he was on a hiding to nothing if he did not bring success similar to Mangnall's – and quickly. United had become a monster of a club, similar to Celtic in Scotland, with their success, their magnificent ground and the demands of their growing army of fans.

Yet in many ways Bentley was a strange choice as Mangnall's successor. His previous employment record hardly singled him out as a potentially brilliant football team manager; rather it pointed to him as being more adept in an administrative role. Let's take a look . . .

James John Bentley was born in Turton, near to Mangnall's beloved Bolton, in June 1860. He was skipper of his town team by the age of 20 and went on to become secretary and treasurer of the club. Bentley also earned several county caps but gave up playing at the age of 25 to become a collector of income tax in Bolton. His love for football remained and, by 1895, he had become the chairman of Bolton Wanderers. He left the club two years later.

By 1903, he was at Manchester United and chairing meetings of the board of directors. Within four years, he held ten ordinary shares in the club and was also controller of the Lancashire FA. He also served on the committee of the Football League, 1888–93 and 1910–12.

They were top admin roles, but did they qualify him to manage a football team? Manchester City did not think so – they had plumped for Mangnall to take their team onwards and upwards. Yet United decided he should be given a chance. It appears Davies was swayed by the service he had given the club in his admin duties. Also, Bentley had been the man who had recommended that Mangnall should succeed James West as secretary-manager. Surely that suggested he was a man who knew his football?

Initially, he appeared an inspired choice, but soon the club were involved in a relegation scrap, eventually finishing 14th – and Davies quickly realised he had dropped a clanger. Bentley was replaced as manager by John Robson on 28 December 1914 but did not leave the club; instead, he reverted to the admin side of things he knew best, resuming his previous role as club secretary.

Robson would stay with the club for seven years. To be fair, it was a tricky time to manage Manchester United, what with the onset of the First World War in August 1914 and taking command when the club's fortunes on the pitch were already declining after the glory years of Mangnall.

Robson had started his career at Middlesbrough, first as a goalkeeper, then graduating to secretary-manager in May 1899. In 1905, he took over at Crystal Palace, where he spent two seasons, and then moved on to Brighton and Hove Albion. He steered the Seagulls to the Southern League championship in 1910, before ending up in his dream job at Old Trafford.

His aim of proving himself after Mangnall and Bentley was dealt an immediate blow when professional football was suspended in England at the end of the 1914–15 season due to the war in Europe. In place of the Football League, a variety of regional divisions were set up. United joined forces with Everton, Liverpool, Manchester City and Stockport County to form a Lancashire League southern section. With many players away fighting, United's situation worsened. Stockport, Oldham and even Rochdale regularly beat them and in March 1916 they could only attract a crowd of 500, as they lost by a single goal to Oldham to slump to the bottom of their regional league.

It was heartbreaking for the club that had come so far so quickly since its formation in 1902. But more agony was to come as the war stretched inexorably on. Just as Celtic suffered fatalities, so too did United. They would lose three players associated with the club in the fighting; Oscar Linkson, Paddy McGuire and Sandy Turnbull were all killed in action. Their deaths sent the club and their fans into mourning.

Linkson had started his career with Barnet FC in 1907. He was then spotted by scouts from United playing for amateur team Pirates FC on a continental tour. He signed for United in 1908 and helped them win the 1909 FA Cup and 1911 league championship. In 1913, he transferred to Shelbourne in Dublin, returning to England at the outbreak of the war and enrolling with the Football Battalion of the Middlesex Regiment, which was formed entirely of sportsmen. On 8 August 1916, Oscar was lost during the battle to seize Guillemont Station. His body was never recovered and he was reported missing, presumed dead, at the Battle of the Somme.

Details are sketchy about the death of McGuire, a reserve-team player, but much more is known about the death in service of Turnbull, a true United hero. He had signed for the club in 1906 and was United's top scorer in the 1907–08 season, with 27 league and cup goals, when the league championship was won. He would also go down in the record books as the first player to be dismissed in a Manchester derby – sent off against his former club, City, on 21 December 1907, after scoring twice in a 3–1 win.

Turnbull, of course, also grabbed the winning goal in the 1–0 FA Cup-final victory over Bristol City in 1909 and won a second championship medal with United in 1911. He scored a total of 60 goals in 119 games for the club and died aged just 33 at the Battle of Arras in April 1917.

The tragedy of Turnbull brings us to another big moment in the evolution of the Red Devils – though an unsavoury one, which would cast a shadow over the player even after his honourable death. The story centres around a Good Friday that would turn out to be a nightmare for Turnbull and United. On that date, 2 April 1915, the Red Devils faced Liverpool at Old Trafford. United were third from the bottom of Division One, battling against relegation, while Liverpool were in a comfortable mid-table spot. It was a surprise that United won 2–0, with two goals from George Anderson – and that Liverpool posed little danger. Soon, it emerged that a firm of bookmakers had taken a large number of bets on that scoreline, which at the time was unusual, as people tended to bet only on a win, draw or loss, not the actual score.

The bookies had been hit hard at odds of 7–1 and made it clear they were unhappy: didn't Liverpool's attitude in the match suggest they were not bothered if the match went against them?

Many in the 15,000-strong crowd also had become suspicious – particularly when Liverpool missed a penalty and centre-forward, Fred Pagnam, having refused to take part in the plot, hit United's bar late in the game and was swiftly reproached by some angry teammates for trying too hard.

Worried by the allegations, the Football League set up an inquiry into the match and it was established that the game had been fixed by a number players from both teams – not to help out United but to line their own pockets. Pagnam would testify against his guilty teammates at the hearing. Three United players (Turnbull, Enoch James West and Arthur Whalley) and four Liverpool players (Jackie Sheldon, Tommy Miller, Tom Fairfoul and Bob Purcell) were charged with match fixing and found guilty.

Sheldon, a left-winger and member of United's championship-winning side of 1911, who was now turning out for Liverpool, was fingered as the ringleader. He admitted as much to the inquiry, saying he had set up the conspiracy among members of the Liverpool team and agreed with United's guilty trio that the score would be 2–0, with a goal in each half. Pagnam had confirmed the 2–0 plan, telling the commission he had threatened to spoil it by scoring a goal, which he almost did when he hit the bar.

All seven players found guilty were banned from the game for life and even from entering football grounds, with only West formally protesting his innocence. He took out a libel suit against the FA but would lose the court case.

The league lifted the ban at the end of the war on all the players except West, who continued to claim he was an innocent man. His suspension thus remained and would do so until 1945, by which time he was 59. Bitter and angry, West refused to visit Old Trafford ever again. He died in a local hospital in 1965, aged 79.

West had been the only United player found guilty who had actually played in the match. The clubs and officials were cleared of involvement, but Chelsea, relegated one point below United, were naturally none too pleased that the Red Devils had not been docked any points.

Individual punishments meant that Whalley and Turnbull were dropped from their army team and West was dropped from United. Sadly for Turnbull, a United hero after his 1909 FA Cup-winning goal, this meant he died with the shame of a lifelong ban from football hanging over him like a dark cloud.

One other interesting aside to the match-fixing scandal is that not all the players found guilty were plunged into dark obscurity. Tommy Miller, one of the four Liverpool bad boys, went on to become a Scotland international and was eventually transferred to . . . Manchester United on 23 September 1920.

The First World War had finally ended by 1918 and a year later league football resumed. United started the new season a pale shadow of the team that had triumphed until 1912 under the brilliant Mangnall. Manager Robson was struggling on, doing the best he could in circumstances that were still, despite the end of the war, extremely difficult. He tried to inject new hope into the club by bringing in a set of young players he had been grooming, along with several modest signings, but the two seasons following the war saw United finish in 12th and 13th position respectively. Robson's seven-year association with the club would come to an end in October 1921, when he retired on the grounds of ill health. Shortly after, in 1922, he caught a heavy cold that led to pneumonia, which took his life on 11 January 1922.

The year of Robson's death would see United's decline in the new decade confirmed, as they were relegated back to the Second Division. And that would not be the end of the dark times: they would be promoted in 1924 but relegated again in 1931.

For United and Celtic, the '20s and early '30s would be a time of joy coupled with disappointment, hope shadowed by misery and tough, sometimes bitter battles to re-establish their footing as the premier clubs in England and Scotland.

6

....

THE RAW '20s AND DIRTY '30s

THE '20s and '30s were two difficult decades for Celtic and Manchester United. After the flurry of success enjoyed by both clubs in the decade before the First World War, there were testing times from 1920 to 1940.

Celtic, of course, had notched their record of six Scottish Division One titles in a row and would follow it with seven more crowns from 1914 to 1926, but they would then enter a period in the wilderness. The club would not win the title for another ten years, as a resurgent Rangers threw down the gauntlet. Celtic's wins in 1936 and 1938 would be followed by an even longer absence – of 16 years – before the league crown was once again deposited in the Parkhead trophy room in 1954. Of course, there would be the consolation of six Scottish Cup triumphs during those two decades – in 1923, 1925, 1927, 1931, 1933, 1937 – but clubs like Celtic and Manchester United are traditionally defined by their league success, rather than the lottery and arguably second-rate nature of mere cup glory.

For United, the two decades would be the most demanding in the club's history, with little to shout about in terms of trophies or financial stability; indeed, at one stage it looked as though United could have gone under. They were once again lucky that a knight in shining armour emerged to save them … this time in the guise of businessman James Gibson. After their league title wins of 1908 and 1911, and the FA Cup win of 1909, United would go off the radar until the advent of the Busby era. They would not lift the FA Cup again until 1948 and the league title four years later in 1952.

Celtic knew what shape the battle of the next two decades would take when Rangers won the first two league titles of the 1920s. In 1921, the Hoops finished a massive ten points behind their bitter rivals. Given this, the way they grabbed the trophy back from Rangers the following year was all the more remarkable – a testimony to the dogged nature and belief of the players and manager Maley. It looked as though Celtic would need a win at Morton on the final day of the season to take the trophy. At the interval, they were 1–0 down, but Andy McAtee's late equaliser took the title back to Celtic Park. Rangers could only draw in their final match.

The Bhoys had needed strong heads on that fateful day at Morton, as the ugly spectre of sectarianism had reared its head on the terraces, with bigots pouring abuse on the visiting team and its supporters. This atmosphere had been simmering over the previous few years but had only taken a hold in Scotland the year before Celtic regained their league title. The establishment of the Irish Republic in 1921 had given those already intent on propagating religious hatred an ideal focal point from which to spew their anger.

Celtic were formed with a noble, peaceful purpose by Brother Walfrid and would over the years go to great lengths to disassociate themselves from religious extremists. The club would also sign up players regardless of their religion; but for all that, it was known as a Catholic club – as indeed was Manchester United – and some Protestants in Scotland now saw a window of opportunity to cause havoc in Glasgow by nailing their colours to the Ibrox mast. They were unhappy at what they saw as an unacceptable burden being placed on the state by Irish Catholic immigrants and voiced their protests while hiding behind the flags of Rangers, the team they had adopted as their own because of its obvious rivalry to Celtic. As the bigotry at Morton would show, the hatred was not merely confined to the banks of the Clyde.

Celtic had difficulties of a different nature to conquer in 1922–23, namely the developing team moulded by new Rangers boss Bill Struth in the '20s. Just a year after that triumph, the Hoops would finish third, trailing in nine points behind Rangers and even losing out on the runners-up spot to Airdrie. It was the first time since 1911 that the club had finished outside of the top two.

It would be the same story the following season, when the top three spots in the league were once again taken up by Rangers, Airdrie and Celtic. It also did not help Willie Maley's mood that, for the second time in two years, his former Hoops charge Willie Orr had inspired the unfashionable Diamonds to the runners-up place at his expense.

The gap between Rangers and Celtic stood at 13 points, but it would get worse: the next season, they finished 16 points behind their Ibrox rivals and ended up *fourth* in the table, languishing thirteen points behind second-placed Airdrie and eight behind Hibernian.

The two Scottish Cup wins, in 1923 and 1925, brought some consolation and soothed worried brows. Joe Cassidy's superb header had won the first of these two trophies, with a 1–0 win over Hibs, and a new kid on the block helped secure a similar triumph in 1925, this time in a 2–1 victory over Dundee. Patsy Gallacher had conjured up an equaliser after Dundee had taken the lead, but it was the 20-year-old centre-forward Jimmy McGrory who would steal the show – his diving header bringing Celtic their 11th Scottish Cup win.

A legend in the making, McGrory would go on to batter down every record put before him. To this day, he remains the club's top scorer of all time – having netted a remarkable 468 in 445 appearances. The fact that Bobby Lennox is second in the club's all-time listings with 273 goals and Henrik Larsson third with 242 highlights the sheer brilliance and magnitude of Jimmy's feat. Of those 468 goals, 397 were scored in the league. In total, he scored a British record of 550 goals in first-class football – even netting eight in one match against Dunfermline Athletic in 1928 and grabbing a hat-trick in three minutes against Motherwell eight years later.

Born in Garngad, Glasgow, on 26 April 1904, Jimmy joined Celtic from St Roch's Juniors in 1922, making his debut in the 1–0 loss against Third Lanark on 20 January 1923. He was sent on loan to Clydebank for the 1923–24 season, but would then play for Celtic for thirteen magnificent years, along the way winning three league championships and four Scottish Cup-winner's medals. He was the Scottish league's top goalscorer in 1926–27, 1927–28 and 1935–36 and would also represent Scotland seven times, scoring seven goals.

When McGrory left Celtic in 1937, he joined Kilmarnock as manager, eventually returning to his spiritual home in 1945 to manage the Hoops – a position he would hold for nearly 20 years before Jock Stein took command in 1965. But his involvement with the club did not end there: at the time of his death in 1982, he held the post of Celtic's public relations manager.

In the 1925–26 season, Jimmy would help Celtic to become champions again. They finished eight points ahead of Airdrie, with Rangers a further six adrift, the Ibrox outfit ending a surprisingly unsatisfactory campaign in seventh position. The unexpected sting in the tail, however, was that this would be Celtic's last title triumph for a decade. The Hoops were expected to complete the double with a Scottish Cup-final win over St Mirren, but slumped to a shock 2–0 defeat. Yet it had been a season of success – the championship had returned to Parkhead – and one achieved largely without the genius of the often injured Patsy Gallacher.

Boss Maley, deciding that Gallacher, at 33 and seemingly injury prone, was pretty well all washed up, allowed him a move to Falkirk in the summer of '26. Patsy would give the Bairns six years of his skills.

Maley's decision to unload him now had the effect of pushing Jimmy McGrory even further into the limelight as the team's key man – and he did not let down those lauding him with great expectations. Jimmy ended the 1926–27 campaign by setting a new scoring record for the Scottish First Division of 49 goals (a superb haul, but one he would better in 1935–36, when he hit 50).

Maley had laid the blame for the cup final defeat at the door of hapless goalkeeper Peter Shevlin, who he felt was culpable with both goals, and replaced him with a man who, like McGrory, would go on to become a Celtic legend – John Thomson. 'The Boy Keeper', as he would always be affectionately known to the club's fans, would come in for his debut in a 2–1 victory at Dundee on 12 February 1927. The 18 year old would keep his place as the team battled to win the cup that season after surrendering their league title in a dismal campaign that saw them finish seven points behind Rangers and three behind Motherwell. Consolation would come as they lifted the cup at Hampden, with a 3–1 win over East Fife, a triumph secured without the injured McGrory.

The outcome the following season brought only despair to Celtic and their supporters, as Rangers stormed to their first-ever double. The Ibrox club finished five points clear of the Hoops in the league and thrashed them 4–0 in the cup final in front of a crowd of 118,115 – the largest-ever official attendance at a club match in the world at the time.

In the summer of 1928, Willie Maley and his directors appeared still punch-drunk after Rangers' double. In an act of lunacy, Maley tried to sell his star man, McGrory, to Arsenal for what would have been a record fee of £10,000. McGrory, a Celt through and through, held up the move by demanding a £2,000 signing-on fee. That killed the deal – much to the relief of Celtic's army of supporters.

Some historians have argued that the board put Maley under pressure to cash in because money was needed to fund a replacement for the Grant Stand. Now in a state of disrepair, its replacement was costed at £35,000. With a capacity of 5,000, it was a move in the right direction for a club like Celtic – but at the expense of the man known to the fans as Parkhead's 'crown jewels'? The stand would still be funded and built without McGrory's sale – eventually opening on the first day of the 1929–30 season.

Jimmy's form – and goals – were the main source of cheer for Celtic in the cup as the 1920s came to a less than satisfactory conclusion. In the 1928–29 campaign, the club finished 16 points behind Rangers, whose title win was their eighth of the decade. The following year, Jimmy's importance to the club was underlined when he was sidelined for a large part of the season with injury and, without his goals, Celtic slumped to fourth in the league, 11 points behind Rangers, who started the new decade as they had finished it . . . as champions. The Hoops also crashed out of the cup early on to St Mirren.

In 1930–31, they again lost out in the race for the title to Rangers – finishing two points adrift and just failing to stop their arch rivals from winning their fifth consecutive title – but Celtic at least lifted their first major trophy in four years by beating Motherwell 4–2 in the cup final, a welcome brace from

McGrory helping them on their way in the replay after also netting in the first match, which ended 2–2.

The next season started with great hope but quickly lost its sparkle when goalkeeper Thomson passed away in tragic circumstances after a league match at Ibrox on 5 September 1931. More of that in chapter ten; suffice it to say, John's death plunged Celtic into mourning. Maley, in particular, seemed to suffer more than most; he had been like a second father to the boy. A season of hope deteriorated into one of gloom. Maley would describe the impact of the tragedy as a 'crushing, staggering blow from which the team never really recovered'. He would in later life add:

> The shock had a tremendous effect on our players – one which we firmly believe was responsible for many failures during the next few years. The team was playing first-class football when the blow fell, and continued to do so, but without any great fire or enthusiasm. It seemed as if they had lost heart.

Celtic would finish the campaign 18 points behind champions Motherwell, then fourth in 1933 and third in 1934. By 1935, Maley and his boys seemed settled again – they finished the season as runners-up to Rangers. The wilderness years, in terms of league success, were finally about to end.

The club had won the Scottish Cup in 1933, McGrory's goal seeing off a determined effort by Motherwell in a 1–0 triumph, and by the start of the 1935–36 season Willie Maley was convinced he once again had a team capable of challenging in the league. He was not wrong. Maley's new Bhoys powered to their first title in a decade, scoring 115 goals and conceding just 33. They beat Rangers and Aberdeen to the crown by five points.

The following season, the three clubs would once again compete for the three top places: Celtic would relinquish the crown to Rangers, who finished on sixty-one points, nine clear of the Hoops, who ended up third, and seven clear of the Dons, who were runners-up. The Bhoys took consolation from winning the Scottish Cup again, this time beating the Dons 2–1 in the final at Hampden. The match would prove to be McGrory's swansong as a player. He had scored nine of the Hoops' twenty goals en route to the showdown and would retire the following season, scoring in his final match for the club, in the 4–3 triumph over Queen's Park in October 1937, before becoming boss at Kilmarnock. His role as a bustling centre-forward would be taken by Johnny Crum, a different type of player. Crum was more mobile and had a defter touch; he was no bull in a china shop.

Crum had sent out his calling card in the final against the Dons on 24 April 1937, nipping in for the opener in the first half and playing his part at inside-forward as McGrory sometimes struggled with the pace due to a niggling injury.

Willie Buchan's goal took the cup back to Parkhead for the 15th time – but he would be rewarded for his winner, and undeniable talents in midfield, by being flogged to Blackpool seven months later, the Celtic board deciding the money was better than his services. Malky MacDonald would take over his role.

It was a controversial sale but one that, in hindsight, arguably paid off, judging by the league table at the end of April 1938. Celtic were once again champions, this time seeing off the challenge of Hearts, who finished three points behind in second place, and Rangers, who staggered to the finishing line in third spot, twelve points adrift of the Bhoys. It was a memorable way to celebrate the 50th anniversary of the advent of the club and Maley's men also lifted the one-off Empire Trophy. This competition was one of many events taking place in Glasgow that year to celebrate the arrival of the Empire Exibition to the city. The contest involved four teams from Scotland and four from England, with a first prize of a solid-silver model of the

Tait Tower, which stands in Bellahouston Park, the site of the exhibition.

Celtic progressed to the final by beating Sunderland and Hearts. Watched by a crowd of 82,000, the Bhoys then saw off the threat of a fine Everton side to win the trophy, Johnny Crum scoring the only goal of the match on 10 June 1938. Maley was delighted with the win – it told him he had created another fine team: one that had been tested by the best of the English league and emerged victorious. Jimmy Delaney's contribution to that historic victory was also immense. He terrorised the Everton backline, leading to the immortal cry from the crowd of 'Fetch a polis man ... Everton's getting murdered!' Yet the glory would come at a price for Maley.

The board had decided to promote the feel-good factor at Parkhead by recognising Maley's 50-year contribution to Celtic with a long-service award of 2,500 guineas. But Maley, at the time resentful of the poor financial rewards he had accrued at the club over the years, sarcastically thanked the directors for their gift.

Maley would remark that while he was grateful enough for the money, it was the first time he had been treated in his long tenure. Then, over the following months, he would bemoan the fact he had to pay tax on the gift, arguing, with some foundation, it must be said, that Celtic should have picked up that tab.

The directors were tiring of him and his arguments, and he was not helped in the 1938–39 season, when Celtic again relinquished the league crown they had fought so hard to win back. Rangers finished top, a full 11 points ahead of the Bhoys, who were runners-up. There was not even the consolation of a Scottish Cup win to ease the pain. By Christmas of the new season, Maley was gone, replaced two months later by former captain Jimmy McStay. He would prove a caretaker in wartime, from 1940 to 1945, as the Bhoys competed in the Western Regional League and then the Southern League.

In July 1945, McStay was ousted for Jimmy McGrory, who would be responsible for the rebuilding of Celtic FC in the tough post-Second World War period. They were a team largely unrecognisable from the side of the late '30s and there would follow seven mediocre seasons in which the best league position the club could manage was fifth. There was even a flirtation with relegation in 1948.

It would be 1951 before they finally regained their winning ways, by lifting the Scottish Cup. Three years later, they won the league again and also the cup – Celtic's first double for forty years.

McGrory was 41 when he took over at Parkhead and, of course, in another remarkable similarity between Celtic FC and Manchester United FC, 200 miles south of Glasgow Celtic-mad Matt Busby was at the same time becoming manager of the Red Devils. Matt was, like Jimmy, another young man with a mission to reconstruct a major football club – he was just 36 when he took the reins at Old Trafford.

The 25 years prior to Busby's arrival in Manchester had been as testing for United as for Celtic, battling to remain the dominant force in Scottish football. English league football had finally resumed in 1919 after a four-year disruption due to the first Great War. United started the 1919–20 season a shadow of the team that had looked destined for great things a year or two before hostilities began. James West was still banned after the match-fixing case, Sandy Turnbull had been killed in action, players had moved on and Billy Meredith would soon be gone as well, disgruntled at the money on offer.

New manager John Robson was hopeful that a group of young players would take the club to the next level, along with a couple of new signings, including Clarence Hilditch from Altrincham and Charlie Moore from Hednesford Town. His team would finish 12th in the First Division in that first post-war season. One consolation was that the fans were still behind the club. Like Celtic, they would turn up in their droves whatever league position the club found itself in. The average gate in the First Division was around the 20,000 mark, but United were drawing 10,000 more – on 27 December 1920, a staggering 70,504 fans turned up to see United beat Aston Villa 3–1. Even in those dark post-war days, the romantic lure of being a fan of Celtic FC or Manchester United FC was a strong one.

The following season, Meredith was given a free transfer and rejoined Manchester City; United ended up one place further down the table than in the previous campaign, 13th in the First Division. But much worse was to follow in 1921–22, as they were relegated back to the Second Division.

John Robson's term at United ended in October 1921 and his successor, John Chapman, a Scot who had formerly managed Airdrie, was unable to stop the rot on the pitch, as the club plunged to relegation. In his first fifteen matches in charge, United won just once – in the league against Aston Villa in November 1921 – and out of its 42 league games that season managed a total of just eight victories. They were relegated after accruing only 28 points.

Joe Spence was the only beacon of hope at Old Trafford at this time. The dynamic winger was born in Throckley, Northumberland, and had played for Blucher Juniors and Throckley Celtic. While with the former, he scored 42 of the team's 49 goals in his first season. Aged 13, he began work as a miner and was conscripted into the army at 17, where he served as a machine-gunner. He guested for Liverpool, Newburn and Scotswood during his years in service and won the Army Cup with his battalion.

Spence joined United in 1919 from Scotswood and scored four in a 5–1 Lancashire Section destruction of Bury at Old Trafford. His official debut came in August 1919, away at Derby, and he remained at Old Trafford until June 1933, when he moved to Bradford City.

Spence would finish as United's top scorer that first post-war season, with fourteen league goals, and again the following season, 1920–21, but this time with just seven goals. In all, he made 510 appearances for the club, scoring 168 goals, and his appearance records would stand for 40 years until being finally surpassed by Bill Foulkes. He was unfortunate to be at United at a time of transition and difficulty, and he would only win silverware after leaving the club – finally clinching a Third Division North championship medal with Chesterfield in 1936.

It would be 1926 before Chapman hauled United back into the big time. Their first season in Division Two for sixteen years started well, with six wins in eight matches, but the team fizzled out and they finished in fourth position. Notts County ended up as champions and secured that coveted promotion spot, which only compounded United's misery, as they had thrashed County 6–1 away during the campaign.

The 1923–24 season was even worse, as United finished 14th in Division Two, with 13 wins, 14 draws and 15 defeats. In 1912, they had won the league title; yet in 1924, Manchester United were fighting to beat the drop to the Third Division. It was one of the lowest moments in the club's proud history.

Incredibly, the next campaign would be Chapman's *annus mirabilis*, as he turned his relegation scrappers around and led them back to the First Division. They would achieve it with a mean streak, scoring only 53 goals in all their matches but winning 23 and drawing 11 of their 42 matches, finishing runners-up to Leicester.

One of the reasons for the shock turnaround in fortunes was

the inspirational leadership of Frank Barson. The big centre-half was renowned as one of the hardest men – if not the hardest – in football in that era and he harangued his teammates back into the top flight. Another Red legend, he joined United in August 1922 for a fee of £5,000 from Aston Villa. Barson was born in Sheffield and played once for England. In his book, *Soccer in the Blood*, Aston Villa legend Billy Walker wrote of his former teammate Barson:

> Perhaps the greatest of all the great characters in my album – he played with and against me – was the one and only Frank Barson. Frank was a Sheffielder, a truly great footballer and personality and a card. He was never ashamed of numbering amongst his friends the notorious Fowler brothers, who were hanged for murder.

United fans were also quickly won over by Barson's unflinching commitment and no-holds-barred aggression. Two stories sum up the nature of this celebrated big hard man. The first relates to a promise, the second a gun. The promise came from United's directors when they persuaded Barson to sign. The 31 year old would be paid a normal wage but would receive a healthy 'bonus of sorts' – his own pub – if he led the club back to the promised land of Division One within three years. Duly, when promotion was swiftly achieved, Barson was handed the keys to a pub but decided, after being swamped when he opened the doors by a rush of punters eager to see him in the flesh, that running a boozer was not the life for him.

The gun story came later in his career, at Wigan, when he felt he was not getting the pay rise he deserved. Legend has it that Big Frank decided it might help smooth negotiations if he turned up to meet his manager carrying a gun!

Barson spent an injury-plagued six years at Old Trafford, but his leadership in the 140 league appearances he made helped the club through a difficult patch. He scored four goals for the Red Devils before joining Watford in May 1928.

United consolidated their position back in the top flight by finishing ninth in 1925–26. Chapman's team also did well in the FA Cup, falling 3–0 in the semis to Manchester City, though their blue neighbours' luck would also run out when they crashed to Bolton in the final and were relegated from the First Division. But the smiles would soon be wiped off the faces of United fans . . .

On 20 September 1926, an FA investigating committee met at the Grand Hotel in Manchester to begin an inquiry into the affairs of United. The committee reconvened in Sheffield the following week and then returned to Manchester in the first week of October. What they were investigating to this day remains unknown, but in October 1926 the FA suspended manager John Chapman with immediate effect for reasons which never became public. The FA simply announced: 'That for improper conduct in his position as Secretary-Manager of the Manchester United Football Club, Mr J.A. Chapman be suspended from taking part in football or football management during the present season.'

Wing-half Clarence Hilditch took over as player-manager while the club looked for a more permanent replacement. He managed to keep the Reds in the top flight that year, finishing 15th in the league, and resumed his playing career when Herbert Bamlett took over. After playing 332 games for Manchester United and scoring seven goals, Hilditch retired from playing professionally in 1932 and took over as coach of the United 'Colts' (the club's youth team).

Bamlett had arrived at Old Trafford in April 1927. He was already known to United fans as the referee who called off the club's FA Cup quarter-final tie at Burnley in 1909 when their team was trailing 1–0 in the midst of a blizzard. United had then gone on to win the cup . . . But Bamlett would bring no success as United manager. The team slowly slipped down the First Division, finishing 18th in 1927–28 and 12th in 1928–29. United had lost fifteen matches before the April of 1929 but survived by winning five and drawing one of their final six games. Their saviour would be Tom Reid, the lively Scottish forward who scored 14 goals that season and went on to score 67 in just 101 games, before he moved to Oldham five years later.

Hopes of competing for the title were a pipe dream, however; as the '30s approached, United were perennial relegation battlers. Finances were also a problem – particularly after the death of the club's founding father, John H. Davies, in 1927.

In the 1929–30 season, United finished 17th. Their next campaign began in similarly nightmarish style, as the Red Devils made the worst start in their history by losing their first twelve league matches in a row. The dozen defeats began with a 4–0 home loss to Aston Villa and included back-to-back thrashings at Old Trafford: 6–0 by Huddersfield Town and then 7–4 by Newcastle United. The game against the Toon truly set the alarm bells ringing for the United board of directors – the crowd had numbered little more than 10,000. It would be November before Herbert Bamlett's team took their first points, beating Birmingham 2–0 at home. It was crisis time.

The supporters had started to make demands a month earlier: they wanted a new manager, new players, better scouting, five shareholders elected to the board and money to be raised through a new share issue. Foolishly, the board snubbed them, saying the Supporters' Club was an unofficial body and unrepresentative of the majority of United fans. By the end of September, with United rooted firmly at the foot of the table, the supporters threatened to boycott matches unless the board took them seriously.

There was no response. In October, at an emergency meeting

at Hulme Town Hall, more than 2,500 United fans voted for a boycott of United's match against FA Cup holders Arsenal. Former United skipper Charlie Roberts had argued against the boycott, but his views were dismissed.

United lost 2–1 at Old Trafford to the Gunners on 18 October 1930, in front of a crowd of 23,000 – without the boycott, it would have been at least double that figure. The rift widened as the horror show continued. By the end of probably the worst season in the history of Manchester United FC, the Red Devils had lost twenty-seven and won just seven of their matches, conceding a massive 115 goals along the way.

It was a sign of the times when in their final game of the campaign at Old Trafford just 3,900 watched them draw 4–4 with Middlesbrough. United were relegated to the Second Division, finishing bottom of the table and staring bankruptcy in the face.

The board finally took a popular decision – sacking the hapless Herbert Bamlett as manager. Secretary Walter Crickmer and the evergreen Louis Rocca took temporary command of a sinking ship. The reason for their elevation was simple and stark: United simply did not have the money to employ a new manager. It would not be the last time the long-serving secretary and his close friend Rocca would step in to steer the club they loved as it edged towards the very rocks of disaster.

Crickmer had joined United as a clerk in 1919 and became secretary seven years later. He would be a loyal servant to the United cause until 1958, when he died in the Munich air disaster. A club official wrote a fine tribute to the man in the *United Review* of 19 February 1958 shortly after Munich: 'How to write an epitaph for Walter? He was more than our secretary – he was a part of Manchester United . . . He'd a hand in everything, from helping with the *United Review* to building the floodlight pylons.'

Crickmer never assumed the official title of manager but took charge of team affairs until Scott Duncan was appointed; in 1937, when Duncan resigned, he once again stepped in until the appointment of Matt Busby in 1945. Crickmer was responsible for the introduction of the Manchester United Junior Athletic Club (MUJACs) in 1938, setting in motion a youth policy which would bring brilliant results under Matt Busby and Jimmy Murphy in the 1950s. The MUJACs built upon the success of the club's A-team and the youth team, the Colts, the brainchild of Clarence Hilditch. During his time in charge of the first team, Crickmer was always grateful for the assistance of Rocca.

Back in 1931, it had quickly become clear that even the sterling efforts of Crickmer and Rocca could not save United from the threat of bankruptcy. Another saviour was needed after the death of John H. Davies and one would miraculously emerge from nowhere to lift the club from the abyss – just as Davies had at the start of the century. Businessman James Gibson assumed the role of fairy godfather, immediately giving the club £2,000 to pay the players' wages and making it clear there was more to come if the board would reconstitute itself. The stubbornness of the directors thankfully fell away at last – Gibson was made president and United survived.

Never a follower of football, Gibson had been attracted to the club out of a sense of civic pride and business acumen after football writer Stacey Lintott asked him to help. Gibson would explain his reasoning for getting involved in this way:

> Manchester is suffering enough today through depression without it being known that she cannot afford to keep a famous club. I do not think it would help Manchester business and Lancashire trade in general if such a famous club as United was allowed to drop out without some definite stand being taken to resurrect it.

The man who had made his fortune producing army uniforms proceeded to turn United around as a business, throwing in another £30,000 to help pay off the club's debts. In later years, he would also fund the rebuilding of Old Trafford after German bombs destroyed it during the Second World War and enthusiastically encourage the United youth system, which would provide a conveyor belt of brilliant players, including the Busby Babes. Along with Rocca in 1945, he would also persuade Busby to come to Old Trafford as manager of then sleeping giants United.

Another in the long line of those who have earned a rightful place of honour in the annals of Celtic United – alongside Brother Walfrid and John Glass, Louis Rocca and John H. Davies – Gibson ruled Old Trafford in the paternalistic tradition of Davies before him.

He witnessed his club winning the FA Cup in 1948 but died a year before Busby took them to their first league title under his tenure in 1952. Gibson remains fondly remembered at Old Trafford and he is commemorated by a plaque on the players' tunnel and one outside the stadium on the railway bridge on Sir Matt Busby Way. He had remained the private club's major shareholder until his death. His son, Alan, inherited the major shareholding from his father, but Harold Hardman was appointed chairman.

Off the field, from day one James Gibson was encouraging United onwards. On the pitch, the team was still struggling, despite the changes at the top. Gibson had provided funds for new players, though new manager Scott Duncan did not use them wisely. By May 1934, United were reliving their nightmare of a decade earlier when, in 1924, they had escaped relegation to the Third Division by the skin of their teeth. Now, a terrible sequence of results had them staring into the abyss once again. Survival depended on the last match on the last day of the season,

4 May. It was a winner-takes-all clash at Millwall; the winner would stay up, the loser would be relegated. The *Manchester Evening News* had already written United off, calling it 'the most heartbreaking season in the history of Manchester United'. The Red Devils were next to bottom on 32 points, with Millwall just above them on 33.

But United won 2–0, with goals from Tom Manley and Jack Cape, and sent Millwall down. In an interesting aside to that breathtaking match, that same week Manchester City won the FA Cup; one of their stars on the day was Matt Busby.

The Scott Duncan years had been a real roller-coaster ride for United's long-suffering fans.

He had been employed on a salary of £800 a year and already had links with United and Celtic, being one of the few to have played for Celtic and Rangers, and having guested for United during the First World War. A tricky winger, he had started to make a name for himself as a manager before joining United, at Hamilton and Cowdenbeath.

The 1934–35 season saw an improvement in United's play and form and they finished fifth in Division Two. The following campaign was the pinnacle of Duncan's five-year spell at Old Trafford: the team went on a 19-match unbeaten run, as he took them to the top of the Second Division. On 29 April 1936, United clinched the Second Division championship, with a 3–2 victory over Bury at Gigg Lane. It was their first silverware of the decade.

Yet the joy was short-lived. A year later, United were relegated. They had won just ten matches. To make matters worse, neighbours City were crowned champions. The relegated United team included Walter Winterbottom, who would go on to manage England and earn a knighthood for his efforts.

On 9 November 1937, Scott Duncan resigned as United manager, with Crickmer and Rocca taking over at the helm.

Shortly after his resignation, Duncan took the manager's role at Ipswich and would carve out the reputation as a fine manager he had wanted so badly to achieve at United. He guided Ipswich into the Football League (Second Division) and it is a reflection of his work there that he remained their manager until August 1955.

Duncan had at least bequeathed two special players to the club, two men who would weave a coveted name for themselves in the rich tapestry of Manchester United's history.

On the recommendation of the club's chief scout, Rocca, he signed Johnny Carey from Dublin club St James's Gate for £250. Born in Dublin on 23 February 1919, the 17 year old would begin life at Old Trafford as an inside-forward but would soon convert to full-back and become one of the position's all-time greats. Carey was an outstanding defender of his time and was as inspirational a skipper as Roy Keane in the modern era, captaining United to the FA Cup in 1948 and the league championship in 1952. Carey played for both the Republic of Ireland and Northern Ireland, a total of twenty-seven and nine times respectively. He captained a Rest of Europe side against Britain in 1947 and was English Footballer of the Year in 1949. Johnny would make 344 appearances for United, scoring 17 goals, before hanging up his boots in May 1953.

Scott Duncan also brought in the great Jack Rowley from Bournemouth for £3,000. Born in Wolverhampton on 7 October 1920, Jack would become one of the game's most feared strikers. He served in the South Staffordshire Regiment, participating in the D-Day landings at Normandy in 1945, before resuming his United career in 1946. Rowley was a key man in the 1948 FA Cup-winning side, scoring twice in the 4–2 final victory over Blackpool. His 30 goals in the 1951–52 league campaign would help the Red Devils to their first title since 1911.

Jack would make 503 appearances for United and score

312 goals. He left the club to join Plymouth Argyle as player-manager in 1955, retiring from playing two years later. He also played six times for England.

The roller coaster continued under Crickmer, as United's fortunes rose and fell again. In the first Second Division match after Duncan's resignation, they thrashed Chesterfield 7–1 and went on to win promotion back to the top flight. The following season, 1938–39, saw United retain their Division One status, with Johnny Carey playing a key role as he grabbed six goals in thirty-two games. United ended the campaign in 14th position and the cake was iced for their long-suffering fans when neighbours City were relegated.

But this was no time for gloating. Just four months after confirming their First Division status, the Second World War was declared. The outbreak of war forced football to the back of people's minds – and it would be seven years before the Football League reappeared.

On 11 March 1941, Old Trafford was bombed during a German air raid. The attack destroyed the main stand, dressing-rooms and offices. It was a devastating blow. The biggest club in England was shrouded in darkness, pessimism and misery. United's crowds were typically around the 3,000 mark during the Second World War. They won the Lancashire Cup in 1941, beating Burnley, and topped their regional league in 1941–42. After the bombing of their wonderful stadium, the team had to play at Maine Road; many fans wondered if United would ever rise again from the ashes.

Their prayers would be answered: a new era of joy, wonder and entertaining, winning football was around the corner. As Celtic's age of success would come with the emergence of Jock Stein, first as a player in 1951, then as manager in 1965, so United would arrive with the entrance in 1945 of another Scottish hero.

The Busby years were about to begin.

7

DELANEY: THE FIRST CELTIC UTD SUPERSTAR

It is better to be a champion sport than a sports champion.

— *Jimmy Delaney*

I could take a rest for five minutes while 'Baldie' waltzed around the place for a time.

— *Johnny Carey on Delaney*

IF WE'RE talking about the man who would play for both Celtic and United and become the *first* superstar in doing so, we surely need look no further than the great Jimmy Delaney. This balding, totally modest, speedy winger – as exemplified by the honourable quotes above – would make his debut for the Hoops in 1934 and move to the Red Devils 12 years later. He would also eventually pack his bags for Northern Ireland, ending up at Derry City, a transfer that would bring him the distinction of becoming the only man to ever win three cup-winner's medals in three different countries in three different decades.

Jimmy would win the Scottish Cup with Celtic before the Second World War and the English FA Cup with Busby's United just after the end of hostilities; after short spells at Aberdeen and Falkirk in the early 1950s, Delaney joined Derry

City in the Irish League and, at the age of 39, won the Irish Cup with them in 1954. He also came close to a fourth cup-winner's medal in the Republic of Ireland, earning a runners-up gong with Cork Athletic in 1956.

The Delaney footballing dynasty is still thriving at Celtic Park: his grandson, the promising centre-half John Kennedy, is taking tentative steps to resume his Celtic career after spending almost three years on the sidelines with a terrible knee injury.

Jimmy's professional career – in which he also won 13 Scottish caps – would span from 1933 to 1957. Like Busby and Stein, he was a product of the villages that made up the mining community of Lanarkshire. Born in Cleland in 1914 just weeks after the outbreak of the First World War, Delaney signed his provisional forms with Celtic in 1933 and would go on to make 305 appearances for the club, many of them in unofficial wartime matches, which explains the official figure of only 160 games played for the Hoops. In those official appearances, he scored an official tally of seventy-four goals and also won two league titles, in 1936 and 1938, the latter of course being the last the club would win until the Jock Stein era. In this sense, Delaney was an integral part of the last truly great side of Willie Maley's reign – the bubbling, vibrant team of the late '30s.

Delaney was signed by Maley from Stoneyburn Juniors and was considered a late developer. Like Matt Busby – many people mistook Delaney for the manager, given their similar looks – he was Celtic mad and it did not take much persuasion for him to sign on at Parkhead. He made his debut aged 20, against Hearts in a league match on 18 August 1934, and was soon exhibiting those dazzling skills and that priceless ability to cross perfect balls into the area for the likes of goal machine Johnny Crum. Their partnership would be the key to Celtic's success. Delaney would stress how he loved lining up with Crum and the other Celtic stars of the day: 'We had a great understanding. Johnny Crum was very tricky when he was playing centre-forward. Malky MacDonald was one of those boys that could hold the ball. You didn't need to beat men: Malky would beat them for you.

'He would give you the pass and you would have nothing else to do but cross it. It was the same with Johnny Divers. He would run into great positions and he was a great header of the ball, too. Frank Murphy was a great winger. He could shoot and put over lovely crosses. We had a great forward line. A great team. To me, it was the best Celtic team I ever played in.'

It certainly was 'a great team', but it appears that boss Maley was worried about success going to his team's – and Delaney's – head, an odd view given the nature of the boy Jimmy. Maley even felt he had to admonish the player after he cracked a brilliant hat-trick against Rangers in the Charity Cup final in May 1936, which Celtic won 4–2. It was hardly warranted and is perhaps an indication of the character of Maley by the end of the '30s. A great servant of Celtic FC, he had nonetheless acquired the character of an early Victor Meldrew: he was grumpy and argumentative and unwilling to see things any way but his own.

To be fair to the great man, he was by that stage 68 years old and had earned the right to moan and groan after close on 50 years' service at Parkhead. His time was almost up. Just over three and a half years after he had brought Delaney down to size, he was gone from the club, a lonely 71 year old sent packing in a ruthless swing of the axe by the Celtic board.

Following the Empire Exhibition victory in 1938, chairman Tom White had summed up the celebratory, warm mood by saying of Maley, 'The history of Celtic is indissolubly the life story of Willie Maley. Through all his years, he has built up one great honour-winning team after another.'

It was rich, generous praise, but as Christmas approached in 1939 the board told him he was out. The Maley era was finally over.

Jimmy McStay was appointed manager in the February of the new year, but he never looked like launching his own dynasty and would also be given the boot five years later. Jimmy McGrory would soon be brought in as his replacement.

Maley would admit in later life that he felt blessed to have been given one final great team – and that he particularly enjoyed working with and watching Delaney. Celtic won the league in '36 and '38 playing superb football and wee Jimmy, who many commentators claim was the prototype of another Jimmy, Jinky Johnstone, was at the fulcrum of the team's play.

In the Scottish Cup win of 1937, in front of a capacity crowd of 146,433 at Hampden (the second highest ever there), Delaney was again the key man, inspiring the Hoops to a deserved 2–1 triumph over Aberdeen. These were the days of wine and roses for the wee man. From 1939, it would not be so glorious for him at Parkhead; first, he was affected by a freak accident that could have led to the amputation of his arm and second, by the onslaught of the Second World War.

Delaney would suffer his arm injury during an otherwise dull league match against Arbroath on 1 April 1939. Celtic were leading 2–0 in a meaningless end-of-season fixture when Delaney challenged Atilio Becci to an aerial ball after a corner kick from Frank Murphy. Both men fell awkwardly, but, in landing, Becci had stood on Delaney's arm. Jimmy was taken to hospital, where it quickly emerged the bone was not broken in one place but shattered. One of the doctors was of the opinion that amputation would have been an option had Jimmy not been a professional footballer.

It would take the best part of two years before this wonderful footballer would be back in business, and then only as a part-timer, as the war ground on. Becci was distraught by the damage he had inadvertently inflicted upon a man he much admired. He was a Celtic fan and would later admit that he would have given anything to turn back the clock and erase the nightmare.

During the period of rehabilitation, Jimmy suffered from depression; ironically, it would be his name that kept spirits high in the trenches. Just as the Scots fighting in the First World War had talked about Patsy Gallacher, so those involved in the second Great War used the name of Delaney to boost morale.

Even back in Cleland, Jimmy's name was an encouragement to the war effort. One local by the name of Joseph Brown, who was 16 at the time, admitted as much when he remembered how things were in Cleland as hostilities continued, as recounted on the BBC's People's War web page: 'The Local Defence Volunteers were formed to defend the country against invaders after the Dunkirk fiasco in 1940. There were only about 20 locals in the outfit and what resistance they would have displayed against the Germans if there had been an invasion would have been interesting to see. Captain Mainwaring of *Dad's Army* would have been proud of the men from Cleland. There were quite a number of local personalities in and around the village at this time – the most prominent was Jimmy Delaney, the star of Celtic Football Club.'

Without realising it, just by being wee Jimmy from Cleland and magical Jimmy from Celtic, he was also playing an important part for his country.

Delaney would also play a role for Celtic after having bone graft surgery on his injured arm. The surgery meant he could not play an active part in the war effort, so he worked part-time down the pit and turned out for Celtic FC in unofficial wartime games in the Southern League and the Summer Cup. Celtic were an average outfit during the war, having let experienced players like Crum, Divers and Murphy go, and at times it appeared as if Delaney was carrying them.

He would be the club's top scorer in the 1942–43 season, but by the time the war came to an end in 1945 a series of injuries had left him feeling financially insecure. Now fit but looking for stability, he asked Celtic for a benefit match. He had been at the club for 11 seasons; however, the reward for his loyalty and efforts during the war was a point-blank refusal from the board. The directors then went one step further and ordered boss McStay to keep him out of the team as part of his 'punishment' for asking for financial help.

Delaney, then 30, would return to the team for half of the 1945–46 season, but the clock could not be turned back. He felt niggled by the board's intransigence over his plea for a benefit and was further insulted when chairman Tom White turned down his reasonable request for a wage rise: from the £2 a week that he had earned during the war to his pre-war agreement of £4.

By January 1946, Jimmy was at the end of his tether and, not knowing what else to do given the board's stance, asked for the transfer he never wanted. The board tried to put a brave face on it in public by slapping him on the transfer list, as if they did not need his services, and even brought in Tommy Bogan from Hibs as an obvious rival for his place in the starting line-up. It was childish but also dangerous. Matt Busby, who had taken over at Manchester United in 1945, had been keeping abreast of developments and moved quickly when he saw his old wartime pal on the list. By 8 February 1946, Jimmy had left his beloved Celtic for good and became part of the dynamic footballing revolution Busby was carrying out 200 miles to the south.

The fee was £4,000 and Jimmy would receive wages of £10 a week. With Busby, he would help turn United around as their 'Celtic-in-exile' combination quickly worked wonders. Seventeen years later, Pat Crerand would likewise switch between the two clubs for the same reason – he also thought Celtic were not paying him the going rate – as would Lou Macari in 1973. The bottom line on the Delaney move from Celtic to United was that the Parkhead board had dropped an almighty clanger: Jimmy still had ten years of football left in him.

Both he and Busby would do little to discourage the Celtic-in-exile idea – the Celtic mad pair would constantly be asking the backroom staff at Old Trafford to keep them in touch with how the Hoops were doing via their transistor radios and every nugget of information about the Parkhead club in the papers was eagerly digested by them both.

Of course, they had a job to do at Old Trafford and the exiled Celts would do it supremely well. Busby – in tandem with Delaney and his new teammates – would find an early recipe for glory. The 1947–48 season saw Jimmy line up in what was a world-class forward line alongside John Morris, Jack Rowley, Stan Pearson and Charlie Mitten. That line-up propelled United forwards after years of underachievement, irrevocably changing their status as Manchester City's poor relations.

In 1948, they lifted the English FA Cup, beating Blackpool 4–2, with goals from Jack Rowley (2), Stan Pearson and John Anderson. Eddie Shimwell and Stan Mortensen replied for the Seasiders. It was United's first FA Cup final for 39 years and the first silverware they would win under Busby. Delaney scored eight goals in United's cup-winning year.

The *News of the World* called the final 'Wembley's finest'. The *Soccer Spotlight* of that season described it in these rather stiff-upper-lip terms:

> It was estimated that bookmakers lost something in the region of £500,000 when Manchester United defeated Blackpool in the FA Cup final. That just proves how impressive the Manchester side proved to be from the commencement of the season.
>
> Under the managership of Mr Matt Busby, the former Scottish international half-back, Manchester United, apart from possessing some of the game's

greatest players, went all out to foster team-spirit. They succeeded wonderfully well and this outlook, plus the extraordinary skill of the many fine footballers on their staff, brought them the FA Cup and position as runners-up to Arsenal for the league championship.

With the United experiencing such a great run in League and Cup it is not surprising to find many of their players selected for international honours. Captain John Carey is 'a regular' for Ireland; his partner, Jack Aston, was selected to go on the FA close-season tour; left-half Henry Cockburn and inside-left Stan Pearson have also been awarded their England caps; inside-right John Morris played for the Football League. Scottish international outside-right Jimmy Delaney also played for Scotland again last season.

The club would win no silverware the following season but finished second in the league for the third time in a row. In 1949, after an eight-year absence due to bomb damage inflicted during the war, they finally returned to Old Trafford, bidding a happy farewell to their temporary home, Maine Road.

The new beginning at Old Trafford signified the start of the end for Jimmy at United. He played his first game at the ground on 24 August 1949, as the Red Devils swept aside Bolton 3–0 in front of a crowd of more than 41,000. He was by now 35 and, although he featured in all of United's 42 league games, was beginning to feel the strain as those years of injuries finally took their toll.

He started the new season of 1950–51 in the first team, but by the fourth match of the campaign his run ended with injury. Jimmy was 36 on 3 September 1950 and by November his reign at United was over. He and Matt Busby would part company that month, with his last game in the red shirt of United a 1–0 loss at Chelsea.

Jimmy would head back to Scotland – even at 36, he commanded a fee of £3,500 – where Aberdeen, who had won the Scottish Cup in 1947, were offering a fair wage. Busby was sad to see his old friend and fellow Celt go and offered this tribute: 'He was just about one of the best signings that any football manager could desire. He was one of the main reasons for the emergence of Manchester United as the most successful team in post-war football.' Reflecting on the fact that United had clawed back £3,500 of the £4,000 they had paid Celtic for Jimmy, Matt would add, tongue firmly in cheek, 'Not a bad effort, considering the deal cost United no more than £500.'

Jimmy spent the next four years in his homeland, first with the Dons and then at Falkirk. He experienced an unhappy few months at Pittodrie, finding it difficult to settle; he at one stage asked if he could train during the week with Celtic and simply turn out for his new side at weekends. He made his debut in a home match against Falkirk on 18 November 1950 but was gone by Christmas the following year. Jimmy was glad to return closer to home with a move to Falkirk, who the previous summer had been relegated to Division B. It was a big comedown for the man who had starred on the right wing for the giants of Celtic and Manchester United, but Jimmy would find a kind of contentment with the Bairns. He liked the club's manager, Bob Shankly, brother of Bill, and felt good to be back near 'his own people' in Glasgow.

Jimmy made his debut at Forfar on 8 December 1951 and helped drag the club into Division A in his first season. On the back of those efforts, he was retained for the following campaign but struggled with a series of injury setbacks. He still had enough in the tank, as skipper at the age of 38, to help keep them in the top league that season, but he found it tough in his final half-season at the club, eventually bailing out for Derry City as 1954 dawned. Now nearly 40, he would win the last of his historic three cup-winner's medals with Derry in the north of Ireland.

After running out for Cork Athletic, Jimmy wrapped up his career with Elgin in the Scottish Highland League. His son, Pat, also continued the family's footballing tradition becoming a pro defender with Motherwell and then Dunfermline.

Looking back on his career, one major regret for Jimmy and his legion of fans was that he did not win more international caps. This, for the most part, was down to the fact that his prime years were interrupted by the Second World War. Jimmy would star for his country when he was picked – earning those 13 official caps – and he also performed well in several unofficial wartime internationals and for League of Scotland teams.

In one particularly memorable match in 1936, he grabbed a brace against Germany at Ibrox – goals which, it was claimed at the time, were 'the goals that put Hitler off his tea'. He also scored the winning goal in the Victory International against England in 1946. But for the war, which had begun when he was 25, he would surely have been one of the all-time great goalscorers and in the list of top players for his high number of appearances.

Delaney also held another noteworthy record: he was one of the few players to appear for his country before and after a world war, starring for Scotland in November 1938, then again in April 1947.

The 1938 international was on Wednesday, 9 November, against Wales at Hampden, with Jimmy scoring the first of Scotland's goals in a 3–2 win. At the time, he was a Celtic player. The 1947 match was on Saturday, 12 April. By then on Manchester United's books, he played his part as Scotland drew 1–1 with England at Wembley.

He had made his debut for the national team on 5 October 1935, in the 1–1 draw against Wales at Ninian Park, and hit his first international goals in the memorable 2–0 win over Hitler's Germany already mentioned. His 13th and final competitive appearance for Scotland came on Saturday, 10 April 1948, when England triumphed 2–0 at Hampden. Jimmy was thirty-three years old and had scored four official goals for his country.

For a man who literally had the world at his feet, Jimmy Delaney was remarkably down to earth and even humble. The trappings of modern-day success would have frightened the life out of him; he was happiest with his family and did not seek out the limelight. This was the man who was voted in a survey among fans the 40th best United player in the top 50 of all time, and the man for whom Celtic fans would set up a unique supporters' club, the Jimmy Delaney Celtic Supporters' Club of Cleland. Founded in 1964, it celebrated its 40th anniversary in 2004 and is still going strong.

Delaney revived Celtic's fortunes in the late '30s and brought about Manchester United's dominance in the modern era in England alongside Busby in the mid-1940s. Celtic United remain deeply indebted to the little winger who brought magic to Celtic Park and Old Trafford; the real-life flying Scotsman who made dreams come true for supporters who had begun to despair in Glasgow and Manchester. Jimmy Delaney was the first superstar of Celtic United – and a real gent too.

8

....

SIR MATT BUSBY: THE GOLD MINER

> Matt Busby's presence will always be at Manchester United. He is Manchester United.
>
> – *Sir Bobby Charlton*

MATT BUSBY was the man who would lovingly and tenderly reconstruct Manchester United, bit by bit, after the trauma and crisis of the Second World War years; the man who would turn them into the biggest club in world football and the man who became so famous he was even immortalised by The Beatles in 1970 in the song 'Dig It' on their final album, *Let It Be*.

United were the proverbial ship heading for the rocks when Busby took command in 1945; urgent action was required to avoid the club capsizing. New blood, direction and leadership were needed if the giant was to rise up and conquer as it had done in similar circumstances after the crisis of 1902.

Cometh the hour, cometh the power: just as Louis Rocca had stepped in to help the club at the start of the century when it was tottering on the brink, so he would now provide the answer to a similar epoch-defining problem – a Scot on Liverpool's books.

Rocca knew all about Busby the player. He'd had the chance to sign the half-back from Manchester City for £150 in 1930, but United had been unable to fund the fee. It meant Busby had gone instead to Anfield. United's chief scout was determined not to lose his man a second time.

Busby was still on the books of Liverpool and was working for the army as an instructor at the Sandhurst Military Academy when he received a letter from Rocca informing him of the managerial vacancy at Old Trafford. It is a remarkable testament to Rocca's vision that he saw something in Busby that others had failed to notice: here was a man with great leadership qualities whom Rocca felt could make a swift, smooth and seamless transition from a player of quality to a manager of quality.

When Rocca approached Busby, the Scot had never managed a football team. Liverpool had recognised his tactical nous – they had offered him a coaching role before Rocca stepped in – but had not seen him as managerial material. Not at that stage, anyway. Again, the pioneering Rocca would get there first.

The two men met in private and the chief scout outlined why he had written to Busby with news of the job. Rocca believed the Scot could easily adapt but also had the feeling that Busby would share his vision of a team built from youth upwards. It was a hunch that would, of course, be proved to be spot on when Busby found his feet and developed his famed Babes.

Busby knew at once that the United job was his destiny and informed Liverpool that he would not be joining their coaching staff. (An interesting sidenote for United fans who love to be ahead in the one-upmanship stakes with their Kop counterparts is that even now Sir Matt remains the only Liverpool player ever to be knighted . . .)

The *Manchester Evening News* reported Busby's arrival at the club on Monday, 19 February 1945:

> Company Sergeant-Major Instructor Matt Busby, Liverpool right-back and Scotland captain, today signed an agreement to become manager of Manchester United when he is demobilised. Only a

few years ago Busby, who has proven himself one of the great half-backs of modern times, was the 'forgotten man' of international football. His thousands of Manchester fans, remembering him as a stylish and attractive player when he turned out for Manchester City, unswervingly believed in his brilliance when Scotland's selectors seem to have neglected and forgotten him. And he justified their faith. After one pre-war international cap in 1934 he was ignored until the 1941–42 season. Since then he has appeared for Scotland in eight games, several times as skipper. In these games he has been outstanding, and today he has made a name for himself in Scottish football.

'Busby has had a number of offers, but he approached us himself as he particularly wanted to come back to Manchester,' Mr W. Crickmer, Manchester United secretary, explained today. 'He will build up the team and put it where it belongs – at the top.' Busby left Manchester City for Liverpool in 1936 at a fee of £8,000 and has been released from his appointment as Liverpool's post-war coach.

Interesting to note how Walter Crickmer – back in his post as club secretary after a brief spell as manager at United following the resignation of Scott Duncan in 1937 – put a bit of spin on the Busby arrival, claiming the great man 'approached us himself'. Rocca had done his job again for Manchester United FC: the recruitment of Busby, along with his scouting work and earlier efforts to get the United bandwagon on the road, certainly earned him a glowing footnote in the club's history.

Busby had come a long way when, at the tender age of 36, he walked into Old Trafford determined to bring revolution and renewed glory. He was born in Orbiston, near Bellshill, in Lanarkshire on 26 May 1909, the first child of Alexander and Nellie Busby. Ninety years later to the day exactly, United would win the treble with a momentous 2–1 European Cup victory over Bayern Munich in Barcelona.

His upbringing in Orbiston helps explain his affection for Celtic FC – while researching this book, I came across many references to Sir Matt supporting the team as a young boy. He also got on well with Jock Stein and Bill Shankly, in no mean part because all three of that holy trinity of great managers originated from the same area of Lanarkshire.

Life was tough for the Busbys in their miner's cottage. Home consisted of two rooms, a kitchen and a living room/bedroom, with an outside tap and communal toilets 75 yards away. The men played football as an escape from the dirty, dangerous work at the coalface, and Matt's father was no exception.

The family was Catholic, but religion did not split the men who worked down the mines – they had enough to worry about, staying alive and surviving – and both Catholics and Protestants lived relatively peacefully side by side in Orbiston. Despite the everyday struggle against poverty, the Busbys were a close-knit, proud family. Matt would be joined by three sisters, Delia, Kathy and Margaret, between the years of 1911 and 1914.

Tragedy struck in 1916 when Alexander Busby was killed in the First World War by a sniper's bullet at Arras; all of the children's uncles would also be lost in the conflict. Matt was just six years old and would in later life admit how devastated he was by the loss of his father; how he felt a hole in his soul when other boys at school talked about their fathers and the activities they had shared. He had also taken his first love of football from his father, watching proudly as he turned out for the village team and spending most of his own spare time with a ball, practising and developing his skills.

The family now had to get by on the meagre pension awarded to Nellie and from the small amounts of money she earned working at the pit head. Matt helped out at home, taking on the male role left vacant by his father's death until his mother remarried in 1919 to a man she had met at the colliery called Harry Matthie. Between the age of 12 and 15, Matt, an academically clever boy, attended Motherwell Higher Grade, the top secondary school in the area. This involved a ten-mile-round walk each day.

But football remained Matt's main love. He progressed at a rate, first of all representing the village team and then the best youth side in the area, Alpine Villa, helping the latter win the Scottish Under-18 Cup. He would then star for the Ayrshire side Denny Hibs and from there his journey would lead him to Manchester, but it would be City, not United, who would be his first love there. His aim was to emulate the success of his hero Jimmy McMullen, who was starring at City and for the Scottish national team at centre-half.

Busby left Bellshill for Manchester in February 1928 at the age of 18. Celtic had also been after him. In another ironic twist, he would sign for City in Glasgow at Willie Maley's Bank restaurant. He went on to make over 200 appearances for the Sky Blues and in his first season City won promotion from the Second Division, but it was a tough baptism. Still hoping to make his name as an inside-forward, Matt debuted against Middlesbrough but played most of his games for the reserves. A permanent place in the first team appeared a mere pipe dream. But this was a boy moulded from the grit of the Scottish pit villages, a boy who would not give in without one hell of a fight. At the start of the new season, he was immediately selected for first-team action by manager Peter Hodge.

Matt then oscillated between the first eleven and the reserves, as he tried to come to terms with the physical and mental demands of the English pro game. He was helped along by the compassionate gesture of his skipper and fellow Scot McMullen. The big defender sensed Busby was struggling and invited him to live with his family until he felt settled. Even then, Matt took time to bed in.

In 1930, it appeared that he would be sold after a spell in which he could not even secure a place in the reserves. It was at this point that he could have ended up at Old Trafford – only United could not afford the £150 City were demanding for his services.

Salvation arrived that same year, however, when Hodge asked him to fill in at wing-half instead of his normal forward role. It was as if fate had struck. Busby was such a revelation that Matt Barrass, who had previously made the role his own, could not get back into the side. The legend of Matt Busby, football hero extraordinaire, was born. His first taste of the limelight would come three years later, when he and City reached the FA Cup final, only to lose to Everton 3–0.

A year later, in 1934, Busby won his first professional honour when City returned to Wembley in the same competition – and this time they beat Portsmouth 1–0.

On 4 October 1933, he had represented Scotland at number 4 in a Home International clash with Wales at Ninian Park in Cardiff, finishing on the losing side as the Scots crashed 3–2. In 1957, he would also briefly manage the national team – but would ask to be relieved of his duties in the wake of the Munich air disaster.

In 1935, Busby's clever, incisive distribution and elegant play led *The Guardian* to comment: 'In Matt Busby, City have at best a player who has no superior as an attacking half-back.' It was a wonderful compliment, and his talents were not going unnoticed elsewhere. Within a year, he had departed from Maine Road for pastures new: an £8,000 fee taking him to his final destination as a player – Anfield.

Manager George Kay immediately made Busby his captain and the Scot repaid his faith by leading the team with distinction.

His career was cut short by the Second World War – Busby was one of several Anfield players who immediately signed up with the King's Liverpool Regiment – but he spent the rest of his playing days at Anfield until he retired in 1945, although during the Second World War he guested for numerous other clubs, including Chelsea, Middlesbrough, Reading, Brentford, Bournemouth and Hibernian.

Liverpool's most successful manager, Bob Paisley, would later pay tribute to the man who had served the Anfield club so well – and to whom Paisley would admit he owed a great personal debt. Busby had taken Paisley, who was signed as a young player from Bishop Auckland in May 1939, under his wing, in much the same way as McMullen had done to him at Manchester City. Busby's kindness elicited this compliment from the man who would go on to lead Liverpool to three European Cup wins: 'He was a man you could look up to and respect. He'd played the game and people like him weren't solely tied down with tactics, which was a valuable lesson for me.'

The club Matt Busby took over in 1945 was in disarray. United were very much the second team in Manchester, having to play their games at Maine Road up until 1949 due to bomb damage at Old Trafford. The raid by the Luftwaffe on Trafford Park industrial estate on the night of 11 March 1941 had left the Main Stand and part of the terracing destroyed. Old Trafford was the worst hit of all English league club grounds during the war and United were awarded £22,278 by the War Damage Commission to clear the debris and rebuild the ground.

A 120,000-capacity stadium was planned, but financial restrictions meant only the Main Stand was replaced. Old Trafford finally reopened for Football League action on 24 August 1949, when a crowd of 41,748 saw United beat Bolton. Charlie Mitten became the first player in eight years to score a goal at Old Trafford, as United ran out 3–0 winners. Allied with the FA Cup win the previous year, it was a rousing moment for United's loyal army of fans: those same fans had had little to shout about for many years before Busby – in the season prior to his arrival, the side had finished 14th in Division One. United had not won a trophy since 1911, a gap of thirty-four years, and now Arsenal were the biggest club in England, following their five league titles and two FA Cup wins in the 1930s.

But the miracle man had arrived. He would manage United from 1945 to 1969 and again for 1970–71, and during his tenure the club would lift eight major trophies: one European Cup (1968), five league titles (1952 – after a forty-one-year absence, 1956, 1957, 1965, 1967) and two FA Cups (1948, 1963).

It was his former club, Liverpool, who won the first post-war league title – their first in 24 years – but it did not take long for Busby to make his mark at United. He was the first of a new generation of managers – tracksuit bosses who joined the players on the training field. And Jock Stein would ensure the tradition prospered in Busby's native Scotland, with Celtic. Another trait the two men shared was their love of football played with a smile and with honour: it was not just enough to win . . . they wanted to win with football that was attacking and entertaining. Busby would later define his footballing mission in these words: 'Winning matches at all costs is not the test of true achievement . . . there is no dishonour in defeat, as long as you play to the limit of your strength and skill. What matters above all things is that the game should be played in the right spirit . . . with fair play and no favour, with every man playing as a member of his team and the result accepted without bitterness and conceit. Played at its best between first-class teams, football is a wonderful spectacle. I love its drama, its smooth playing skills, its carefully laid rhythm, and the added flavour of contrasting styles. Its great occasions are, for me at any rate, unequalled in the world of sport. I feel a sense of romance, wonder and mystery, a sense of beauty and a sense of poetry. On such occasions, the game has the timeless, magical qualities of legend.'

Interestingly enough, Eric Cantona would also echo these types of sentiments in *La Philosophie de Cantona: A Bilingual Celebration of Art and Beauty through the Eyes of Cantona*:

> I feel close to the rebelliousness and vigour of the youth here. Perhaps time will separate us, but nobody can deny that here, behind the windows of Manchester, there is an insane love of football, of celebration and of music.

Busby's first trophy came with the 4–2 triumph over Blackpool in the 1948 FA Cup final. The team was one forged from an impressive youth policy and prudent buys. Stanley Matthews had tried to inspire the Seasiders to victory only to find stronger adversaries in United skipper Carey, who drove his side on, and goal heroes Jack Rowley and Stan Pearson.

Busby had few other choices but to plump for youth and bargain buys, having arrived at a United in debt, surviving on a £15,000 overdraft. His first signing was a brilliant one: Jimmy Murphy, who would serve as his assistant manager until 1971. The Welshman had been his opposing number when he won his only cap at Ninian Park in 1933. Together they constructed United's first great post-war team, building from the back, with Jack Crompton in goal, Johnny Carey, John Aston and Allenby Chilton. Up front there was Jimmy Delaney and the attacking skills of Charlie Mitten, John Rowley and Stan Pearson. In the first year under Busby and Murphy, United hit 95 goals – Rowley leading the way with 26, followed by Pearson on 19.

An important development to that first season was the retirement of Bert Whalley as a player. The half-back took on the job of coaching the youth teams at the club and would help nurture the skills of the boys who would become known worldwide as the Busby Babes.

By 1949, Busby's obvious abilities as a manager brought Tottenham Hotspur to the doors of Old Trafford. They wanted Matt to take over as their manager – and offered him £50 a week. He refused: nothing would now tear him away from his beloved United.

The early 1950s saw the first fruits of Busby and Murphy's youth policy, as Jackie Blanchflower and Roger Byrne broke into the first team. It was *Manchester Evening News* journalist Tom Jackson who came up with the phrase 'the Babes'. It stemmed from the debut of Blanchflower and Byrne against Liverpool at Anfield on Saturday, 24 November 1951. 'United's "Babes" were cool and confident,' wrote Jackson, after the match.

Busby was spurred into action after the title win of 1952. He was not a man to stand idly by if he thought things were not right: he was a definite man of action and felt that his league winners had reached their peak that season and had lost their edge and hunger for glory. His answer was 'out with the old and in with the new'.

By 1953, a new team was being blooded in the First Division, as Bill Foulkes, Mark Jones, David Pegg, Liam Whelan, Eddie Colman and Duncan Edwards all broke through. Two league titles followed, in 1956 and 1957 (with an FA Cup final appearance in '57), and the visionary Busby entered United into the European Champions Cup.

Then came Munich. More of this chapter in United's history later, but, from Busby's point of view, everything changed after the tragedy of 6 February 1958. The manager suffered injuries so severe that he was twice administered the last rites. He also had to live with the cruel knowledge that he had lost many of his young players. Busby was absent from his desk for six months.

When he returned to work, with the astute Jimmy Murphy at his side, he began to assemble a new United. Busby would build up his third great team – which included the transfer of 'the

King', super-striker Denis Law, from Italian side Torino, for a record fee of £116,000. David Herd, Paddy Crerand and Noel Cantwell were also drafted in. United won the FA Cup again in 1963, narrowly missing relegation the same season, and the league championship in 1965 and 1967.

Murphy had missed out on that fateful trip to Munich. When the United party flew to Belgrade in 1958, he was on international duty with the Welsh team for a World Cup qualifier at Cardiff. After the tragedy, he took charge of United and led them to the 1958 FA Cup final, which they lost 2–0 to Bolton. He welcomed Busby back in the August of that year and would serve the club loyally as assistant manager until 1971, and then as a scout until his death on 14 November 1989.

When Matt took command again, it seemed he was being driven on by an astonishingly powerful inner force – and in many ways he was. After Munich, he had made it his life's work to rebuild a team that would go on to become the first English side to win the European Cup. Achieving that aim would become his personal holy grail for ten years. Winning it would finally put to bed his demons from Munich: it would bring closure to the guilt he felt at the tragic deaths of eight of his young players.

United's first competitive European encounter took them to Anderlecht in September 1956, in a first-round first-leg European Cup tie which the English club won 2–0, a month before a certain Bobby Charlton made his first-team debut. By the end of that campaign in April 1957, a 19-year-old Charlton had forced his way into the first team and made his European bow, scoring in a 2–2 draw in the semi-final second leg against Real Madrid at Old Trafford, which saw United go out 5–3 on aggregate. Bobby had joined United as an apprentice in 1953, turning pro a year later, and would go on to become one of the club's greatest players. He was from a famous footballing family – his mother (a Milburn) had four brothers who were all pros. Bobby made his debut for

United on 6 October 1956, in an amusing coincidence against Charlton at Old Trafford, grabbing a brace in a 4–2 win. In that match, he had worn a pair of Roger Byrne's old boots. Bobby's first hat-trick was also against Charlton, in a league game at the Valley on 18 February 1957.

Now a United director, Charlton would make 759 appearances for the club in a 17-year playing career, scoring 249 goals. He won three First Division championship-winner's medals, in 1957, 1965 and 1967, and an FA Cup-winner's medal in 1963. Bobby was named the Football Writers' Association (FWA) Footballer of the Year and European Footballer of the Year in 1966. He went on to play a starring role as Alf Ramsey's side won the World Cup that year, scoring twice in the semi-final win over Portugal. His total haul of international caps would eventually reach 106 – and he is still England's record goalscorer with 49 goals.

Charlton would also score 22 goals in 45 European ties for United, in the Cup-Winners' Cup, Inter-Cities Fairs Cup (the forerunner of the UEFA Cup) and four further European Cup campaigns, which included winning the trophy in 1968 with a 4–1 victory over Benfica after extra-time at Wembley. Of course, he also followed in the great Billy McNeill's footsteps by lifting the trophy as skipper – a year after Billy had done so for Celtic.

Looking back, Bobby can understand that while, in one sense, Busby was the great pioneer, in another, his vision condemned him to what would become a personal purgatory following Munich – until United finally lifted the champions' trophy. He remains convinced that Busby's insistence that United and English clubs play in Europe is one of his greatest legacies for the club and football in general. 'It was a great adventure back then,' Charlton commented in 2007, 'an exciting time. Having to go to places you had never been before, having to alter the food you took, the medical side, everything. Nothing was available as it is now, but that didn't matter, from a playing point of view.

'People forget, we played our first few "home" matches at Maine Road and, you ask anybody who was there, the floodlights weren't great. We had to play in silky shirts so that what little light there was would reflect off them.

'It was still a great, great time and if you are a big club, like we always assumed we were, the place you had to be was in Europe and beating those teams. We all thought the English game was good, but you can't measure yourself properly until you have played the very best.'

Charlton had certainly proved himself one of the best – along with Georgie Best – in that 4–1 win over Benfica on a balmy May night in 1968 as United followed Celtic into the record books. Celtic, of course, had beaten them to the elite European crown by a year, but United had at least the satisfaction of becoming the first English team to win the European Cup. It would be the one thing the fans could throw back at their Scouse counterparts as Liverpool went on to win it four times during United's wilderness years to 1999.

It also once again served to highlight the eternal link between Busby and his two major Scottish peers: Stein and Celtic had become the first British side to lift the trophy the year before and Bill Shankly had looked like beating them both to it in 1965 with Liverpool until Inter Milan, with the aid of a corrupt referee, put them out in the semi-finals. Liverpool would have to wait until Busby's great friend Bob Paisley steered them to glory in Rome in 1977.

In the 1968 final, United skipper Charlton had scored twice to kill off Eusebio's dream of taking the cup to Lisbon, his goals instead making his mentor Busby's dreams come true.

Another footballing legend, Jimmy Armfield, believes that the ultimate redemption Busby felt after that 1968 Wembley win led to United becoming the legendary club they are today.

'Matt was the man who laid the foundations for Manchester United with the Busby Babes,' he said. 'Back in the 1950s, they had to overcome losing most of their players in Munich. A lot of people felt for them and out of the ashes came the phoenix of the flames of Manchester United under Busby.'

And another footballing great, Don Howe, is keen to stress Busby's achievement in renewing United after Munich, one he believes will never be matched. 'He was phenomenal. He not only brought in players and let them play, but he introduced a lot of young players. The Busby Babes were innovative and he really knew how to nurture the likes of Duncan Edwards,' Howe said. 'He was interrupted by the Munich plane crash and then he went and did it again. He did it under circumstances that no one else has had to do before or since. He had to completely start again and then led them to the European Cup. He was a wonderful, wonderful man.'

Busby himself was in tears after the win. He said of his victorious team, 'They've done us proud. They came back with all their hearts to show everyone what Manchester United are made of. This is the most wonderful thing that has happened in my life and I am the proudest man in England tonight.'

Busby, who had already been awarded the CBE in 1958, was knighted in 1968. A year later he announced that he would be retiring from Manchester United as manager. He had had enough: he had achieved his aim and admitted he felt worn out. The years since Munich had taken their toll. 'It's time to make way for a younger man,' Busby said, 'a tracksuited manager.' He admitted the job had become too much for a man of his age – he was then 59 – and said he would take on the role of general manager, adding, 'United is no longer just a football club; it is an institution. I feel the demands are beyond one human being.'

Busby had created the world-renowned legend of Manchester United FC. Naturally, his successor, the wet-behind-the-ears

Wilf McGuinness, aged just 31 and a former United wing-half, never stood a chance. Busby's shadow loomed large and the big man would often overrule his decisions – especially if they went against Georgie Best.

By December 1970, the board had persuaded Busby to step in once again – to steer the club away from relegation. It was a shambolic situation: United were like a punch-drunk boxer reeling ever more chaotically from round to round. The quietly ineffective Frank O'Farrell took over for the 1971–72 season but also failed to turn things around. United's freefall would continue until they finally plucked up the courage to send for the Doc in 1972. Even then, they had to go down to come back stronger. Just six years after their greatest moment, the Reds were at their lowest point since the 1930s, when they had been relegated to Division Two.

Busby had been in the United manager's chair for a quarter of a century and would become the club president in 1982, while also holding a senior role on the Football League management committee. He died on 20 January 1994 at the age of 85, but he knew the red empire he had created was now in safe hands. The previous year he had witnessed the exciting development of Alex Ferguson's first great team. They had won their first Premiership title the year before Busby's death, ending a 26-year barren spell.

That year, Warwick Road North, the approach road to Old Trafford, was renamed Sir Matt Busby Way in tribute. And in 2002, he became an inaugural inductee of the English Football Hall of Fame in recognition of his impact on the English game. Directly outside the stadium stands proud a bronze statue of the great man. It was erected in 1996 and was made hollow to allow for the two bales of scarves left as a tribute by fans at his death. The club's annual Player of the Year award is named after him and the recipient is still presented with a small replica of the statue.

Sir Matt even has the distinction of being the man who struck on the nickname for his beloved United. In the early 1960s, Salford Rugby Club were known as 'the Red Devils', but Sir Matt liked the sound of it so much that he adopted it for his own football club.

Our final tribute to the man who created the foundations of the modern-day Manchester United comes from one of the group of people who mattered most to Busby: the fans. It was for them he came up with the blueprint of winning football that also had to be attacking and exciting. It was for them that he produced three wonderfully entertaining teams in his 25 years at the helm. Contributing to the excellent manutdzone.com website, one United supporter sums up the Busby legend in this way: 'The legacy of Busby is that he provided the foundation, philosophy, style and passion that turned a once ordinary club from the grim industrial north of England, into today the most famous, glamorous, richest and now undoubtedly biggest team in the world. Sir Matt Busby created the Manchester United legend and, in doing so, has himself become a legend forever in footballing history.'

Well said that man.

9

··

JOCK STEIN: THE BIG DEAL

John, you're immortal now.
> *– Bill Shankly to Jock Stein following Celtic's*
> *European Cup victory, 1967*

We did it by playing football. Pure, beautiful, inventive football.
> *– Jock Stein, Lisbon, 1967*

Celtic jerseys are not for second best. They don't shrink to fit inferior players.
> *– Jock Stein*

IF SIR Matt set the tone for the new style of tracksuited boss, Jock Stein was the big man who took up the baton with relish – and although he would not start work as Celtic supremo until some 20 years after Busby had taken his job at United, he ended up beating him to the coveted finishing post by becoming the first British football manager to lift the European Champions Cup.

Even now these very achievements raise the question: why was one knighted (Busby) and the other (Stein) not? Jock received the CBE in 1970, but surely, given the way he matched Matt trophy by trophy, he deserves equal official recognition now?

Stein would return to Celtic Park as manager on 9 March 1965, but there was no fanfare for the former player and reserve-team coach. The club were in the doldrums, and if his appointment was not exactly a gamble it was hardly one that had the fans hanging out the bunting. Yet within two years he had pulled off a footballing miracle: taking Celtic FC from relative mediocrity – in their terms of reference, at least – to the undisputed title of the best team in Europe, arguably the world.

That March, Big Jock had arrived with a handshake from chairman Bob Kelly and what at the time might have seemed a poisoned chalice, as Kelly told him, 'It's all yours now, Jock lad.' Billy McNeill, who went on to become Stein's inspirational captain and a fine future manager at Parkhead, admitted he and his teammates were excited by his return. They knew the nucleus was there for a wonderful team – a team Stein had in no small part helped produce when he was appointed reserve-team coach in 1957 – and they also knew all they needed was an inspirational conductor to help them produce the sweet soul music they were capable of playing.

McNeill put it this way: 'Everything was, more or less, in place; all of the players who were to become the Lisbon Lions, Willie Wallace apart, were already there. It needed someone to make it gel, to give us confidence and belief in ourselves.'

Like Busby, John 'Jock' Stein was a native of Lanarkshire, born a few miles away from Sir Matt on 5 October 1922 in a mining village called Burnbank. He was the only son of George and Jane Stein but, unlike Sir Matt, came from Protestant stock. He first attended Glenlee primary, moving on to Greenfield secondary at the age of 12.

He was no genius, but also no fool: Stein knew football would be his only escape from a life down the Lanarkshire coalmines. His father was a staunch Rangers fan and insisted young Jock turn out for the local juniors club, Blantyre Victoria, even though his son wanted to play for Burnbank Athletic. George told him to forget Athletic because they did not play in blue, unlike Victoria. Jock himself was never swayed by religious beliefs like his father; throughout his Celtic career, Jock made it clear that he abhorred the sectarian divide – it is worth pointing out that Jean Toner McAuley, the girl he married in 1946 before he joined the club, was a Catholic.

His tolerant attitude created divisions between himself and his father and friends, particularly when he signed for Celtic as a player, then as their manager. George never congratulated him on his Parkhead appointment and Jock revealed that his best pal, a devout Protestant, went one step further by never speaking to him again.

By 1937, Jock had left Greenfield School in Hamilton and had worked briefly as a labourer in a carpet factory, plus had spent some time down the mines. On 14 November 1942, aged 20, he made his debut as a professional player for Coatbridge club Albion Rovers at centre-half, ironically against Celtic in a 4–4 draw at Cliftonhill. Stein turned out for the Wee Rovers for the next eight seasons, notching up a total of 236 appearances and scoring nine goals, while remarkably still working down the Lanarkshire pits as a miner. He also briefly appeared on loan at Dundee United in 1943.

His spell at Rovers was the beginning of a story of tremendous determination, dedication and optimism against a tough backdrop: these were characteristics he maintained throughout his career as a player and manager and would help him surmount the odds to eventually become a valued player at Parkhead – where, in many eyes, he was seen as a mere journeyman – and one of the greatest managers in football history at the same club.

Stein left Cliftonhill in 1950 after helping Rovers win promotion to the First Division in 1948. That season and the subsequent one in the top flight were undoubtedly the highlight of Stein's time at the club. That year in Manchester Busby was also celebrating, as United won their first trophy under him, the 1948 FA Cup.

Big Jock then surprisingly headed for non-league football in Wales with Llanelli Town. He would later admit that he moved for the money and the prestige of becoming a full-time pro footballer. He was 27 and, as he saw it, time was running out for him to make his mark and secure some financial security.

At Llanelli, he was paid £12 a week – as opposed to the £4 a week that Rovers had offered him to stay at the club as an amateur. But the move to Wales was a disaster: the transfer had been acrimonious and was then declared illegal, as he did not have clearance from the Scottish FA to play under the auspices of the Welsh FA. When that problem was finally resolved, Stein's wife Jean started to suffer from homesickness. She and their daughter, Rae, had only moved down a few weeks when their council home in Hamilton was twice burgled. Jean told Jock she had had enough and that they had to return to Scotland. She would, of course, have a big say when Manchester United came calling for his services 20 years later.

Jean ruled the roost and so Stein returned home to Lanarkshire in 1951 with the intention of giving up football entirely in favour of a life down the pits.

Out of the blue, in December 1951, Celtic stepped in for him and saved him from a life of grime at the pit head. On the recommendation of the club's reserve-team trainer, Jimmy Gribben, they bought him for £1,200, essentially as a squad player. The move left the big man flabbergasted. He would later say, 'I thought they were kidding me. I just didn't believe it. Celtic, after me? It was laughable.'

Yet fate would bring about a further twist, with injuries to key first-team players meaning that the man signed as a reserve was soon in the starting eleven and, within a year, had been promoted to vice-captain.

No sooner had destiny smiled on Stein twice, with the intervention of Gribben and a spate of injuries at his new club, than it smiled again. Skipper Sean Fallon broke his arm and Stein became club captain, an honour he would retain until his Celtic playing career ended in 1956. He had suffered a career-ending injury to his ankle after an accidental collision with Billy Simpson in a League Cup match at Celtic Park in August the previous year and would never recover. Ironic that the match was against bitter rivals Rangers – and at Celtic Park on 31 August 1955.

During his Celtic playing years, Stein was a fine example of what could be achieved with the right frame of mind. He was an inspirational skipper but would modestly describe his talent and impact in this way: 'I was fairly good in the air and at that time Celtic needed someone there at the back, but I had good players around me. I wasn't a bad positional player, but I wasn't exceptional as a player; just ordinary, very ordinary.'

Stein may have been a grafter and a journeyman, but his success was rooted in his understanding of his limitations and his strict Presbyterian work ethic. He made the best of his talents, and his impact on Celtic as a player was immediate and immense. He arrived at the club at a time when it had just one trophy to show for its efforts in thirteen years: the 1951 Scottish Cup, secured after beating Motherwell. It was the Hoops' first glory since the league title victory back in 1938. When Stein arrived, even that cup triumph looked as if it was a one-off in what had become routine mediocrity. They were 12th out of 16 teams in the First Division.

He was on the princely sum of £16 a week and made his debut against St Mirren four days after joining the club, as the injury list began to bite. By 1953, he had established himself as a talker and an organiser, and he proved how effective he was at both as

Celtic FC won the Coronation Cup. This success would be the precursor to a spectacular 12-month period for both Stein and the club.

The Coronation Cup was a one-off to celebrate, as the name suggests, the accession of Princess Elizabeth to the throne. With other competitors including English champions Arsenal and Matt Busby's Manchester United, the winners would proudly be able to proclaim they were the best team in Britain. An eight-team tournament based at Ibrox and Hampden, the cup also featured talented teams from Aberdeen, Hibernian, Newcastle and Spurs.

Celtic and Stein had to prove themselves from the very opener – and did so, beating the Gunners 1–0. Five days later, on Saturday, 16 May 1953, it was the turn of the Busby boys. A crowd of 73,466 turned out at Hampden, and again Celtic would emerge triumphant – this time with a 2–1 victory. At the end of the match, Matt made a point of seeking out and congratulating Big Jock – it was the start of a major mutual appreciation society and, some would claim, the real beginning of the ties of affection that would bind the clubs to the present day.

The win over United put the Bhoys in the final against an excellent Hibernian side that had won the Scottish League in 1951 and 1952 and pushed Rangers so close in '53 that they only lost out on goal average. Again, a Stein-inspired Celtic would seize the day, winning 2–0, with goals from Neil Mochan and Jimmy Walsh.

Mochan would go on to play a major role, as the Hoops won the Scottish league crown in 1954, scoring 20 goals, to help bring the title back to Parkhead for the first time in that barren 16-year spell. Billy McNeill stresses that Stein's role was just as vital, saying, 'A lot of it was down to Stein. Not that he was the greatest player in the world, but he was a good captain and a good leader.'

Indeed he was . . . so good, in fact, that he also inspired his men to victory over Aberdeen in that year's Scottish Cup final – a win that meant they had also secured their first cup and league double for 40 years. It was quite an achievement for the man who could have ended up down the pit for life but for the timely intervention of the brilliantly perceptive Jimmy Gribben.

The following season, Celtic would finish runners-up to the Dons in the league and lose the cup final to Clyde. And worse was to follow. Stein suffered an ankle injury in August 1955 after the clash with Rangers forward Simpson and would miss 17 matches, returning in the 5–1 romp against Partick Thistle on 17 December but then playing only intermittently.

At the start of the campaign that year, he had written a poignant message to the Celtic Supporters Association, saying, 'I cannot, like other Celts, claim that Celtic was my first love, but I know it will be my last and most enduring . . .' Now, without their leader, his team would finish fifth in the league and lose the Scottish Cup final 3–1 to Hearts. Jock's last match as a player was in May 1956, in a friendly in Coleraine, Northern Ireland. He was finished at just 34.

Down, but certainly not out . . . The following summer, his chairman and mentor Bob Kelly set him on the road to what would be managerial immortality by offering him the job of reserve-team coach. It was 1957 – ten years off that glory night in Lisbon – and now Stein would get the chance to nurture the boys who would become men that wonderful night. He worked his magic with the group of emerging youngsters, dubbed 'Kelly's Kids', among them McNeill, Murdoch and John Clark, and confirmation of his good work came in 1958 when Celtic beat Rangers 8–2 on aggregate to lift the Reserves Cup.

At the same juncture in time, Matt Busby was recovering from the Munich air disaster. The two men, who would be the first to bring the European Cup back to Scotland and England, were slowly approaching their destiny but in acutely different circumstances.

Fast-forward two years and Big Jock is forced to face up to a personal dilemma. While he was clearly religiously tolerant, he felt the board of directors did not share his views: in short, he was resigned to the fact he would have to leave Celtic Park to further his career because he believed they would not at that time employ a Protestant as manager.

His wife, Jean, would admit as much in 1988, saying, 'He was more or less told by the chairman that he had gone as far as he could with Celtic . . . coaching the second team . . . I know the old chairman used to suggest that he had simply let John go out for experience and that it was the case that he would go back to Celtic, but I don't think that was right. John didn't think so either . . . He thought the fact that he was a Protestant meant he would never be manager of Celtic. That's why he made up his mind to try elsewhere.'

Elsewhere would end up being Dunfermline. Stein became manager at East End Park, his first stab at a No. 1's job, in March 1960, aged 37. The club were languishing third from bottom of the First Division, but in his first game his new team, with some poetic justice, beat Celtic 3–2, the first goal of his managerial career coming after just ten seconds, courtesy of centre-forward Charlie Dickson. It was merely a sign of what was to come: under Jock, Dunfermline won all six of their final matches of the season to stave off the threat of relegation and the next season would finish fourth. They would also reach their first-ever Scottish Cup final, which almost inevitably, given the way Stein's scripts seemed to play to the galleries, was against Celtic. The first match ended 0–0, but the Pars went on to win the second match 1–0 – and the trophy with it.

The managerial legend of 'the Miracle Men' was now truly taking shape. It was the first time in Dunfermline's history that the club had won the trophy. Recognising the changes and improvements he had brought to the club in his first year, the Pars' chairman, David Thomson, and his board moved quickly to tie Jock down to the club. They offered him a five-year contract, which he signed on 2 May 1961, and also bought him a house in Garvock Hill.

It was a wise move. The big man had also been offered a double-your-money deal from Newcastle United to become their manager but had turned down the £4,000-a-year deal – and a £3,000-a-year deal at Hibernian – because he still felt he had work to do at Dunfermline and could not turn his back on the club that had given him his big chance.

In the 1962–63 season, Stein showed he could 'do the business' in Europe too, as his Pars team knocked the mighty Everton out of the Inter-Cities Fairs Cup 3–1 on aggregate and then, remarkably, pulled back a four-goal deficit from the first leg of their encounter with Spanish giants Valencia, and notched up an incredible 6–2 scoreline at East End Park to take the match to a play-off in Lisbon. They lost that match 1–0, but it was now clear that European competition did not frighten Stein. On the contrary, he thrived upon it.

In 1964, Stein decided it was time for the next stage of his managerial career and Easter Road was his destination. Again, he arrived at a club that was struggling and transformed its fortunes. Hibernian were lying in 12th place among the 18 clubs of the First Division and were starved of success. Stein swiftly changed that by winning the Summer Cup at his first attempt, as Hibs beat Aberdeen 3–1. It was the club's first trophy in ten years.

But that wasn't enough for Big Jock – he wanted to give the club's loyal fans something to shout about in European terms. Neighbours Hearts had qualified for Europe and their fans were ramming it down their rivals' throats, so Stein arranged a game against Real Madrid, the most famous club in the world. It was a move that typified the big man's brash, extrovert public persona.

In this way, he differed greatly from Busby. While Sir Matt preferred to do his talking behind closed doors and keep any disagreements in the dressing-room, Big Jock liked things out in the open. He was not afraid of the press; indeed, he relished ringing journalists up at home and berating them if he did not agree with their judgements. Busby would never have done that: he kept a distance between himself and the media.

Yet there was a mutual respect between the big man and the press. At one stage of his career, Stein had been worried that the press might expose his compulsive gambling. It could have cost him his job, but they left him in relative peace. Martin Hannan, in the *Scotland on Sunday*, wrote: 'It says much for the respect in which he was held that, even today, former colleagues and bookmakers will only acknowledge that Stein was a heavy gambler but will not state the scale of the financial losses he incurred.'

Stein was more of a Ferguson in his dealings with the media. He would have no hesitation bollocking them if he felt they were out of order and would also ban them, just like Ferguson at Manchester United. Television commentator and Stein biographer Archie MacPherson was a favoured friend of the big man but that did not save even him from the lash. 'As a fledgling commentator, I got the rough end of his tongue many times,' he said. 'They were bollockings to end all bollockings. But there was always something about a roasting from him that was educational, part of your growing up and maturing in the job.'

Jock was loud and overbearing, Matt was quiet and would whisper. There was quite a contrast between the two managers who would dominate British football at the back end of the 1960s.

Hibs defender Pat Stanton said that Stein's coup in bringing in Real Madrid for that friendly in 1964, which reportedly cost the club upwards of £15,000, worked wonders in that it lifted morale. But Stanton also admitted he was a little shocked when Jock told him it was he who would be man-marking the legendary Ferenc Puskas. 'I got a wee insight early on into Puskas when he went over the top on me,' Stanton said. 'I was a bit taken aback. Here was the world-famous player sorting out me, a young laddie from Niddrie. Anyway, we won 2–0 and did a wee lap of honour afterwards.'

The fans and the players loved Stein for his confidence, his showmanship and the belief he instilled in his players that they were winners, but his spell at the Edinburgh club would be short-lived.

Just one year later, in 1965, he was approached by Celtic to return to the club as their manager and saviour. It was an offer he simply could not refuse. Like Busby, he had been brought in for a specific task: to sweep away the cobwebs of mediocrity that had engulfed a great club and lead them forward to the top, where they belonged.

His impact was immediate at Parkhead: a phase of unequalled success followed for the next 13 years, beginning with the winning of the Scottish Cup, his new charges seeing off his former club, Dunfermline. It was Celtic's first big trophy since 1958 and the beginning of a staggering haul of 25 competitive trophies that would arrive at the club under Stein.

The big man had quickly shown his abilities in that first final, and he had needed to, as the Pars had gone in 2–1 up at the interval. By the end of the 90 minutes, the Hoops had won 3–2. Stein's encouragement to Billy McNeill to wander upfield more during set pieces and corners had made all the difference: the big defender had connected emphatically with Charlie Gallagher's corner to win the game.

It was the launchpad for an unprecedented era of glory, as Stein then went on to secure the club's first-ever domestic treble and set a phenomenal Scottish football record of nine successive league championship titles in a row, from 1966 to 1974.

That first full season under his command, in 1965–66, had ended with Celtic winning the double of league and League Cup. The first trophy to fall was the League Cup, as they beat Rangers 2–1 in the final, then they lifted the championship after seeing off a consistent pursuit by the Ibrox outfit. But Rangers would have the final say, ending their treble bid by beating Stein's men 1–0 in a replayed Scottish Cup final.

In 1966, Celtic again reached the semi-finals of the European Cup-Winners' Cup but were eliminated by Liverpool. Still, it had been a fine start by Stein and was a proud, loud clarion call for the success he was demanding from his players and for the football he wanted to keep the fans happy – always of the fast, attacking, entertaining variety.

Of course, the next season, 1966–67, would be the greatest in the club's history as, just two years after returning to Parkhead, Stein would prove he was indeed the Miracle Man by bringing home the European Cup as part of an unprecedented quadruple of trophies that included the league title, the Scottish Cup and the League Cup.

The first to fall was the League Cup, when Rangers were beaten 1–0 in the final in October 1966, thanks to a Bobby Lennox goal. Then came the FA Cup: two goals from Willie Wallace secured the trophy in a 2–0 win over Aberdeen. A week later, the Bhoys travelled to Ibrox and earned the 2–2 draw that secured a second successive Scottish Championship, Jimmy Johnstone grabbing the vital second goal.

Then it was on to Lisbon and the big one. Thousands of Celtic fans converged on the Portuguese capital and dared to dream. They knew that under Stein those dreams had a habit of coming true, but first they had to overcome the tough defensive fortifications that Inter Milan and their dour, cynical Argentine manager, Helenio Herrera, were planning to erect.

They did just that in their first attempt to lift the European Cup: on 25 May 1967, at the Estadio Nacional, Celtic became the first British and northern European club to win the trophy, overcoming the Italian giants 2–1. Goals by Tommy Gemmell and Stevie Chalmers secured the ultimate glory. It remains a formidable feat: no other Scottish side has ever even reached the final.

Afterwards even Herrera was forced to admit the better team had triumphed. 'We can have no complaints. Celtic deserved their victory,' he said. 'We were beaten by Celtic's force. Although we lost, the match was a victory for sport.'

Not a bad compliment from a man who had won the European Cup twice for Internazionale, in 1964 and 1965 (they also won the World Club crown in both those years), and would rack up a total of 16 major club titles in his coaching career. The man who would also coach three national teams – France, Spain and Italy – knew he had met his match, that he had been outfoxed by Big Jock. Flair had overcome the dull defensive football he had lived by – as he himself pointed out, the result was good for the sport. It was a triumph for attacking football over the ultra-defensive Italian style that at the time was threatening to suffocate the game on the Continent. It set the scene for Busby 12 months later, when he would lead Manchester United to the same trophy, with the same style of cavalier play from the likes of Best and Charlton.

After the final whistle, all hell broke loose in Lisbon, as joyful Celtic fans invaded the pitch. It meant the Celtic players could not be presented with the trophy out on the pitch, so club captain Billy McNeill was ushered around the outside of the stadium under armed escort, then climbed the stairs to the presentation podium, where he was handed the large-handled trophy and held it aloft.

Later that night he would present the other players with their medals after a celebration meal in a local restaurant.

It seems to me that Stein's victory marginally overshadows Busby's the following year – and I say that as a United fan – for two prime reasons. The first being that the Celtic team was made up 100 per cent of home-grown, local players (they were all born within a 30-mile radius of Celtic Park), a feat that has never been repeated in European football and can be viewed against United's winning of the trophy with players from England, Scotland and Northern Ireland. The second reason is that the Bhoys won it at their first attempt while Sir Matt had had many opportunities to learn the ropes before realising his ultimate triumph.

After the Celtic win, Stein would famously pronounce: 'There is not a prouder man on God's Earth than me at this moment. Winning was important, aye, but it was the way that we won that has filled me with satisfaction. We did it by playing football: pure, beautiful, inventive football. There was not a negative thought in our heads. Inter played right into our hands; it's so sad to see such gifted players shackled by a system that restricts their freedom to think and to act. Our fans would never accept that sort of sterile approach. Our objective is always to try to win with style.'

In an appreciation at the time of his death, BBC Scotland would sum up his achievement in Lisbon with this excellent tribute: 'It was the ultimate achievement in an ongoing success story generated by Stein's presence at the club. The early success of Celtic under Willie Maley was completely overshadowed by Stein's unstoppable progress and innovation. Before him, Celtic were not recognised outside of the UK, and barely noticed outside of Scotland. In the three decades before Stein took over, Celtic had won only three league titles, and had not picked up a single piece of silverware since 1958. As many observers have commented over the years, Jock Stein was Celtic; he made the club what they are today and his legacy remains as relevant in the modern era as it did 40 years ago.'

No sooner was the European Cup back at Celtic Park than Stein turned his attention to the next challenge: winning the World Club Championship in a similar style, with exciting, adventurous football. He would confidently proclaim: 'Whoever we have to play from South America, we shall attack. We want to show South America, as well as Europe, that defensive soccer is finished.'

It would be one sermon too far for the man who was the first to preach the gospel of total football – certainly years ahead of the Dutch, who are usually associated with its conception. Celtic's opponents in the world clash would be another cynical Argentine side, Racing Club of Buenos Aires.

Stein had made such an impact by lifting the European Cup that even Prime Minister Harold Wilson ventured up to Hampden for the first match in a two-legged affair against Racing. He did not like what he saw. Celtic would triumph 1–0, thanks to a Billy McNeill-headed goal, but the match would be remembered for the kicking, spitting and punching tactics of the shameful Argentines.

In the return leg, the Hoops were disadvantaged even before the first whistle when keeper Ronnie Simpson was sidelined after being hit by a missile, John Fallon stepping in. A penalty goal from Tommy Gemmell gave Stein hope that it would end in triumph, but Racing scored twice to take it to a play-off in Montevideo, Uruguay.

This time Celtic had had enough of the roughhouse antics of their opponents and gave as good as they got. Four Celts were dismissed – Lennox, Johnstone, Clark and Auld – and two Argentinians.

Racing went on to win 1–0. Uncannily, the match and the team's unsavoury tactics would be mirrored 12 months on when Manchester United played another Argentinian outfit, Estudiantes La Plata, in the same competition. The Red Devils lost the first leg 1–0 in Argentina and drew the return 1–1 at Old Trafford. George Best would later admit that, with a quarter of an hour gone in that first leg, he simply ceased trying to play because the Argentines' endless, largely unpunished, fouling made it impossible. In the return match at Old Trafford, his temper snapped and he was sent off.

The fortunes of Celtic United were tallying again – the years were passing, but the clubs were still progressing in a strangely similar manner.

Stein had worked his magic in '67 by turning a squad of underachievers into the champions of Europe and, like Busby a year later, he hoped it would be only the first of many European Cup wins. Again, both men would end up disappointed, their expectations never met.

Yet while Busby would not take United into another Champions Cup final after '68, Stein would bring Celtic back in 1970, when his team were matched with Feyenoord of Holland in Milan. It seems that, for once, the big man seriously underestimated his opponents, initially believing they would present few problems. Astutely, his opposite number, Feyenoord coach Ernst Happel, had suggested this before kick-off, saying, 'Celtic had better not underestimate us. We are a good team and we believe we can win in Milan. Our team are playing very well and we are afraid of no one. Of course we know all about Celtic. All Europe knows about their two victories over Leeds United and their win in Lisbon. But, although it will be hard, those victories do not make us afraid of them. We have fine players in our team, too, and we are looking forward to the final.'

Happel was born in Austria and joined Rapid Vienna as a 13 year old in 1938, making his debut in the first team three years later. He won seven Austrian championships with the club and represented his country in the 1954 World Cup, reaching the semi-finals with them. This was just the base camp of his achievements, however: as a manager, they were so extraordinary that some pundits claimed he was the greatest coach of all time. After his death in 1992, of cancer at the age of 66, the biggest football stadium in Austria, the Praterstadion in Vienna, was renamed Ernst Happel Stadion as a tribute.

The man who would plot Celtic's downfall also took Holland to the runners-up spot in the 1978 World Cup and lifted the Champions Cup with German club, Hamburg, in 1983. This win also earned him a permanent place in the record books – as one of only two men to win the European Cup with two different clubs (the other being Ottmar Hitzfeld).

This was the brilliant coach Stein would, uncharacteristically, underestimate as Celtic set out for their second tilt at the European crown in Milan. Big Jock could have been forewarned had he read an interview with Feyenoord's general manager, Guus Brox, the week before the final. Talking to the *Daily Record*, Brox made it clear his men were not going to Italy merely to make up the numbers. He talked about money, big money, incentives for his men – and dismissed out of hand the idea that Dutch football was in any way inferior, given it had only turned professional 16 years earlier.

'The days of Feyenoord being a part-time team are long gone,' Brox said. 'I am certain that the wages that we pay are as good as what Celtic pay or any of the other Scottish teams. Our players are earning an average of around £5,000 a year without any bonus payments being added. For the game against Celtic, we have decided to pay the players the biggest bonus that they have ever earned from the club [£1,000 per man]. In fact probably the biggest that any Dutch club had been offered . . . We are determined that we will win.'

It appears Stein's assistant, Sean Fallon, may have suspected Celtic could be up against it. Having watched Feyenoord play in the run-up to the final, he admitted to the *Glasgow Evening Times* that he was stunned by what he had seen. 'A first-rate team in every way. We couldn't spot any weaknesses,' Fallon said. 'Did you know that they haven't been beaten [in the league] this season? They'll take a bit of watching in Milan.'

Stein seems to have waved away his fears. Certainly Celtic's approach to the final suggests Big Jock was not unduly worried. As one of the final warm-ups he decided, instead of a tough workout against a pro outfit, to send his men up to Fraserburgh to play in an exhibition match in aid of the Fraserburgh Lifeboat Disaster Fund. The Bhoys strolled their way to a 7–0 win.

That year Manchester City had already won the European Cup-Winners' Cup and Arsenal had beaten Anderlecht to lift the Fairs Cup, and it was generally accepted that Stein's boys would complete the clean sweep of European trophies by British clubs. Even the Prime Minister, Harold Wilson, spurred them on in a pre-match telegram that read: 'Best wishes for your success in Milan. Make it a European hat-trick for British football. Harold Wilson, Downing Street.'

It was not to be. Even Stein, finally sensing the danger, appeared to wise up a day or two before kick-off. 'You know, I have the feeling we are being overrated and the Dutch underrated,' he said. 'That's dangerous. I don't like it. It's 1967 in reverse. Then we went to Lisbon starry-eyed, the underdogs not expected to win. Now Feyenoord are in that position and we are the fastest gun in the West. We are the target everyone wants to see knocked over.'

And knocked over they surely were, losing 2–1 after extra-time, the consolation goal coming from Tommy Gemmell.

After the match, Stein admitted, 'We played badly. That sums it up. They won and they deserved to win. You can carry a team with two, or even three, of the players off form. We had too many out there who were just not with it. They played as a team without a weakness. Unfortunately we had too many players off form, too many bad players tonight. But I don't want to take anything away from Feyenoord. They played well, better than us. Naturally, I am disappointed.'

In the following years, the idea that Jock had fatally underestimated the Dutch would gain more credence. In his autobiography, *Lion Heart*, Tommy Gemmell wrote:

> We were maybe a wee bit overconfident. I would say we probably underestimated Feyenoord, as we were the hot favourites to win. The team talk and the information that we got from Jock about Feyenoord weren't up to the usual high standard. He played it a bit too low-key, I felt, and never really built us up in the way you would expect before a European final.

Then, in an interview with *The Scotsman* in 2003, Gemmell was even more candid about Celtic's lax approach to the final, saying: 'There was a fatal underestimation of Feyenoord, and I mean from top to bottom, at Celtic. That kind of complacency is not a good thing to take into a European Cup final. When we saw them knocking the ball about even in the early stages, we thought, "Aye, aye, what have we got here?"'

Of course, there was the Leeds factor: the belief that the Hoops had already won the competition after their magnificent semi-final win over Don Revie's side. At the time Leeds were viewed as the best club team in Britain – arguably, the world – such was their dominance and sheer brutal power. Certainly, they were hot favourites to beat Celtic over two legs in the semis and then go on to win the trophy. Yet Celtic won the first leg in Leeds 1–0, thanks to a goal from George Connelly just 40 seconds after the game had started, and then went on to triumph 2–1 in the return leg at Hampden Park.

A crowd of more than 134,000 witnessed the brilliant win, which stunned the English press, who had expected Leeds to walk it. Leeds had even scored first, thanks to a fine strike from Billy Bremner after 14 minutes. But an equaliser from Murdoch forced the journos from across the border to eat humble pie. Afterwards Jock Stein would make it doubly indigestible by saying, 'Scottish football has been laughed at long enough. Now maybe they'll take it seriously.'

They did. The only problem was that Stein and his men also seemed to believe their own publicity: that they only had to turn up in Milan for the final to claim what was rightfully theirs. Bobby Lennox would be another who would put that poor performance against the Dutch down to the wins over Leeds. He told Eugene MacBride in his book, *Talking with Celtic*, 'I think, probably at the back of our minds, we thought, "We've beaten Leeds, that's us!" But to be fair, Feyenoord on the night were brilliant.'

In Graham McColl's book, *The Head Bhoys*, Davie Hay also points to the Feyenoord debacle as a rare night of blunder by the big man. He comments:

> The only one time when he probably failed in all his time, and we played our part in that, was the European Cup final against Feyenoord, where I think we all underestimated the opposition after doing so well against Leeds.
>
> Strangely enough, despite the fact that we didn't play well, we could almost have won that game – not that we would have deserved it. I think we were all to blame for losing that game. It was maybe the one error in his [Jock's] long career.

Hay would talk further about the aberration in an interview with the *Sunday Mirror* in August 2006, saying, 'Strangely, I really believe we should have won the European Cup that season. We beat Leeds United home and away in the semi-finals and probably thought that was the job done.'

Alan Herron, writing in the *Sunday Mail* after the match at Hampden, put Celtic's success at almost legendary level, saying, 'Scotland is no longer associated with haggis, bagpipes, Rabbie Burns and the River Clyde alone. It is associated with Celtic and successful attacking football.'

The Hoops would fall back to earth with a bump in Milan – and two years later, when they reached the European Cup semi-finals for the third time, only to lose in heartbreaking fashion at Parkhead to Inter Milan when Dixie Deans missed the first spot kick during a penalty shoot-out. It was the same story of heartache in 1974, the year Celtic won the league championship for the ninth season in a row – at the time a joint world record for success in domestic titles – but lost 2–0 in the semis of the European Cup to Atletico Madrid.

Still, most fans of the Bhoys would argue it was better to have loved and lost than never to have loved at all . . . at least they had the honour and pride of seeing their beloved team making those four European semi-finals.

A year later, Big Jock was almost killed in a car crash as he returned from a holiday on the Spanish island of Menorca. He returned to Celtic in 1976, but many believe he never fully recovered mentally or physically from the accident. Nonetheless, back under his command the Hoops won the double in 1976–77 of the inaugural Scottish Premier Division title and the Scottish Cup.

By 1978, the dream was over – and Stein was gone. Billy McNeill, captain of the 1967 team, succeeded the big man as manager. During Stein's 12-year tenure (excluding 1975–76, when he was recuperating from injuries received in his car accident), the club had enjoyed those 25 successes in major competitions: the European Cup, ten championships, eight Scottish Cups and six League Cups. It is a haul that will surely never be matched at the club, a lasting testament to the man and his work.

It is a pity the club did not look after him when he stepped down in '78. He had lost the services of Kenny Dalglish to Liverpool a year earlier and there were rumours that his relationship with the Celtic board was in tatters. It certainly appeared that way when, instead of offering him a place on the board, they effectively insulted him with the 'lure' of managing their pools ticket sales. Inevitably, he declined, and moved south to England to succeed Jimmy Armfield as manager of Leeds. That would be a prickly stepping stone, one he certainly did not enjoy, and he was gone within 44 days, happy to be returning to Scotland as head coach of the national team.

On 10 September 1985 in Cardiff, Wales, Jock Stein died while leading the Scots to the 1986 World Cup finals. His final decision as Scotland manager was to take off Gordon Strachan and send on Davie Cooper in the World Cup qualifier against the Welsh. It was an inspired move: Cooper would score the penalty that took the Scots into a play-off against Australia and towards eventual qualification. A few moments after the penalty goal, Stein collapsed. He died in the dressing-room of heart failure, aged 62. His record as Scotland boss is second only to Craig Brown's: 68 games played, 30 won, 13 drawn and 25 lost.

His funeral took place on Friday, 13 September 1985, with thousands lining the streets of Glasgow. The big man was gone – yet is never forgotten. Nine years later, Sir Matt would be similarly mourned in Manchester.

The fans of both clubs will forever remember the men who cheered their worlds or, as Billy McNeill said of Stein, in a sentiment that both sets of supporters can easily adapt for their beloved Busby and Jock, 'He gave me my dreams . . .'

10

··

WHEN THE TEARS FELL:
MUNICH, THOMSON AND DOYLE

All flights cancelled. Flying home tomorrow.
Duncan.

– Telegram sent by Duncan Edwards to his landlady,
delivered on 6 February 1958

You can keep all your Bests, Peles and Maradonas,
Duncan Edwards was the greatest of them all!

– Tommy Docherty

'I COULDN'T understand how I could have been 50 yards away
from the aeroplane, still strapped in my seat, without suffering
anything but a bang on my head. How could that be? How could
I feel myself all over and find out that I was all right, completely
whole, and my pals were dead? . . . I think about this every day of
my life.' These moving, tender words from Sir Bobby Charlton
only begin to sum up the tragedy that befell Manchester United
FC on 6 February 1958, but they are as worthy a starting point
as any as we start to examine the tragedies that have afflicted
Celtic and United over the years.

Of course, the Munich air disaster will forever live in the

memory of lovers of football everywhere, but as the 50th anniversary of the crash looms, the tears will flow more poignantly than ever in Manchester.

The first full account of Munich from Sir Bobby was given for the publication in 2007 of the *Manchester United Opus*, an 850-page compendium charting the history of the club. Talking after it was published, the 69 year old summed up the effect the crash had on the club in this way: 'Looking back on it now, I know I was so lucky. It was one of the greatest tragedies in sport simply because this great team was on the threshold of being the best.'

Lucky he was, indeed. Almost half a century after the plane carrying the Manchester United team home from a European Cup match broke apart on the outskirts of Munich airport, the memories still bring tears to Sir Bobby's eyes. Just 20 at the time, he still has nightmares about the crash, when, after two aborted take-off attempts, the twin-engine airliner finally sped down the runway. 'It was taking so long to get off the ground, and I suddenly realised that everyone felt the same,' he recalled. 'Then it went really quiet, and as I looked out of the window we hit a fence. We knocked it flat, and then everyone knew this was really serious.'

He would not talk about what he saw in the Munich snow because, he says, 'I looked round and saw injuries I will never describe.' Surrounding him was devastation: mutilated bodies lay in the snow; Matt Busby, the team's manager, was in agony, clutching his chest; teammate Roger Byrne was sitting, dead. Almost 50 years on, Sir Bobby told *The Times* he can feel the same painful emotions Busby felt in the late '60s and early '70s. He put it this way: 'And you know, you feel a bit guilty. I do feel guilty, even now, even as I say this.'

The Munich air disaster would claim the lives of twenty-three people, including eight of the world-famous Busby Babes, the boys who would surely have found true greatness in world football. Sir

Bobby, who had been knocked unconscious, was one of the lucky ones. He came round 15 minutes after impact, still strapped into his seat but 50 yards from the burning plane, teammate Harry Gregg having saved his life by lifting him to safety.

It had all started so differently that fateful night. The Babes were making their way home to Manchester after beating Red Star 5–4 on aggregate, the match in Belgrade ending 3–3. The BEA aircraft had stopped off at Munich's Riem Airport to refuel on the way back from Yugoslavia. As Captain James Thain had flown to Munich, his second in command, Captain Kenneth Rayment, now took over the controls.

Captain Thain would later describe the first attempt at take-off. 'Ken opened the throttles, which were between us, and when they were fully open I tapped his hand and held the throttles in the fully open position. Ken moved his hand and I called for full power.

'The engines sounded an uneven note as the aircraft accelerated and the needle on the port pressure gauge started to fluctuate. I felt a pain in my hand as Ken pulled the throttles back and said, "Abandon take-off". I held the control column fully forward while Ken put on the brakes. Within 40 seconds of the start of its run, the aircraft was almost at a halt again.'

The aircraft was suffering from a technical fault, 'boost surging', which meant the wrong mixture of fuel was causing the engines to fluctuate when accelerating.

A second take-off attempt also failed at 2.34 p.m. and the players disembarked and headed into the coffee lounge and it was now that Duncan sent his famous telegram to his landlady in Stretford. Like the rest of the Babes, he feared they would not get out of Munich that day. He was to be proved grimly correct.

Fellow United defender Bill Foulkes further explains, 'We'd

been playing cards for most of the flight from Belgrade to Munich, and I remember when we left the aircraft thinking how cold it was. We had one attempt at taking off but didn't leave the ground, so I suppose a few of those on board would start to worry a little bit, and when the second take-off failed we were pretty quiet when we went back into the lounge.'

Fifteen minutes later, the passengers were told to climb back aboard, but by now there was a general feeling of anxiety as the snow continued to fall. 'We got back into our seats, but we didn't play cards this time,' Foulkes said. 'I slipped the pack into my jacket pocket and sat back waiting for take-off.'

Captain Thain admitted he knew almost immediately that they were in for trouble as they attempted a third take-off: 'I glanced at the air-speed indicator and saw it registered 105 knots and was flickering. When it reached 117 knots, I called out "V1" [Velocity One, the point on the runway after which it isn't safe to abandon take-off]. Suddenly the needle dropped to about 112 and then 105. Ken shouted, "Christ, we can't make it," and I looked up from the instruments to see a lot of snow and a house and a tree right in the path of the aircraft.'

It had been third time unlucky when, at 3.04 p.m. local time, the aeroplane careered off the runway, smashing into the house before bursting into flames. A build-up of slush at the end of the runway was subsequently identified as the cause of the crash – it prevented the plane from gathering enough speed to lift off. Foulkes described the immediate build-up to the crash in this way: 'There was a lot of slush flying past the windows and there was a terrible noise, like when a car leaves a smooth road and starts to run over rough ground.'

Foulkes and United keeper Harry Gregg would visit the hospital in Munich the following day and be shocked by what they saw: Busby was in an oxygen tent, Edwards and a few others were seriously injured. But it was only when they were about to leave that the full nightmare of what had happened that night in Munich finally began to sink in. 'We came across Frank Taylor in another bed,' Foulkes explained. 'He was the only journalist around and he asked if we'd like to have a beer with him. Like us, he didn't know the full implications of what had happened the afternoon before. We were about to leave the hospital when I asked a nurse where we should go to see the other lads. She seemed puzzled, so I asked her again, "Where are the other survivors?"

'"Others? There are no others. They are all here."

'It was only then that we knew the horror of Munich. The Busby Babes were no more.'

Gregg had been convinced he was going to die when the plane veered off the runway. 'I braced myself and waited for the end,' he said. 'In the blackness, I thought I had died, but then I felt something trickling down my forehead and in my nose. I put my hand to my face and felt the warmth of blood.

'I began to crawl towards the hole in the aircraft. The first person I saw was Bert Whalley, lying in the snow, eyes wide open. He was dead. I thought, my God, I'm the only one alive, but then the captain appeared with a little fire extinguisher and bellowed, "Run, you bugger, she's going to blow." At that moment I heard a child cry. I crawled back into the plane, scrambling over the bodies in the dark, before I found the baby. Suddenly, a pile of rubbish erupted and out of it the child's mother appeared. I shoved her past me and out of the plane.'

Back in England, news of the tragedy was relayed via teleprinter: 'Manchester United aircraft crashed on take-off. Heavy loss of life feared.' The BBC interrupted its afternoon programmes to broadcast news flashes. It said that Sir Matt had suffered fractured ribs, a punctured lung and leg injuries. A hospital statement said, 'We do not have much hope of saving him,' and the last rites were administered.

Nobby Stiles, who would later became an England World Cup winner with Sir Bobby Charlton, was at the time a 15-year-old youth-team player at United. He was told about the crash while training but said neither he nor anyone else realised the full tragic nature of what had happened – and that it only sank in when he bought a newspaper that had the faces of Roger Byrne, Geoff Bent, Eddie Colman, Mark Jones, David Pegg, Tommy Taylor and Billy Whelan on the front page.

It was Nobby's job to clean 'Coly's' boots and he could not believe he was dead. In the *United Opus*, Nobby explained, 'I felt sick. We'd been laughing about this crash back in the dressing-room, saying maybe somebody had broken a leg, maybe the big chance had come for one of us. I got on the Collyhurst bus, and now I didn't hear anything going on around me. Everything seemed normal enough. The streets and the shops looked just the same. The sun was presumably still up there behind the low, leaden sky, and I guessed the moon would take its place in a few hours' time.'

There had been a total of thirty-eight passengers and six crew on board the flight. United lost their captain Roger Byrne, Mark Jones, Eddie Colman, Tommy Taylor, Liam Whelan, David Pegg and Geoff Bent. The great Duncan Edwards would also die in hospital 15 days later. Eight British sports journalists and several club officials were also killed.

It was the first fatal accident for this type of aeroplane since it had begun service six years earlier. The *Lord Burghley* had also taken the United entourage to Belgrade for the match. United had chartered their own plane after a problem in the previous round, when they had played in Prague. They had been delayed on the return and had landed back in England for their league game at Birmingham City with only hours to spare. This time they were scheduled to play Wolves, the league leaders, on the Saturday and Busby wanted to be home as quickly as possible.

After the tragedy, as United fans mourned the loss of their team, Red Star suggested United should be made honorary champions in the 1958 European Cup. Some supporters put up in their front windows black-edged copies of the *Manchester Evening News*, showing pictures of the team that had flown to Belgrade. Others were too upset to go to school, college or work.

Years later some have still not fully come to terms with the tragedy. Malcolm Wood, of Manchester, says, 'I'm a grown man of nearly 70, but it still brings tears to my eyes when 6 February comes round each year. That team was my team and, as well as watching them whenever I could, I would often see some of the players getting off the bus as some, including Matt, lived in Old Trafford.' Joe Cooke, of Birmingham, comments, 'I had just got home from school with my mate and I was ready to open my birthday cards – I was ten. Then it was outside with the ball. I was going to be Duncan Edwards. Then a news flash came on the radio – even now I can still remember the hurt. I still visit Duncan's grave. Bobby Moore was a great player, but how many caps would he have won if Big Dunc had lived?'

United supporter Aldo Hanson, once of Manchester, now living in America, says, 'When the news of the Munich air crash came through late that afternoon, I cried for hours. Younger football fans may not realise that before the 1990s supporting Man U was always something of a roller coaster: much success, often very emotional, but disappointment and sadness too – notably Duncan Edwards surviving the crash but dying of injuries days later and reaching the next cup final to be beaten by Bolton.'

The team that lined up in the final game with Red Star Belgrade before the fatal crash was Gregg, Foulkes, Byrne, Edwards, Jones, Colman, Morgans, Charlton, Taylor, Viollet and Scanlon. Of them all, legend would best preserve the memory of Duncan Edwards – 'Big Dunc' – the man-boy who had sent the telegram to his landlady the day before the Munich crash believing he would have to stay an extra day in Munich because of the snow. Many other people still believe the late great Bobby Moore would never have lifted the World Cup for England in 1966 had Duncan survived Munich, that the boy from Dudley would have had that honour, consigning Bobby rather to a footnote in history than the main story.

Duncan Edwards was born on Elm Road, on the Priory Estate, in the Black Country town on 1 October 1936 and died in Munich's Rechts der Isar hospital 15 days after the crash. He was just 21 years old. Doctors were 'amazed' at his fight for life. Sir Bobby Charlton once famously said of the big defender, 'If I had to play for my life and could take one man with me, it would be Duncan Edwards.' While Charlton was recovering from the crash back in Manchester, he would read the newspapers each day looking for news of his teammates and how their battle for life was going back in Munich. On the day of Duncan's death, he knew the big man had died when someone hid the paper from him in the morning.

The following are the bare facts of a career that turned the man into a legend: between 1952 and 1958, Duncan made 175 appearances for United, scoring twenty-one goals and winning two championship winner's medals, in 1956 and 1957. Between 1955 and 1957, he won 18 caps for England.

Duncan had proved he was a natural-born leader from his early days – his sports master at junior school is famed for commenting that at the tender age of 11, Duncan 'told all the other 21 players what to do and where to go and that included the referee and linesmen!'

In a similar way to the legendary telegram United's Northern Ireland scout Bob Bishop sent to Busby about Georgie Best, saying, 'I have found you a genius', so Duncan's teacher wrote to a friend with the immortal words, 'I have just seen a boy of 11 who will one day play for England.' In 1950, that prophecy went some way to being fulfilled, as Duncan turned out for England schoolboys at Wembley in a match against the Welsh.

Sir Matt Busby swooped to bring him to Old Trafford. He would make his debut for the first team on 4 April 1953, against Cardiff City: unfortunately, United crashed out 4–0. He was 16 years and 185 days old.

At 18 years and 183 days, he was at the time the youngest player to be capped by England, making his debut as his national side crushed Scotland 7–2 at Wembley. Yet Duncan hardly lived the high life. He was a quiet, conscientious boy who lived for his football – he devoted himself to United. It was hardly as if he earned the money to live like a king anyway; he was on just £15 a week during the season and that fell to £12 a week in the summer.

Duncan is buried in Dudley's Borough Cemetery. His tombstone reads:

> A day of memory,
> Sad to recall,
> Without farewell he left us all.

On the day of his funeral, more than 5,000 people stood in silence outside the cemetery and lined the streets. In 1961, Sir Matt Busby proudly unveiled two stained-glass windows at St Francis's church in Dudley to commemorate the life of Duncan, the boy who Matt would one day admit was, along with George Best, his favourite player ever. On that day in 1961, Busby would pay this tribute: 'There will only be one Duncan Edwards and any boy who strives to emulate Duncan or take him as his model won't go far wrong'.

Jimmy Murphy, United's assistant manager and the man who was key to Duncan's development, described his lost star as 'the Kohinoor diamond among our crown jewels'.

Murphy would later give this remarkable tribute in a statement to the press, emphasising Duncan's powerhouse play, his tackling and his majestic distribution skills: 'When I used to hear Muhammad Ali proclaim to the world he was the greatest, I used to smile. You see, the greatest of them all was an English footballer named Duncan Edwards. If I shut my eyes now I can see him. Those pants hitched up, the wild leaps of boyish enthusiasm as he came running out of the tunnel, the tremendous power of his tackling, always fair but fearsome, the immense power on the ball. The number of times he was robbed of the ball once he had it at his feet could be counted on one hand. He was a players' player. The greatest? There was only one and that was Duncan Edwards.'

In 1999, a statue of Duncan, resplendent in his England kit and created by renowned sculptor James Butler, was unveiled by his mother, Sarah, and Sir Bobby Charlton in Dudley's market place, as a permanent tribute to the boy who would have been king.

Busby was sure he had a team on the verge of greatness. As he recovered in Munich, United were third in the league, through to the fifth round of the FA Cup and into the last four in the European Cup. 'I felt I was in a position where I could have sat back for ten years while they played,' Busby said. 'They were that good.' In the event, Busby would spend the next decade on a personal mission of redemption: one that would only sweep away the guilt he felt at the death of his babes when United finally won the European Cup in May 1968.

It is a cruel irony of Munich that on the one hand it broke the club, while on the other it helped make Manchester United what it is today. It brought the club into the lives of many who had previously not felt an allegiance and added to its legend and history. Rob Hughes, writing in the *International Herald Tribune*, sums this up, noting the club had already established its character in rising from ashes after the bombing of Old

Trafford: the club, he writes, was now 'to attract global sympathy for the refusal of Matt Busby and other survivors to quit ... They became a worldwide symbol of the spirit of man, embodied in a simple, irresistible game.'

* * *

At Celtic, there were two tragedies also involving the club's players that jump out and demand investigation. The first involves the brilliant young goalkeeper John Thomson, who died tragically in the 1930s; the second centres on a great, fiery character of 1980s Celtic, Johnny Doyle.

> So come all you Glasgow Celtic
> Stand up and play the game
> For between your posts
> There stands a ghost
> Johnny Thomson is his name.

Celtic fans still sing the above folk song – called 'Johnny Thomson's Ghost' – in deference to the man who would surely have gone on to become Scotland's greatest ever goalkeeper had he not died at just 22 after an accident at Ibrox, home of Celtic's greatest rivals, Rangers.

Johnny made his debut for the Hoops in 1926 at the age of 17 and by the time of his death he had made 211 appearances. He was also established as the No. 1 in his country, having made four appearances for the national team, and had turned out the same number of times for the Scottish league side.

Born in Kirkcaldy in 1909, Johnny lived with his parents and his brothers and sisters at Balgreggie Park, Cardenden. He would die in Ward 5 of Glasgow's Victoria Hospital at 9.25 p.m on Saturday, 5 September 1931. One Cardenden local, writing in 1993 for the Cardenden local history group, would sum up the tragedy in this succinct, factually correct way while paying tribute to Johnny:

John Thomson put Bowhill on the map. As Celtic's goalkeeper he is remembered to this very day for his goal-keeping prowess. I was only nine years old when that tragic accident happened at Ibrox. Rangers were playing Celtic. It was during the second half and five minutes had gone from the restart when the ball was swung into the Celtic goalmouth. John Thomson left his goal and dived to a 50/50 ball with Sam English, the Rangers' centre-forward. Tragically, John lay still on the field and had to be carried off, badly injured. Later that evening, he died in the Victoria Hospital, Glasgow. The game ended with the score, Rangers 0 Celtic 0.

Thomson had suffered a fractured skull in the clash – one pressman would later describe him as 'a casualty of his desire to triumph and his determination to prevent a goal'.

English was absolved of any blame for Thomson's death, but he would never recover from it. The big Irishman was tortured by guilt and within a year had left Scottish football for good, joining Liverpool. As the keeper was being stretchered off, a section of the home support were unaware of the seriousness of the injury and cheered until they were silenced by one of the Rangers players.

Charlie Geatons took over in goal as John was rushed to hospital. Many fans did not wait around long enough to see him play in that unusual role that day: realising something was seriously amiss, thousands of Celtic supporters left the ground almost immediately. They, like their footballing idols, did not seem to have the stomach for a match which had previously seemed so important. A crowd estimated to be 1,000 strong assembled outside the Bank restaurant, owned by Celtic manager Willie Maley, awaiting any developments.

The *Dunfermline Journal* reported the situation in this way:

Mr Maley and all the Celtic directors were there. They were constantly in touch with the infirmary. Mr Maley, whose interest in his young players is that of a father, was deeply moved. Phone calls at the Infirmary were at the rate of 150 per hour. These came from all classes of people: Celtic supporters, club managers and officials throughout the country, and personal friends.

Talking of those who showed deep concern, it is only fair that Rangers get a vote of respect here . . . or at least their manager of the time, Bill Struth. He was the man who quickly helped sort out an ambulance to take John to the hospital and arranged for a car to bring his parents down from Fife. Struth also had the strength of mind to show compassion to a young woman who had screamed out loud from the Ibrox stands after John was injured. She had gone to the home dressing-room by mistake, asking to see him; Struth had taken her by the hand and compassionately directed her to John. It would later emerge that her name was Margaret Finlay, a 19 year old from Uddingston, and John's sweetheart.

John died a few minutes after his parents arrived to see him for the last time. His funeral was attended by over 40,000 mourners. A Cardenden local remembered it this way:

> The funeral at Bowhill Cemetery took place on Wednesday, 9 September, and was the largest I have ever seen. Two special trains left Glasgow for Cardenden; people walked all the way from Glasgow and slept the night on the Crags and along by the bing just to be there on the day of the funeral; football supporters came from all over the country. The Bowhill Pipe Band and the Bowhill Silver Band were in attendance. An aeroplane landed in the Daisy Park. I think it belonged to one of the national newspapers.
>
> The crowd along the route from 27 Balgreggie

> Park to the cemetery was packed tight, some even clambering up on to the rooftops. The coffin was carried by Celtic players. Even to this day I remember one of the wreaths, which was a piece of green turf with white goalposts made of white flowers. Celtic has never forgotten John Thomson. When they are playing in Fife, they make a point of paying their respects at his grave and usually they lay a wreath.

It is certainly true that Hoops fans will never forget him; they still pay tribute when the anniversary of his sad death arrives each year.

Thomson was snapped up by the club after scout Steve Callaghan saw him impress in goal for Wellesley Juniors against Denbeath Star in 1925. At the time, he also worked down the pits in Cardenden. Celtic paid £10 for John, who would go on to become known as 'the Prince of Keepers'. His debut for the club arrived in 1927, against Dundee at Dens Park. John would win two Scottish Cup medals: in 1927, when East Fife were defeated 3–1, and in 1931, when Celtic beat Motherwell 4–2 in a replay, after the first game had ended 2–2. It would take a long time for the club to get over the tragedy. Boss Maley would suffer in particular; it was as if he had lost a son, which in a way he had, given his close relationship with the boy. He seemed to withdraw into a shell. Results suffered, too, as the club tried to come to terms with it all. And further tragedy would follow: just two years after John's death, Peter Scarff, who had also played in the match that cost John his life, died from tuberculosis at the age of just 24.

In 1993, a street was named after John (Thomson Court) and a memorial erected in his name, funded by worldwide public subscriptions. It reads: 'They never die who live in the hearts they leave behind.' In the old part of Bowhill Cemetery, there is another memorial to him, whose inscription reads:

In memoriam, John Thomson,
Scotland's international goalkeeper,
who died 5th September 1931, aged 22 years.
The result of injuries received at Ibrox Park.
Beloved son of John and Jean Thomson.
'Honest and upright he played the game,
Beloved and respected he made his name.'

James Hanley, in his book *The Celtic Story*, sums up the appeal of the boy who was the Prince of Keepers in this way:

It is hard for those who did not know him to appreciate the power of the spell he cast on all who watched him regularly in action. 'A man who has not read Homer,' wrote Bagehot, 'is like a man who has not seen the ocean. There is a great object of which he has no idea.'

In like manner, a generation that did not see John Thomson has missed a touch of greatness in sport, for which he was a brilliant virtuoso, as Gigli was and Menuhin is. One artiste employs the voice as his instrument, another the violin or cello. For Thomson it was a handful of leather. We shall not look upon his like again.

In *The Story of Celtic*, Willie Maley would pay the following tribute to the boy he loved but lost, emphasising the particular goalkeeping skills Thomson had in abundance:

Among the galaxy of talented goalkeepers whom Celtic have had, the late lamented John Thomson was the greatest. A Fifeshire friend recommended him to the club. We watched him play. We were impressed so much that we signed him when he was still in his teens. That was in 1926. Next year he became our regular goalkeeper, and was soon regarded as one of the finest goalkeepers in the country.

But, alas, his career was to be short . . . Yet he had played long enough to gain the highest honours football had to give. A most likeable lad, modest and unassuming, he was popular wherever he went.

His merit as a goalkeeper shone superbly in his play. Never was there a keeper who caught and held the fastest shots with such grace and ease. In all he did there was the balance and beauty of movement wonderful to watch. Among the great Celts who have passed over, he has an honoured place.

Johnny Doyle was another Celt destined to forever hold feelings of affection within the club and its supporters. Like John Thomson, he would die young in tragic circumstance, being electrocuted at the age of 30 in October 1981. Ask any Celtic fan who has been following the club since the late '70s or earlier and he or she will tell you that Doyle is one of their favourite players ever.

Why? Celtic fan Stevie Murray explained to me: 'Because Doyley was one of us – he was a fan who was living the dream of playing for Celtic, the dream we all have. He was like our representative out on the pitch; he would get stuck in – particularly when we were up against Rangers. He always gave 100 per cent for the club. We loved him for it. He always made time for us, signalling to us and bowing and grinning when we chanted his name. There will probably never be another like him.'

Johnny Doyle arrived at Celtic Park as a 24 year old in March 1976 from Ayr United. He was born in Bellshill, Lanarkshire, on 11 May 1951 and moved with his parents when he was five to Fallside, the same area of Lanarkshire where Jimmy Johnstone grew up. A big Celtic fan from an early age, Johnny was influenced by his father William, a miner. He would also die young, when Johnny was just eight.

Johnny joined his local Celtic supporters' club in his teens but signed for Ayr in 1970 for the grand wage of £4 a week. His fiery temperament soon came to the fore even in his early days as a part-time player: he was sent off four times while playing for Ayr.

By 1976, he had had enough of 'being kicked around for £30 a week' and turning out in his day job as a clerk at the Clydesdale steelworks. He admitted, 'I want to go to Celtic.' His dream would swiftly come true that year, but it would cost the Hoops a fair packet to secure his signature. He became their record signing on 15 March 1976, costing £90,000. Like his hero, Jinky Johnstone, Johnny was also a wee winger (about 5 ft 4 in.) and, like Jimmy, was fearless and brave. He would play for Celtic until 1981, making 143 appearances and scoring 37 goals. He was a league winner in 1977 and 1979 and a Scottish Cup winner in 1977 and 1980.

The fans loved him for his struggles with officialdom and frequent run-ins with refs and other players. The chant, 'Johnny, Oh Johnny Doyle, Oh Johnny Doyle on the wing', would reverberate around Celtic Park during the late '70s in reverence to the uncontested hero of the Jungle.

One particular incident cropped up time and again when I talked to Celtic aficionados about Johnny boy: when he was sent off in the 4–2 title-winning game against Rangers on 21 May 1979. That was the day the famous Jungle chant of 'Ten men won the league' was born.

The match was Celtic's last game of the season, but Rangers still had two games to come. For Celtic, a win was vital; it would mean Rangers could not gain enough points to secure the title. To rub salt into the wounds, if Rangers won they would have been celebrating their first title win at Parkhead. With 25,000 of their fans on the terraces, it was a prospect the Jungle Bhoys were not savouring one bit.

Doyle was devastated when he was sent off after an incident with Alex MacDonald, the Rangers goalscorer, ten minutes after the interval. Johnny thought MacDonald was feigning injury after a tackle and tried to get him to stand up. MacDonald kicked out and Doyle responded with his own kick. Johnny would later say, 'Alex hit me on the leg and I hit him back, but there was nothing to it.' Trailing 1–0, Celtic now had to play with ten men for thirty-five minutes.

They clinched the title after a storming comeback inspired by the brilliant skipper Danny McGrain, the driving efforts of Roy Aitken and boss Billy McNeill's tremendous encouragement to his men to keep pressing forwards. Afterwards, his teammates would tell a still apologetic Doyley to stop fretting; it had all turned out all right on the night, after all, and the street parties were beginning in earnest in the east end of Glasgow.

Johnny admitted in a newspaper at the time:

> I was nearly spewing by the time I got to the dressing-room. I thought we had lost the championship because of me . . . If Celtic had lost, I had visions of collecting my boots and going. I thought I had reached the end of the road.

In the summer of 1981, there was speculation that Johnny would leave the club, but he turned down approaches from Hearts, Dundee and Motherwell, commenting, 'I don't want to leave Celtic – it took me long enough to get there.' His last appearance for the club was in a Glasgow Cup match against Queen's Park in which he scored. A week later he was dead. He had been electrocuted while rewiring his loft.

In May 1982, eight months after Doyle's tragic death, the faithful would celebrate winning another title with the immortal chant of 'We won the league for Doyle'. The victory over St Mirren had brought Billy McNeill and his men their third league championship in four seasons.

McNeill himself paid this tribute to Doyle, pinpointing Johnny's special relationship with the fans he adored and who, in return, loved him: 'The openness of his love affair with our club endeared John Doyle to the Celtic fans in a very special way and the rapport between them grew to a level that most players never achieve.'

Johnny's best pal at Celtic, Tommy Burns, summed up the unique nature of the friend he would mourn long and hard, saying, 'There were only two things that acted as any form of consolation to me after I came back from Johnny's funeral: the realisation that, at last, he was truly at rest and that he had died while still a Celtic player . . . In life he was a Celtic man through and through and it seemed fitting to me that he should meet his death while still a Celtic man, and I know that would have been important to him, too.'

That could have been the epitaph for all those who died while playing for Celtic and United: heroes all – and each one still terribly missed but always revered.

11

JINKY AND GEORGIE: SIMPLY THE BEST

Jimmy, O Jimmy Johnstone,
O Jimmy Johnstone down the wing,
Seven in heaven,
Lest we forget.

– Celtic fans' lament after Jinky's
death in March 2006

I spent a lot of money on booze, birds and fast cars.
The rest I just squandered.

– George Best on George Best

OK, LET'S get personal: in my considered opinion, Roy Keane shades it from Henrik Larsson as the best ever footballer to play for both United and Celtic, and Jimmy 'Jinky' Johnstone and George Best are the greatest footballers – certainly my favourites – ever to grace the stage individually at Celtic Park and Old Trafford respectively. In terms of this book's theme, how Celtic and United have mirrored each other in remarkable ways both off and on the pitch over the last century, Jimmy and Georgie are further prime examples of the links that will never die.

No other two players highlight so gloriously the very nature of Celtic and United than Jimmy and Georgie: a reliance on flair and attacking football that brought European Cups and glory galore, and a devil-may-care mischievousness that marked them out as bohemian rebels and firm terrace favourites. Both epitomised what Celtic and United meant to the fans, both delivered on the pitch and were the equals of any other player in any other era at their peak. Both were legends the like of which we may never see again.

Both men were divinely gifted players and emerged and starred during the same era; both made the number 7 shirt iconic at their respective clubs; both had problems with the demon drink and died young, a tragic genius, within months of each other; and both will live forever in the hearts and minds of the clubs and fans that adore them and are eternally grateful for their contributions.

* * *

James Connolly Johnstone was born on 30 September 1944 to Sarah and Matthew Johnstone in Viewpark, Lanarkshire. The village, which stands on the north side of the River Clyde and is about seven miles to the south-east of Glasgow, was the home town of Celtic ace George McCluskey and goalkeeper Lindsay Hamilton, who played with Stenhousemuir, Rangers, St Johnstone and Dunfermline. David Kettle, who won numerous Scottish swimming titles in the late 1970s and early 1980s, was also born there. But it remains best known for Jinky – and its wonderful castle, the largest and finest thirteenth-century stone castle in Scotland, much fought over during the Wars of Independence. Young Jinky would often visit the castle during his school days and he would admit to having enjoyed growing up with a loving mother and father on Old Edinburgh Road.

From an early age, he was obsessed with football and would spend happy hours kicking an old leather football around the streets with his young mates. In later life, he would relate how football was just something to help keep spirits up during hard times. 'Football was no big deal,' he said, 'not in the way that it is now, with all the hype. You would just pick up a ball and be practising against a wall and in no time at all a team would have formed around you and yet another football match would start.'

Jimmy was fortunate to have a trio of teachers at his primary school, St Columba, who were also football crazy. He remembered with fondness the impact John Crines, Mr Milligan and Mr Travers had upon him, encouraging him to caress the ball and practise as much as he could. Of course, he was a star player for the school team and by the age of ten he and his young teammates had swept all before them: the league cup, the county cup and the John Lee trophy.

His father, Matt, who worked in the local colliery, was also a massive influence on his development as a footballer. From an early age, Jimmy was a Celtic fan, but he would later admit his hero was an Englishman: the great Sir Stanley Matthews, a legend whose autobiography he read aged 12.

Jimmy would tell how he used to dribble around milk bottles for three hours every day in his hallway to perfect his skills. He used one of Matthews' tips to strengthen his leg muscles: after reading that Stanley would make his way to Blackpool's ground in heavy boots for that very purpose, Jinky employed a similar practice to build himself up when he was a 17-year-old lad at Celtic. He wore pit boots for football training and claimed it 'probably added about three yards on to my pace'.

A few years beforehand, at his next school, the junior secondary St John the Baptist in Uddingston, Jinky had got what appeared to be his lucky break. Tommy Cassidy, the PE teacher, was a friend of Celtic star Sammy Wilson and had engineered a place for him at Parkhead as a ball boy. Remarkably, Celtic would initially allow him to slip from their clutches (although he starred for their youth team) because he wanted to play on Saturdays rather than work on the sidelines. Jinky would explain it this way: 'It was great to be at Celtic, to see all the great players, your heroes, but we all wanted to be playing on a Saturday and that was with the Boys Guild, so I left.'

When the Boys Guild headed for a game in Manchester in 1957, Celtic could easily have lost the services of the boy who would one day be hailed as their greatest player – to United. Jinky, aged 13, turned on his silky skills for the match and afterwards he was approached by one of the club's scouts with an offer to join the Old Trafford giants. Celtic were alerted and their head scout appeared at the Johnstones' home within two days of his return. Jinky chose to sign with Celtic and he played his first game for the senior team at the age of 19 on 21 March 1963, becoming an instant favourite with the Celtic fans.

Asked how he and his family felt about being approached by the two biggest clubs in the world and about putting pen to paper at Celtic, Jimmy, with his natural humility, remembered it in this modest way:

> Aye, Dad was delighted, for sure. But, you see, we played all the time, it was our life, the biggest part of your life, and so when Johnny came round it was just sort of, 'Oh aye, that's great,' and then on with the next thing. Maybe that's what kept my feet on the ground. I mean I look back now and think, 'Bloody hell, what did we achieve?' and I guess they were great things, but at the time we were just a bunch of ordinary lads.
>
> We never bragged or talked about things, we just got out there to win, we were confident that we could take anyone on, and we did. You've got to remember times was hard then, football was the biggest part of our lives, just like for the boys in Brazil and Spain. They lived in poverty like us and that's where all of the great players come from, the streets.

Johnstone's contribution to the Celtic cause was immeasurable: he would more than pay them back for the faith they had shown in him. Although he made his first-team debut in 1963, it wasn't until the great Jock Stein arrived as manager two years later that he and the Celtic of the era finally took off in a big way. Jimmy would say of Stein and the debt he owed him, 'Jock was good with tactics, but his real talent was with people. Big Jock wasn't just a manager. It was as if he could read your mind. He knew if you had a problem.'

Jinky would make a total of 515 appearances for the club, scoring 130 goals, and would be a key member of the side that won nine successive Scottish league titles and a European Cup in 1967. He would also play in the 1970 European Cup final that Celtic lost to Feyenoord and in two semi-finals.

He stood at just 5 ft 4 in. and had a skinny frame, but his low centre of gravity and marvellous balance meant he was a twisting nightmare for defenders. The Celtic fans would dub him 'Jinky' for that reason, as he could so easily dribble past – jink past – hapless opponents. The true measure of his contribution to Celtic FC would come in 2002, when the club's supporters voted him their greatest ever player.

Georgie Best would be similarly skinny and slight of frame when he finally arrived at Old Trafford. Born 20 months after Jimmy on 22 May 1946, he would make just as swift an impression on big-time football. He grew up in a council house on the Cregagh estate in Belfast, Northern Ireland, the eldest of six children and, like Jimmy, enjoyed a happy childhood. His father, Dickie, worked in the Harland and Wolff shipyard, his mother, Ann, in a tobacco factory.

Like Jimmy, he took what was then the usual route to a footballing future by investing hour upon hour in kicking balls about in the local streets. A bright lad, he earned a place at the local grammar school, Grosvenor High, but did not last long there, quickly becoming disillusioned with a school that practised rugby over football.

He played truant often and eventually his parents agreed that he could leave Grosvenor for the local secondary modern, where football was king. He soon made a name for himself – at 14, George scored 12 goals for Cregagh Boys in a match they won 21–0. A year later, George headed to Manchester United after the club's Northern Ireland talent scout, Bob Bishop, sent that now legendary telegram to Matt Busby, saying, 'I think I have found you a genius.'

Best was subsequently given a trial and signed up by chief scout Joe Armstrong in 1961. When he finally joined United, aged 15, as an amateur on 16 August 1961, George still was only 5 ft 1 in. and weighed just 8 st. 7 lb and so Busby ordered his staff to fatten him up.

Just as Jinky lit up Celtic Park and left a lasting legacy with his European Cup and Scottish title wins, so Georgie would lift United to the pinnacle of English and European football. After turning professional, he went on to make 466 appearances for United in all competitions, scoring 178 goals (including six in one game against Northampton Town). Best was United's top scorer for six consecutive seasons. During this run, he also topped the First Division scoring charts in 1967–68 with 28 goals, a remarkable achievement when you consider he was not an out-and-out striker like, say, Denis Law.

George won two English league championship-winner's medals, in 1965 and 1967, and in 1968 gained a European Cup-winner's medal and was named European Footballer of the Year. He still holds the record for the most goals by a United player in a single match: his six against Northampton in the FA Cup fifth round on 8 February 1970, a tie United won 8–2.

In his early career, George was nicknamed 'the fifth Beatle' and he certainly had more to contend with than Jinky in terms of press interest and intrusion into his private life. He was the first pop-star footballer, receiving thousands of fan letters a week after making his name worldwide in the 1966 European Cup quarter-final away leg to Benfica. United had won the first leg 3–2 at Old Trafford and after just 12 minutes of the return in Portugal Best had scored twice: once with a header, the second, in a moment of magic, as he beat three men before shooting past the goalkeeper. His brace in the 5–1 triumph brought about Benfica's first-ever home defeat in the competition – they had been unbeaten in 19 matches – and propelled him to world fame. His boss, Busby, would in public be seemingly forever admonishing George for going AWOL or missing training, but in private he admired the resilience of the man who had to face a constant barrage of media pressure. Indeed, later in his life Busby would pay this tribute to 'the Belfast Boy': 'George was gifted, with more individual ability than I have seen in any other player; he was certainly unique in the number of his gifts. He was skinny looking but strong, and courageous to a degree that compensated amply. Every aspect of ball control was perfectly natural to him from the start, and he had more confidence in his ability than I have seen in any other sportsman.'

Busby would also later admit in a melancholy way that he had a soft spot for George – and that was why he allowed him to get away with things that would have seen other less talented players straight out the door marked 'exit': 'Every manager goes through life looking for one great player, praying he'll find one. Just one. I was more lucky than most. I found two – Big Duncan and George. I suppose, in their own ways, they both died, didn't they?'

As Busby nurtured and threw a loving, forgiving arm around Best, so Stein would adopt a similar role with Jinky. One of the big man's first moves as manager was to install Jinky on the right wing at the expense of Jim Brogan, immediately showing his admiration and support for the little man. This confidence boost meant a lot to Johnstone. Like Best, he was someone who needed to be loved, who needed a pat on the back rather than a kick up the backside for motivation. 'What an influence he had on me!' Johnstone would admit in later life. 'He made me feel wanted; as if I was someone special.'

Who were the real George Best and Jimmy Johnstone? Well, like Jimmy, George was an essentially shy person who did not like the limelight. He would also use booze, like Jimmy, as a crutch to deal with his fears and to help him compensate for cripplingly low self-esteem and the feeling that he was never quite big enough, never quite good enough. I remember seeing George at Alcoholics Anonymous meetings in London and was surprised at how he lacked confidence in the flesh. The man who had perfected the 'couldn't give a f**k' attitude in public was actually a softly spoken man, plagued by self-doubt and low self-worth. The 'real' Georgie boy was the man you would find in his local boozer near his flat in Chelsea, alone in the corner working his way through a newspaper crossword.

The public conception of Georgie remains best summed up by the most famous anecdote about him. Yes, the one that has him opening his hotel-room door to a waiter bringing him a refill of champagne and caviar. The waiter looks around the room, sees a crumpled bed with 20 grand in notes lying on it and Miss World, Marjorie Wallace, lying in it. As he leaves the room, the waiter turns towards Georgie and asks sadly, 'Where did it all go wrong, Mr Best?' Yet, for someone who never appeared without a blonde on his arm in public, he was actually a very private man who enjoyed his own company.

Similarly, although he enjoyed a laugh with the lads when away from home with Celtic and appeared happy-go-lucky and outgoing, Jinky was equally uncomfortable with fame and had turned to alcohol for consolation and support. Both Busby and

Stein would use a network of 'spies' – fans eager to snitch on their heroes – to find out where Best and Jinky were holed up. It is said that Jinky's face would turn white when he received a call at whichever pub he was in when he sussed out it was Stein on the other end of the phone.

Again like Best at United, Johnstone's relationship with drink deteriorated as his Celtic career came to a close in 1975. His 'where did it all go wrong?' anecdote concerns a trip he made out to sea with the Scotland squad in May 1974, just days before a game against England. Jinky and the boys had sunk a few at their hotel in Largs, Ayrshire, and thought they might take an early morning dip at 5 a.m. – but Jimmy decided he would be a little more adventurous and headed out in a rowing boat. Soon he was adrift in the Atlantic. The Scotland boss at the time, Willie Ormond, did not join in the laughter the next morning when the escapade was all over the newspapers – after the coastguard was called to rescue him. 'I don't know what all the fuss is about,' Jinky had said at the time, 'I thought I'd go fishing!' But in later years he admitted, 'I never thought it would attract the attention it did and I do regret the publicity, because that hurt my family.'

At international level, Jimmy and Georgie would again tally, both hardly enjoying illustrious careers at that level. George was capped thirty-seven times for Northern Ireland, scoring nine goals, but never got to perform on the world stage. He called for a united Ireland football team several times.

Some pundits use his lack of international success to make a case for him not being in the same league as Pele and Maradona, yet it was hardly Best's fault that the players around him were not of his ability – Pele and Maradona were lucky enough to be surrounded by world-class stars in the Brazil and Argentina sides respectively. It is also worth pointing out that Maradona has frequently named Best as his all-time favourite player and that Pele once said Georgie was the best player he had ever seen. He was also quick to name him as one of the 125 best living footballers in his 2004 FIFA 100 list.

The peak of Best's international career, given its lack of glory, was, perhaps inevitably, one that involved mischief. On 15 May 1971, he scored the cheekiest and one of the most famous 'goals' of his career at Windsor Park in Belfast against Gordon Banks. The England keeper was about to kick the ball downfield and had dropped the ball towards his left foot, however Best had anticipated the move and, with his right boot, knocked the ball up in the air behind Banks. The duo both scrambled towards the net, but Best outpaced the keeper and headed the ball into the empty goal to the delight of the home supporters. His effort was disallowed for ungentlemanly conduct, but Banks would admit he was not so sure – and he was forever embarrassed at being so emphatically outwitted.

Jinky would endure a similarly bleak time of it at international level with Scotland. He would earn just twenty-four caps and score just four goals. His problem was not so much a lack of talent in the Scottish squad – indeed, you could argue that the 1974 World Cup squad was Scotland's strongest ever – but the feeling that he did not belong. In those 1974 finals in West Germany, he never played a game. He would later try to explain his international career in this way:

> I preferred playing for Celtic. I had a couple of bad experiences playing for Scotland, when I was booed by our own fans. I may have been playing a stinker, but I didn't feel right after certain fans booed me because I was a Celtic player.

Again the need for a friendly arm around the shoulder is apparent, for a Jock Stein-like figure to nurture him and help him feel part of the set-up. Both he and George were sensitive creatures who required compassion and love if they were to thrive. On the rare occasions he did feel part of it at international level, defenders would suffer, as England's Emlyn Hughes – and indirectly Sir Alf Ramsey – would once testify after the Liverpool man was run ragged by Jinky. 'Scotland beat us 2–0 one year and I was embarrassed to come off the pitch. Jimmy Johnstone absolutely crucified me,' Hughes said. 'But Alf Ramsey came up and said, "You've just played against a world-class player today. He can do that to anybody."'

The highlights of both men's careers would again run in remarkable parallel, coming within the same 12-month period and in the same competition: the European Cup. Jinky and Celtic were, of course, the first British club to lift the trophy in 1967, and Georgie and United the first English club a year later.

Johnstone was one of the 'Lisbon Lions', the Celtic team that beat Inter Milan 2–1 in Lisbon to lift the European Cup. Jinky admitted after the match he had expected that Celtic would 'get gubbed': 'There they were [Giacinto] Facchetti, [Angelo] Domenghini, [Alessandro] Mazzola, [Renato] Cappellini; all six-footers with Ambre Solaire suntans, Colgate smiles and sleek-backed hair. They even smelled beautiful. And there's us lot – midgets. I've got no teeth, Bobby Lennox hasn't any and old Ronnie Simpson's got none, top or bottom. The Italians are staring down at us and we're grinning back up at them wi' our great gumsy grins. We must have looked like something out of the circus.'

But they did not play like a freak-show act; no, Celtic were class and clever that unforgettable day. With Jimmy running intelligently at the Italians and spraying the ball about, the Bhoys gained control of the match and left their opponents bemused and befuddled.

Stein had told his men to go out and enjoy themselves – but they suffered an early setback when Jim Craig felled Cappellini and Mazzola netted the resulting penalty, sending Ronnie Simpson the wrong way with eight minutes on the clock and giving Milan an early lead. The equaliser came after 65 minutes, when Tommy Gemmell rifled home an unstoppable shot after brilliant link-up play from Jim Craig and Bobby Murdoch. A deflected Stevie Chalmers goal after a Murdoch piledriver won the match and the cup for the Bhoys, leading to delirious celebrations among the vast army of Celtic fans in the crowd.

It was a marvellous victory. For Jinky, it would be the pinnacle of his career in football. That year, at the age of 23, he also received wider recognition for his gifts when he finished third in the European Footballer of the Year award. The following year, Best would follow in Johnstone's footsteps and lift the trophy.

After narrowly overcoming Real Madrid 4–3 on aggregate in the semi-finals, Best and United once again faced Benfica, this time in the final, taking on the two-time winners at Wembley. It was all-square at 1–1 after 90 minutes, with the match heading into extra-time after Jaime Graça cancelled out a Bobby Charlton header.

Two minutes into extra-time Best left Benfica captain Mário Coluna in his wake to put United ahead again, majestically slipping the ball around the keeper and gently tapping it over the line. He danced away in triumph, his blue shirt – a special one-off kit for the final – dangling over his blue shorts. Two more United goals, the first from 19-year-old Brian Kidd and the other from skipper Charlton, taking the final score to 4–1, followed his moment of personal joy.

Ten years after the Munich air crash, United and Best had reached the pinnacle of European football. 'The players have done us all proud,' Busby said. 'After Munich, they came back with all their hearts to show everyone what Manchester United are made of. This is the most wonderful thing in my life and I am the proudest man in England. The European Cup has been the ambition of everyone at the club: now we have it, at last.'

Best had been United's star player on the night and, just a fortnight after being chosen as the FWA Footballer of the Year, he was also named European Footballer of the Year. Later he would say, 'That night at Wembley we knocked it about as well as any of the great sides I've ever seen. That night, at least, we were as good as the Real Madrid of the '50s, the Spurs double team – anyone you care to mention.' Truly, in May 1968 Best and Busby had the world at their feet . . . but this would be the last footballing prize ever for both men.

At 22, it should have been the start of it all for Georgie – not the end. He had announced his retirement from the game by 1972 but returned to United a year later; however, by early 1974 he had left Old Trafford for good. Twenty-nine years later, he would even sell off those two precious Footballer of the Year trophies at auction.

At Celtic, Jinky still had one more worldwide audience to whom to show off his skills before he too drifted away from the club in 1975. He tormented Leeds United in the aggregate European Cup semi-final victory of 1970, leaving the brilliant full-back Terry Cooper almost a broken man.

'Wee Jinky was out of this world at Elland Road,' teammate Tommy Gemmell has commented. 'Terry Cooper, the Leeds left-back, must have nightmares every time somebody mentions Jimmy Johnstone because he gave him a total going-over. Norman Hunter was shouting to Cooper, "Kick him!" Cooper turned around and said, "You come out and kick him." Hunter came out and tried to stick it on wee Jimmy. Wee Jimmy just waltzed round about him and nutmegged him.'

But Jinky, dubbed the 'Flying Flea' by the French press after an inspired display against Nantes in a European Cup tie, would, again like Best, miss out on becoming a two-time European Cup winner. Celtic, as we know, lost 2–1 to Dutch side Feyenoord in Milan, but at least Jimmy could claim to have played in two European Cup finals.

After leaving Celtic at the age of 30, Johnstone moved to Sheffield United, Dundee and even Elgin City in a series of brief pitstops that mirrored George Best's career after Manchester United. Like George in his no-man's-land days, Jinky played for San Jose Earthquakes. He eventually returned to Celtic Park in the mid-1980s to coach younger players.

Best 'enjoyed' spells with Stockport County, Fulham, Hibernian, Los Angeles Aztecs and San Jose before finally retiring from the game in 1983 after a brief stint with Bournemouth. Ironically, given both he and Jinky turned out for San Jose, George would claim his goal for them against Fort Lauderdale in 1981 was his finest ever. George was 35 by then, but he took on a swathe of defenders, swerving around them all as if they were invisible, before lifting the ball over the hapless goalkeeper.

Johnstone was diagnosed with motor neurone disease in November 2001. To raise funds for charity and awareness of the disease, Jimmy, together with Jim Kerr of Simple Minds, launched a new version of the classic Pogues single 'Dirty Old Town', but the wee wizard would lose his battle with the disease on 13 March 2006. He was just 61. The last person to call him was his old Rangers rival, Willie Henderson, who had become a firm friend.

Jimmy's son, James Johnstone, 35, announced his death, saying, 'My dad passed away at 6 a.m. this morning. It hasn't even begun to sink in yet for the family.' Johnstone's family later released a statement on the Celtic's website that noted: 'Although Jimmy was one of the finest footballers ever, he was also a great man off the field as a husband, father and grandfather. Despite serious illness, the courage, strength and appetite for life which Jimmy

HUMBLE BEGINNINGS: The Celtic FC team line up for the 1887–88 season:
(players only, middle row, left to right) Willie Groves, Tom Maley, Paddy Gallagher,
Willie Dunning, Willie Maley and Mick Dunbar; (front row, left to right) Johnny
Coleman, James McLaren, James Kelly, Neil McCallum and Mick McKeown.
(© Getty Images)

WELSH WIZARD: Billy Meredith of Manchester United (left) in action during the
first-ever FA Charity Shield match against Queens Park Rangers on 28 August 1908.
Following a 1–1 draw, United won 4–0 in the replay. (© Getty Images)

THE FIRST CELTIC UNITED SUPERSTAR: Jimmy Delaney in his United days,
starring at outside-right during a match against Arsenal at Highbury on 30 August 1948.
(© Getty Images)

THE BABE WHO HAD IT ALL: Duncan Edwards of Manchester United
in December 1956. Fourteen months later, he would tragically perish in the
Munich air disaster. (© Getty Images)

THE BIG MAN: Celtic manager Jock Stein pictured on 12 May 1967 during a training session before Celtic's European Cup final match against Inter Milan. (© Getty Images)

BILLY THE HERO: Billy McNeill of Celtic receives the European Cup trophy from the President of Portugal after the Scottish side's 2–1 victory over Inter Milan in Lisbon on 30 May 1967. (© Getty Images)

MISSION ACCOMPLISHED: Manchester United captain Bobby Charlton and manager Matt Busby celebrate their European Cup victory over Benfica at Wembley Stadium on 29 May 1968. The victory represented the end of a ten-year obsession to win the cup for Busby after the death of his Babes in 1958. (© Getty Images)

BOB'S THE JOB: Bobby Charlton holds aloft the European Cup, after his team's 4–1 victory at Wembley. (© Getty Images)

WHERE DID IT ALL GO WRONG, MR BEST?: George Best in action for
Manchester United in September 1970. He was still the star of the team,
but the decline had set in. (© Cleva)

NEVER FORGOTTEN: Fans gather to watch the funeral cortège of Celtic and Scotland legend Jimmy Johnstone as it makes its way past Celtic Park on 17 March 2006. Thousands of mourners turned out to bid a final farewell to their hero, who died after a brave battle with motor neurone disease. (© Getty Images)

SWEDE DREAMS: Celtic's Swedish forward Henrik Larsson celebrates after scoring for his team during the UEFA Cup final against Porto in Seville on 21 May 2003. He would go on to help Manchester United to their ninth Premiership title during a loan spell in 2007. (© Getty Images)

ROY'S THE BOY: 'Keano' takes on Cristiano Ronaldo in the Irishman's testimonial match at Old Trafford between Celtic and Manchester United on 9 May 2006. (© Getty Images)

THE WEE MAN: Celtic manager Gordon Strachan looks on during his club's Champions League match against AC Milan at the San Siro on 7 March 2007. Despite his success, some of the club's fans remain unconvinced he is the man to take Celtic forward. (© Getty Images)

THEATRE OF DREAMS: Manchester United's Old Trafford ground dwarfs the
surrounding Trafford Park area. The stadium has been constantly redeveloped and now
boasts the largest capacity of any British club ground, 76,212. (© Getty Images)

BHOYHOOD DREAMS: Glasgow's eastern necropolis forms a backdrop to the home of
Celtic Football Club, Celtic Park, the finest stadium in Scotland, with a capacity of 60,832.

(© Getty Images)

showed was an inspiration to everyone who met him. Jimmy will be sadly missed by so many people, but the memories he gave us all will live on forever.'

Thousands of Celtic fans, and fans of many other clubs, including those of Manchester United and rivals Rangers, paid tribute to his memory outside Celtic Park on St Patrick's Day, the day of his funeral service. Tributes were also paid before the Scottish League Cup final on 19 March 2006. There was a minute of applause before the game and the entire Celtic squad wore the number 7 on both the front and back of their shorts in his honour. When the match ended, as part of the celebrations for winning the match, they all put on tops displaying JINKY and number 7. And Celtic Park itself bore witness to some of the most moving scenes in modern football as Jimmy's fans bade a final farewell to a legend. Supporters laid hundreds of shirts, tributes and personal messages outside the stadium which had become their hero's spiritual home.

Billy McNeill, Jinky's long-time team captain, summed up the feelings of those who had played with him for the Hoops when he said, 'Jimmy Johnstone could terrorise any defence. He was among the greatest players this game has seen. However, I have as much respect for him as a man and the courageous way in which he handled his illness as I have for him as a footballer.'

Tommy Gemmell had no doubt that Johnstone would go down in history as the club's finest ever player. 'It's a tragedy. We've lost a great pal and a colleague,' he said. 'He fought the disease with great courage and he stood up to it well. On the pitch, he had the heart of a lion and the ability of a maestro. He was an unbelievable player, as good as any you will see.'

Another ex-teammate, Bertie Auld, commented, 'You know what a player he was, but what a person. He was the kindest guy in the world. All the time he was lying there, he never complained. I saw him on Friday and, like any time you met him, you left feeling a stronger person. Jimmy was so desperate to help other people with the same disease, he wanted a cure for it even though he knew he couldn't be helped.'

Former Scotland winger Pat Nevin says he copied Johnstone's style on the field when he was learning how to play the game. 'I never met him, but my dad got a book signed by him and he wrote a message in it that was positive about how I played, which meant a lot,' Nevin said. 'I have no doubt there will be a lot of Rangers fans mourning Jimmy Johnstone.'

Lou Macari broke into the Celtic side in the 1960s and has said what a fantastic role model Johnstone was for youngsters. 'It was wonderful to have played alongside Jimmy and he looked after me,' said Macari. 'He trained well, worked hard and had a great attitude towards the game.'

Celtic manager Gordon Strachan said Johnstone would never be forgotten. 'Jimmy was a wonderful player and a wonderful character and we will always have the memories – they will never die,' he said. 'He radiated. If you were down, he made you feel better, that's the kind of guy he was. He was a great advert for Scotland.'

Henrik Larsson also paid tribute to the man who, like himself, wore the Celtic number 7 shirt with such distinction. 'I didn't understand what an honour it was to wear the same number jersey as him when I first arrived at the club, but by the time I left I knew exactly why it was so special,' the Swede said. 'Most people will remember him as an incredible player, but, to me and a lot of other people, it was just as important that he was a really fantastic guy.'

Rod Stewart knew Johnstone personally – and admitted, 'He was the reason I became a Celtic fan in 1971. At the end of his life, he couldn't move his body but that face still had a beam on it.'

Celtic hero Tommy Burns, who was the club's first-team coach at the time of Johnstone's death, said that Jinky enjoyed the same iconic status as George Best. He said that he had 'a God-given talent but he also worked very hard in terms of stamina, strength and speed in order to use that talent at the highest level. Jimmy was everyone's favourite player because of the magical things he could do with the ball.'

Similar affectionate tributes poured in for Georgie Best, who had died just three months earlier than Jinky, on 25 November 2005, of multiple organ failure. In 2002, owing to consistent alcohol abuse over 25 years, the condition of George's liver had deteriorated to the point where a transplant had become necessary to save his life. But the immuno-suppressive drugs given to prevent rejection of his new liver had caused him to develop a serious kidney infection, which his doctors were unable to redress. In 2005, the infection caused him to fall into a coma.

In his final days, he was watched over by his father and other family members and by former football colleagues, such as Denis Law. He died at the age of fifty-nine, two years younger than the tragic Jinky.

At this point, I think I should point out that there were notable differences between the two men. Jimmy would remain a one-woman man throughout his life, a proud husband to Agnes and father to young James, Marie and Eileen. George, of course, could never settle, getting involved in relationships with numerous women, including three Miss Worlds, and marrying twice, first to Angela James in 1978 and then to Alex Pursey in 1995. Angie would give him a son, Calum, but the marriage ended in divorce in 1986. Alex also divorced him, in 2004.

And while Jimmy would, for the most part, keep his drinking under wraps, George's would be carried out in the full glare of the media spotlight. As he himself would quip in later life, 'I was the one who took football off the back pages and put it on to page one.' Many of his scrapes were documented on camera; many times he would suffer the ignominy of humiliation and shame in public. Chief among his 'crimes' was his arrest for drink-driving, assaulting a police officer and failing to answer bail in 1984, for which he received a three-month prison sentence. He spent Christmas 1984 behind bars and turned out as a player for Ford open prison. (On 2 February 2004, Best was convicted of another drink-driving offence and was banned from driving for 20 months.)

In 1991, George appeared on prime-time BBC chat show *Wogan* while drunk. He talked sleazily and swore at the presenter. A few days later, plagued by remorse and guilt, he apologised and said it had been one of the worst episodes of his alcoholism.

Yet despite his indiscretions – there were also claims of abuse by some of the women with whom he had relationships – it was difficult not to love Georgie. He was like a naughty child and, having met him on several occasions during the late '80s and early '90s, I must say that he could be a very kind, generous and compassionate man. When sober, he was never tight or mean-spirited. It was only when the demon alcohol kicked in that he would change from Dr Jekyll into Mr Hyde.

In his defence, he was suffering from an illness which he could not control. Alcoholism has long been recognised as such by the World Health Organisation; it is a cancer in its own way, as it insidiously takes a hold of the individual, ultimately controlling their whole being and character. It had even snatched away the life of his beloved mother Annie, who was also a victim of its ugly claws. I know those affected adversely by George's bingeing would perhaps find it difficult to accept, but in hindsight we should perhaps feel compassion for a man who was himself suffering so much under the hammer of such an incomprehensible, morally bankrupting illness.

Best and Johnstone also differed in another area of life: George, a Belfast Protestant, would in later years never publically comment on his religion, preferring to keep his own counsel. He did once tell me in the '80s that he still believed in God but, as he battled to overcome his alcohol addiction and saw the suffering in his own world, and the world in general, he would voice doubts about 'the Big Man' – but he did not want to get involved in a debate about it. He did not like the arguments it could bring up; the fires of hatred it could stoke. Contrary to the traditional picture of him as an aggressive man, he was actually a shy person who much preferred his own company.

George never got involved in such public controversies over religion, although Jinky, on the other hand, would open up about his religious beliefs in his later life, admitting he sometimes had doubts about God and his Catholic faith. In 2002, he told *The Scotsman* that he was no saint, that he had been 'in a deep, dark place' largely due to his battle with alcohol. He still attended mass daily but felt anger as a result of his battle with motor neurone disease. It was not a selfish anger that he had become a victim. That was not in his nature. No, his resentment was centred on the Church's opposition to stem-cell research using cloned cells or cells taken from embryos. This opposition, he felt, was holding back possible breakthroughs in research to beat his illness. 'I just can't see why the living should suffer when there's a chance for a cure,' he said at the time. 'It's a mystery why anyone would want to hold back science.'

A year later, he would reveal more specifically how his religious beliefs had been tempered by his illness. 'I am a Christian, a Roman Catholic who believes in the Ten Commandments. However, I also believe that the Man upstairs put scientists here for a reason, and if we can find a positive use for these cells, then it will be because He wants that to happen.'

There would be an outpouring of grief and sympathy after it was announced George Best had died in London's Cromwell Hospital in 2005. There was to have been a minute's silence before all Premiership games to be held over the weekend of his death, but this tradition was ignored in favour of a minute's applause in his honour. Many football fans travelled to pay tribute to Best, outside Old Trafford, Windsor Park in Belfast and at Belfast City Hall, and outside his father Dickie's home, where signed shirts, scarves, flowers and messages were left.

Manchester United's greatest ever footballer was even afforded a statesman-style funeral in Belfast on 3 December 2005. His body left the family home at Cregagh Road, east Belfast, shortly after 10 a.m. with the cortège travelling the short distance to Stormont. The route was lined with around 100,000 mourners. There was an 11 a.m. service in the Grand Hall relayed to 25,000 mourners inside the grounds of Stormont and live on BBC1, UTV, RTÉ, ITV News, BBC News 24, Sky News, Sky Sports News, EuroNews and MUTV. Afterwards, Best was buried beside his mother in a private ceremony at the hilltop Roselawn Cemetery, overlooking east Belfast.

The tributes were generous and far-reaching. Sir Alex Ferguson led the way, saying, 'He was a fantastic player. Everybody at United regarded George as being one of the greatest of all time. It's very sad because he was a wonderful person, who was very likeable.'

Sir Bobby Charlton, who played alongside Best at his peak but was never close as a friend, said, 'He was on a par, at least, with anyone you can name. We at Manchester United have learned from our experience with Eric Cantona: we had to treat him differently, make allowances. If, instead of being hostile to George, which I was, we had leaned a bit his way and tried to help him, who knows?'

Denis Law, who had been at Best's bedside the day before

he died, said, 'From 1964 to 1969, he was the best player in the country. It's sad as hell, but I don't think we saw the best of him. He went on the blink at a time when he could have got even better.'

Former Northern Ireland team and room-mate Pat Jennings, who made his international debut in 1964 alongside Best, commented, 'He was not only a fantastic player, to me he was also a fantastic bloke. The George Best I met then is the same George Best I knew later.'

Republic of Ireland and Leeds midfielder Johnny Giles described Best as 'the most naturally gifted player I have ever seen'. Giles added, 'He had the lot: balance, pace, two good feet; he was brave, strong and a good header of the ball. Pele wasn't as gifted as George Best and I would definitely put George above Johan Cruyff because he had more heart.'

In a *Sunday Times* interview, Celts legend Tommy Gemmell was one of the few who would offer a direct comparison between Georgie and Jinky and say who he thought the better player was. 'George Best was the greatest player I ever faced and, drunk or sober, he could take you to the cleaners,' he said. 'At his peak, George was a better all-round player than Jimmy Johnstone, but for individual skill Jinky was streets ahead. Bestie was like the great Alfredo Di Stefano, similar in the way he could see things happening, but for pure ability there was no one like wee Jimmy. At his greatest, he was unstoppable. I'm glad I only had to face him in training games. However, I count myself fortunate to have seen both in action when they were at the top. They were both incredible.'

Tributes for George also flowed in from those outside of the game. Belfast City Airport was renamed George Best Belfast City Airport, and Flybe, the airport's biggest operator, named one of its planes *The George Best*. The specially branded aircraft was used to carry Best's family across to Manchester for a memorial service for him. On the first anniversary of his death, Ulster Bank issued one million commemorative £5 notes. They sold out within three days.

On what would have been his 60th birthday, on 22 May 2006, an auction was held to raise funds for the George Best Foundation at a special gala dinner held in George's honour at Belfast City Hall. The foundation raises money for research into liver disease and alcoholism and one of the items featured was the 'Genius' egg designed and created by Sarah Fabergé, of the world-famous jewellers. Only 68 of the gold eggs were made. Their creation again linked Georgie to Jinky Johnstone.

A year earlier, Sarah had created a similar egg for Jimmy Johnstone's charity in his bid to raise funds for motor neurone disease research. So even in late life and in death, the two men would find common ground through their altruistic desire to help other sufferers of the illnesses that would cost them their lives.

Two great footballers, a shared passion. We will never forget them.

12

RED AND GREEN GIANTS: CRERAND, McCLAIR AND CO.

He's my television wife, but we do have a great understanding after commentating together for over ten years. It's never dull with Paddy and his style is irrepressible.

– Former MUTV commentator Steve Bower
on his former co-presenter Paddy Crerand

Mark Hughes – Sparky by name, sparky by nature, and the same applies to Brian McClair.

– The late TV commentator Brian Moore

I DON'T think we are being too out of order here in claiming that Paddy Crerand was a '60s version of Roy Keane, the man who would go on to become one of United and Celtic's greatest legends. Keane, thanks to his all-action, snarling play and inspirational captaincy skills, would be voted in at No. 3 in the *Manchester United Opus's* 'Top 50 Players of All Time'. Yet Crerand would also get a favourable mention – hitting the ground running at No. 21.

Both men played for Celtic and United. Both possessed a

similar never-say-die attitude: hard tacklers yet with the vision, creativity and ability to dictate a game. And both remained as controversial as ever after hanging up their boots – Keane as a manager of supreme potential, Crerand as a TV pundit who gives it to you straight.

Patrick Timothy Crerand was born in Thistle Street in Glasgow on 19 February 1939. Brought up in the tough Gorbals district of the city, Paddy quickly made his mark at the one thing he could do better than his schoolmates: playing football. He became a regular for his school teams, first at St Luke's Primary and then at Holyrood Secondary, and then went on to play for Duntocher Hibs in 1957.

Paddy is remembered by friends and neighbours from the time of his Gorbals upbringing – the Crerands eventually moving to Crown Street. One former Gorbals resident, Hughie Carey, summed up the fondness with which Paddy is viewed when he commented: 'Paddy Crerand played for Duntocher Hibs, I watched him as a lad. I was born in 1938 and served my apprenticeship in Singers in the '50s, I was in the same department as Paddy. Paddy's brother-in-law was big John Ferry – I often wonder where big John is. He was a great guy from the Gorbals. I played a game of football for Yoker with Charlie Gallacher and we beat Blantyre Celtic 4–1. I remember Paddy's wife; she was a bonnie lass with red hair . . .'

Tommy Deehan, who moved from the Gorbals to Newmarket, Ontario, Canada, is another who remembered the young Paddy with joy. Tommy said: 'Gorbals memories 1938–55 – yes, I remember "The great one – Paddy Crerand". I have very fond memories of playing with Paddy as early as his first days in the playground at Holyrood Secondary in Crosshill.

'I also remember playing with his future brother-in-law, John "Jumbo" Ferry with the Secondary Juvenile football team, sponsored by Rancel Rangers/Celtic Supporters Club, for two or three seasons. The coach-manager then was Hugh "Shug" Wiseman.'

From such humble beginnings, Paddy was destined for greatness. He signed professional forms for Celtic in 1957, making his debut the following year. He would stay at Celtic Park until January 1963, when Sir Matt Busby, a long-time admirer, finally lured him south to Old Trafford. In his time at Celtic, Paddy would make a total of 120 appearances in all competitions, scoring eight goals, but win only a runners-up medal from the final of the 1961 Scottish Cup – which the Hoops lost 2–0 to Dunfermline in a replay after the first match had ended 0–0.

Dave Thomson had put the Pars ahead at sixty-seven minutes and, ten minutes later, it looked as if Crerand would equalise – but his powerful shot was brilliantly saved by keeper Eddie Connachan. Steady Eddie would prove to be the bane of Celtic – just as he was to the rest of the teams, who had been unable to beat him as he made winning the cup appear a one-man crusade. Before the replay, he had not conceded a goal in 360 minutes of cup games and had worked his shifts in the coalmine, on the Monday and Tuesday before the match. A goal from Charlie Dickson two minutes from time wrapped up a memorable win for the Pars – and a day of heartache for Paddy boy.

Paddy was known as something of a bad boy during his Celtic days – and this helped ease through his transfer to United. Tom Campbell and Pat Woods sum up Crerand's reputation in their book, *Dreams, And Songs to Sing*:

> [He] was transferred to England – to Manchester United – in 1963 after a record of falling foul of referees, and for arguing violently with the first-team coach, Sean Fallon, in the dressing-room at Ibrox during the interval of the most recent Old Firm match, which had resulted in a heavy defeat for Celtic.

Yet they admit that Crerand, the player, was, on his day, a

remarkable attribute to the club, saying, 'Pat Crerand at right-half drew gasps of admiration for his inch-perfect passing.'

Crerand moved to Old Trafford on 6 February 1963, the fifth anniversary of the Munich air disaster, for a fee of £56,000 – a record transfer fee for a wing-half at the time. He was delighted to join the likes of his hero and friend Denis Law at United but sad to be leaving his beloved Hoops. Yet he knew there was a special magic with both clubs and the special relationship – and he was proud to be one of those who would be a member of the Celtic United club, as he noted in *United: The Legendary Years*:

> The team I supported as a kid in Scotland was Celtic. I knew about Manchester United even in those days because of the great players they had. And everybody knew about Matt Busby because he had wanted to play for Celtic at one time and he came from a place not far from Glasgow. As well as that there has always been a good relationship between Celtic and Manchester United. Jimmy Delaney was a great Scottish winger from the 1940s and he went down to Manchester from Celtic in 1946 – he was one of Matt Busby's first signings. Lou Macari and Brian McClair also came down from Celtic to play for United, so it has been quite a steady connection.

The Denis Law connection also helps explain how Paddy ended up at Old Trafford, in a move he admits came right out of the blue. Busby had asked the Lawman whether he should sign Paddy or Jimmy Baxter of Rangers, and Denis told him that while Baxter was a more skilful player, Crerand was a better long-term bet and more of a team player.

While Paddy had struggled for medals to fill his cabinet at Celtic, he had no such problem at United; indeed, he had the first one on display within three months. In May 1963, Paddy helped his new club to a 3–1 win over Leicester City in the FA

Cup final at Wembley. The United team that day read: Gaskell, Dunne, Cantwell, Crerand, Foulkes, Setters, Giles, Quixall, Herd, Law, Charlton. David Herd scored two of the goals – and Paddy set up the Lawman with a fine pass for his goal.

That doyen of Manchester United correspondents over the years, David Meek, analysed Crerand's initial impact at the club in his book *Legends of United* like this:

> Crerand had arrived too late in his first season to do much about the league position. Indeed, he struggled to fit in at first, but in the FA Cup that season there developed a pattern and a glimpse of better days ahead. The final was the match that saw Crerand come into his own and he destroyed the Leicester midfield in a link-up with Law that was a firm indication of things to come. Manchester United and Pat Crerand were on their way . . .

It would be merely the start of the glory years: in a distinguished career at Old Trafford, Paddy made a total of 392 appearances, scoring fifteen goals, and won two league championship medals and a European Cup-winner's medal to add to that early FA Cup honour. He was also an ever-present in the European Cup-winning campaign of 1968 and retired in 1971, an all-time United legend and a definite fans' hero. Capped sixteen times by Scotland, Crerand also earned one Under-23 cap, and he had represented the Scottish league as a Celtic player.

Of course, that '68 European Cup final win was the pinnacle of Paddy's glittering career. He admits Celtic winning the competition a year earlier was a great spur for him to emulate the triumph at United. In the book *United: The Legendary Years*, he tells how his mother and father-in-law, both great Celtic fans, went to Lisbon to see the great victory over Inter Milan. He admits he was delighted for his former club, but that a wee bit of jealousy was the catalyst for United's all-out assault the next season. He also reveals how when Busby presented Stein with the Team of the Year trophy at the BBC Sports Personality of the Year awards in '67, Jock said to Matt, 'Well, hopefully I'm presenting this to you next year.'

'Once Celtic had won the trophy, it had the effect of making us believe that United could definitely win it too,' Paddy says, 'and this cleared away a lot of inhibitions and gave us confidence as well.' The fortunes of Celtic and United were moving along in natural tandem.

After winning the trophy at Wembley, United were awarded a civic reception back in Manchester. Paddy's stock at the club by then can be gauged by the fact that he was one of those chosen to address the masses of fans from the town hall. In most of the pictures of the celebrations, Busby is flanked by George Best on his right . . . and Crerand on his left.

Fan website RedCafe.net sums up the club's debt to Crerand, the man who would become a legend in the great United team of the era with players such as Best, Law, Stiles and Charlton, in this astute way:

> An extrovert Glaswegian, raised in the Gorbals, Paddy allowed his fervour to get the better of him at times and occasionally he landed in trouble with referees. Indeed, it's been said that he never moved so fast as when headed for a mêlée 40 yards away! But his fiery nature was as much a part of Crerand the player as Crerand the man. It would be hard to find a United follower who would have wanted him any other way.
>
> And if part of that huge heart will be forever at his beloved Parkhead – the home of Celtic, his first club – it would be a rare Stretford Ender who wouldn't forgive him. His loyalty to Old Trafford was never in doubt, his contribution to the club's cause colossal. It was a red-letter day, indeed, when Matt Busby crossed the border to claim him for Manchester United.

Crerand and Stiles were the midfield glue – the solid cement base – that allowed the likes of Charlton and Best to thrive and prosper.

A taster of where Paddy's future would lie after hanging up his boots came in 1970 when, in the twilight of his career as a player, he was part of ITV's famous World Cup pundits' panel. The TV channel's famous four was made up of Paddy, Manchester City coach Malcolm Allison, Wolves ace Derek 'The Doog' Dougan and Arsenal full-back Bob McNab – with commentator supreme Brian Moore and prickly co-host Jimmy Hill spearheading the programmes.

Paddy's performances were hailed as astute and passionate – and he enjoyed the critiques on his showings so much that when he ended his career he would eventually become a regular TV pundit and a United ambassador. One critic 'bigged up' Paddy and his five World Cup TV co-stars in the Watney Cup semi-final programme, when United took on Hull on Wednesday, 5 August 1970, saying, 'Now, especially for the Watney Cup, the sextet will be together again when ITV exclusively screen highlights of the matches. Once again the bluntness of "Big Mal", the eloquence of "The Doog", the passion of "Paddy" Crerand and the astuteness of Bob McNab will be seen and heard throughout the country. During their three-week session with ITV's World Cup team, these four top soccer names became TV's wonder team.'

David Meek sums up Paddy's new role as a TV pundit and the new status as a cult figure with United fans that it brought him:

> Pat Crerand, once the heartbeat of Manchester United out on the pitch, is now their passionate advocate on television. He has become as integral to the commentary team on Manchester United TV as he was to the glory side of the '60s when it was said that if Crerand played well, United played well . . . He

still avidly follows Celtic's results but is now a firmly adopted Mancunian, living in Sale, just a few miles down the road from Old Trafford.

Crerand also tried his hand at football management in the years between the end of his playing career and his more recent TV role – not all together successfully, it must be said. He was assistant manager to Tommy Docherty in the early '70s but left the club in 1976 to become manager of Northampton Town, where he lasted just six months. The club had won promotion from the Fourth to the Third Division but struggled under Paddy; his resignation was accepted after a 2–0 defeat to Brighton in the new year.

Docherty and Crerand – two forthright figures – were probably never made to work as a team. Docherty initially appointed Paddy and Bill Foulkes to look after the United youth team but claims that when he promoted Paddy to be his assistant, 'I was to have monumental problems with him ... We just weren't compatible in terms of our working practices – time keeping, how to present yourself in a managerial capacity, that sort of thing. We had different ideas on it.'

Docherty revealed that Paddy remained at United for a few weeks on the same salary before leaving for Northampton – and that he was unwilling to recommend his former assistant for the job of team manager at the Cobblers when their chairman Neville Ronson rang for a reference.

Docherty feels vindicated in his assumption that Paddy was not cut out to be a manager, adding, 'The fact that, following Pat's voluntary departure, I then guided United to two FA Cup finals, to within four points of winning the championship and into Europe didn't serve to make him warm to me any the more.'

I asked Paddy to give his side of the story, but he did not get back to me. He is a busy man still with his TV work. He also contributes regularly to the club programme, the *United*

Review, and his staunch backing of the club, especially when it is under fire, becoming a 'rent-a-quote' United spokesman when required, has earned him a cult following among the supporters, who regard him as a United legend.

Another former Celtic ace who became loved at United over the years is Brian McClair. Nicknamed 'Choccy' by former Celtic boss Tommy Burns, simply because 'McClair rhymes with chocolate éclair', Brian proved himself as a centre-forward of some note at both Celtic and United before joining Sir Alex Ferguson's backroom team at Old Trafford.

Brian was born in Airdrie on 8 December 1963. He played for his school, St Margaret's High in Airdrie, and Coatbridge FC. Of his childhood, he says, 'As a boy, I dreamed constantly about becoming a professional footballer, but the future I imagined for myself would have had a hard time matching the reality.'

But before the glory days would come, there were some hard knocks and learning curves. In 1980, McClair would head south to take up an apprenticeship, somewhat surprisingly, at Aston Villa – there were no clear links between Scotland and the top club in the English Midlands back then (or even now, for that matter). It was a brave move and a brave start for a 16 year old, but McClair could not settle. He was back up in Scotland within a year. He joined Motherwell on a free in August 1981 and scored 15 goals over the next year, eventually making it to the big time at Celtic Park in June 1983 for a fee of £70,000. He was signed by Billy McNeill just ten days before 'Caesar' abruptly left for Manchester City. Some critics were surprised by the signing of McClair and questioned McNeill's judgement, but Billy would dismiss their fears, saying, 'I had felt convinced that this boy would be a scorer.'

McClair would easily justify the big man's faith in him. He spent four happy seasons at Parkhead and was the club's leading scorer in each of them, grabbing a total of 99 goals in 145 league appearances. He was hardly a like-for-like replacement for the departed Charlie Nicholas: he had neither the grace nor the slick movement of the man who had abandoned ship for Arsenal in the same summer that McClair signed on at Celtic Park. But he could score goals, and that was all that mattered.

David Hay had been appointed as McNeill's replacement and that pleased McClair, who had had a good working relationship with him at Fir Park, when Hay was manager at Motherwell. In their joint debut season at Celtic Park, the bond between the two men enhanced McClair's fine form: he scored 31 goals. OK, his predecessor Nicholas had found the net 46 times the previous season – but his haul had included 14 penalties.

No, Brian was doing good and in the 1986–87 season he would claim 35 goals in 44 league appearances and win both the Scottish FWA Footballer of the Year award and the Scottish Players' Player of the Year prize.

Three years after joining Celtic, he also won the first of 30 Scotland caps in a match against Luxembourg.

It was his top-class scoring rate that alerted Sir Alex Ferguson down in Manchester. Fergie knew a natural-born scorer when he saw one and, in McClair's debut season at Old Trafford in 1987–88, he would become the first United player since Georgie Best to hit the net more than 20 times in a season.

While at Motherwell, McClair had also studied for a degree in mathematics at Glasgow University and in later life Brian would sum himself up by saying, 'I was always kicking a ball about when I was a kid, but I also believed education was important. I'm often seen as an atypical player, because I began a degree, have left-wing politics and read books.'

At Celtic, he would win a Scottish Cup-winner's medal in 1985 and a Scottish championship-winner's medal the following year, and play four times for Scotland. The key matches in which Brian earned those honours, and three in Europe, which brought an unexpected link-up with Manchester United are arguably the most memorable of Brian's reign at Parkhead.

The first of the European games involved Rapid Vienna – and some cheap gamesmanship by the Austrians. Celtic went down 3–1 in the away first leg of their second-round European Cup-Winners' Cup clash, with McClair grabbing their consolation goal. In the return, the Hoops stormed into a 3–0 lead, with another goal from McClair and one from Murdo MacLeod, Tommy Burns lashing the third home past the goalkeeper.

Rapid appealed against the eventual 3–0 result, claiming one of their players was struck by a missile thrown from the Jungle, and UEFA weakly gave in to their demands, overturning the result, fining Celtic and ordering the game be replayed at least 100 km from Parkhead. This decision would bring McClair and co. to what would eventually become his second home: Old Trafford. Celtic had wisely chosen the venue of their English mates, as it was the one that would most closely allow their fans to replicate the passionate atmosphere they brought to Parkhead on big European occasions. Only this time the outcome would not go to script . . . on 12 December 1984, in front of a crowd of over 51,000, they exited the Cup-Winners' Cup in a 1–0 loss to Rapid.

Consolation would come at the end of the season when Celtic duly triumphed in the 100th Scottish Cup final at Hampden. After a goalless 45 minutes, Stuart Beedie gave opponents Dundee United the lead. Davie Provan equalised on the three-quarter mark and Frank McGarvey's headed winner five minutes from the end took the trophy back to Celtic Park.

Twelve months later, Brian McClair would land the second of his medals while playing for Celtic – this time at the rather less celebrated surroundings of Love Street, home of St Mirren – on the final day of the 1985–86 campaign. The Bhoys were second in the league table, two points behind Hearts. The Edinburgh outfit were unbeaten in the league since the new year and needed just a point against Dundee to be crowned champions.

Brian scored twice as Celtic romped home 5–0, and the lads learned they had won the league after Hearts conceded two late goals to lose to Dundee. It was the first time Celtic had topped the table in the season – but it brought McClair a well-earned championship medal to take with him to Old Trafford.

McClair finally made the move south in July 1987 for a fee of £850,000 and quickly made his mark at United, playing both inside-forward – alongside Mark Hughes – and centre-forward. It is also worth mentioning that when Eric Cantona arrived, Brian would prove adaptable as opportunities became limited – he even cut it in the centre of the park as an attacking midfielder. When asked why he had chosen United, with a wry smile he explained one of the central tenets of this book, as he replied, 'Why does anyone come to United? They are the biggest club in England. I always liked them and Celtic when I was younger.'

At Old Trafford, Brian would be rewarded for his efforts with FA Cup-winner's medals in 1990 and 1994, a European Cup-Winners' Cup and European Super Cup winner's medal in 1991, a League Cup-winner's medal in 1992 and Premiership winner's medals in 1993, 1994, 1996 and 1997. In total, Brian made 471 appearances for the club, scoring 127 goals – including 24 in his debut season. He scored the only goal in the 1–0 League Cup final win over Nottingham Forest and also, as a substitute, claimed the last goal in the 4–0 win over Chelsea in the 1994 FA Cup final.

On Tuesday, 15 April 1997, Brian travelled the route well known by many associated with Celtic United: he enjoyed a testimonial at Old Trafford between United and Celtic.

At the end of the 1997–98 season, he was given a free transfer and returned to Motherwell. It did not work out as well as first time around, and in December 1998 he took the job that would eventually help open the door to him returning to Old Trafford in a backroom-staff capacity as he became Brian Kidd's assistant at Blackburn.

The duo failed to keep Rovers in the Premiership and within a year both were sacked, but soon afterwards he returned to Old Trafford as a reserve-team coach. Sir Alex Ferguson was now determined to keep him at the club – he liked the boy: his tenacity, hard work and measured opinions – and had a plum role lined up for him. At the start of the 2006–07 season, Ferguson appointed him the new director of Manchester United's youth academy, a vital job in a club that, like Celtic, has long believed in nurturing young talent.

Brian spent a year preparing for the role, shadowing the previous director, Les Kershaw, and admitted it was his dream job. 'I enjoyed my time here as a player and I enjoyed being part of the coaching staff,' he said, 'but we've got a buoyant Academy that we want to keep improving and hopefully I'll be able to do that. It's a job and role that I've had in my head as something I'd like to do at some point, so when the chance came up I was delighted to be given the opportunity.

'We will look at players from all over the world but are still very hopeful that we'll get local boys. That is still very much part of our motivation, that there are still the opportunities there for local boys to follow in the footsteps of the Nevilles, Paul Scholes, Nicky Butt, Wes Brown and now Phil Bardsley.

'Of the jobs I've had at the club, this is simply the closest to playing in terms of enjoyment. There is great enjoyment in seeing young players growing into top footballers but, more than that, it's great to see them become top people too.'

Other notable men who played for both Celtic and United over the years, or played for one and had a backroom role at the other, include Joe Jordan, Tommy Bogan and Liam Miller. Here's the rundown on them . . .

JOE JORDAN joined Manchester United from Leeds on 4 January 1978 for a fee of £350,000. He had scored 48 goals in 220 appearances for the Whites and would hit the net 41 times in 126 appearances for the Red Devils before moving to AC Milan in July 1981 for £325,000. Joe would end his playing career with spells at Verona, Southampton and Bristol City before turning up at Celtic Park as assistant to Liam Brady in 1983.

Born in Carluke on 15 December 1951, Jordan had to make the big time the hard way, but went on to represent his country on fifty-two occasions, playing in three World Cups (1974, 1978 and 1982) and earning the distinction of becoming the only Scotsman to score in three World Cup finals. For the record, he scored in a 2–0 win over Zaire in the first group game in 1974; in the opening 3–1 defeat by Peru in 1978; and in the 2–2 draw against the USSR in the group stages in 1982. With sheer bad luck, he got injured in the same match, missed the rest of the tournament and never played for his country again.

It had been a long, hard journey to that stage – and a permanent history in Scotland's footballing Hall of Fame. Ignored by the big clubs when he left school, Joe had played for junior side Blantyre Vics before moving on to Morton, while working as a draughtsman to pay the bills. Bobby Collins alerted Leeds boss Revie to the raw talent in the 18-year-old Jordan and Revie was not fazed when Morton asked for £15,000 for their star man's services.

An old-fashioned bull in a china shop, a big bustling number 9, Joe also had a trick to make his opponents even more wary of him. Like Nobby Stiles a decade earlier, he would turn out first for Leeds and then Manchester United without his false teeth to frighten the life out of those unlucky enough to mark him. His fellow Scot defender Gordon McQueen joined him at Old Trafford a month after Joe signed – much to the consternation of the Leeds loyalists.

Nicknamed 'Smokin' Joe' and 'Jaws', he won a league championship medal with Leeds in 1974 and appeared in two European finals, the 1973 European Cup-Winners' Cup 1–0 loss to AC Milan and the 1975 European Cup 2–0 defeat at the hands of Bayern Munich. At Old Trafford, he played in the 1979 FA Cup final, which the side lost 3–2 to Arsenal.

His backroom career began with a short spell as manager of Bristol City in 1988, before he moved back to his native Scotland to become manager of Hearts in 1990. In a three-year spell at Easter Road, he took the club to runners-up spot in the Premier Division and two Scottish Cup semis but lost his job in 1993 after a poor run of results – including a 6–0 battering at Falkirk.

He would end up at Celtic as Hoops manager, Liam Brady, tried desperately to turn around a nightmare reign by changing his backroom staff. The Irishman had taken over the reins in 1991 and his appointment marked a break from tradition at Parkhead – he was the first Celtic manager never to have played for the club. He brought in Jordan as his assistant, but the pair's unsuccessful tenure came to an end in October 1993, when Brady finally bowed to the inevitable and resigned. For a very brief spell, Jordan was Celtic manager – albeit in a very temporary caretaker role – before he also resigned, saying he had been brought in by Brady and felt it would be wrong to step into his shoes. His critics said it was a facesaver: that he would not have been given the job anyway.

Jordan returned to England for stints with Stoke, Bristol City and Huddersfield Town. Ironically, he would join Stoke after their then manager, Lou Macari, took over at Celtic and would become Macari's assistant at Huddersfield in 2000. He has become a respected coach in the game, and in recent years worked at Portsmouth under Harry Redknapp.

TOMMY BOGAN was born in Glasgow on 18 May 1920, and is famous – and in the record books – for having the shortest ever international career in football. He represented the Scottish league in a wartime international against England at Hampden in April 1945 – and lasted just 60 seconds, after colliding with visiting keeper Frank Swift. England won 6–1.

Bogan played for three Scottish clubs and four in England between 1938 and 1954, beginning with Hibernian, then Celtic – he scored eight goals in forty-seven appearances from 1946 – then Preston and joining Manchester United in 1949 for £3,500. The chirpy inside-forward scored seven goals in twenty-nine games for United before returning north, to Aberdeen.

LIAM MILLER made an acrimonious move from Celtic to United in July 2004 amid much talk of him being the new Roy Keane. Having joined the club as a 16 year old in 1997, the Irishman had made his name as a combative midfielder. Like Keane, he hails from Cork and, also like Keane, he had dreams of making it right to the top. That is where the similarities end. After moving to United on a free transfer, his game seemed to fall apart; he looked a shadow of the player who had starred for Celtic. The move appeared to have gone to his head. I remember on Boxing Day 2004, after watching United beat Bolton 2–0 at Old Trafford, walking back to the car and seeing Miller acting the big star.

It was freezing cold and two lads who had not been able to afford a ticket to the match were waiting patiently for those players who had not made the team to drive out. Miller was the first, but from what I saw it took some persuasion to get him to wind down his electric windows and sign the poor lads' autograph books.

It had not been like that when he had arrived five months earlier in the warmth of summer. A star product of the Celtic youth set-up, he had been bigged up as if United were landing a world-class talent: Celtic's loss seemed to be their gain. A.B. Murdoch, writing in the brilliant Hoops fanzine, *Not the View*, summed up the feelings of loss and betrayal at Parkhead: 'The really galling thing about this departure is that he was meant to be one of our own. He was a product of the youth set-up, and when no one else would touch him because of injuries we saw him through.'

Miller had made nineteen starts for the Hoops and twenty-four as a sub, scoring five goals. By 2005, United fans were also on Miller's back, after a series of ineffective displays led him to sign for Leeds on loan. He would eventually be shown the exit at Old Trafford – after making eleven starts in two years (he also came on eight times as a sub and scored a total of two goals) – and would swap the red shirt for the red-and-white-striped shirt of Sunderland in August 2006.

The irony, of course, was that the man who signed him was Keano – the very same Keano who had moaned about the quality of the likes of Miller, Darren Fletcher and John O'Shea before leaving United in November 2005. To be fair to Miller, he has shown glimpses of the form that marked him out as top-class potential at Parkhead since settling at the Stadium of Light. And he played his part in Keane's remarkable wizardry in transforming the Black Cats from relegation candidates to a team that would go on to win the championship in just one season.

But I retain the view I had at the time of Miller's crossing from Celtic to United in 2004 . . . that the real jewel in the crown lay elsewhere within the Hoops' ranks. In the shape of the magical Aiden McGeady, who had been somewhat in Miller's shadow while he was at the club but who quickly showed his worth when he left. Five years younger than Miller, he was the man United should have been in for. Martin O'Neill certainly knew what he was talking about when he described the quick-thinking midfielder as having 'enormous potential'. He is now turning it for the Bhoys – and good luck to him.

Others who played for Celtic and United include:

JOSEPH CASSIDY, who netted exactly one hundred goals for United's first incarnation, Newton Heath, in two spells, in

1893 and from 1895 to 1900. Cassidy also played for Celtic from 1893 to 1895.

JAMES CONNACHAN, who played for Celtic in 1897 and Newton Heath in 1898, and JOHN CUNNINGHAM, who was a triallist at Celtic in 1890 and Newton Heath in 1898.

SCOTT DUNCAN, who we have already mentioned in an earlier chapter as being United's secretary-manager from 1932 until 1937, also played as an outside-right for Celtic and United in wartime during the First World War.

BILLY GRASSAM, who played for Celtic briefly in 1903 before joining the newly formed United that same year. He spent two years with United.

GEORGE 'GEORDIE' LIVINGSTONE, who played for Celtic in 1901 and for United eight years later. Equally at home at wing-half or outside-right, he was also an FA Cup winner with Manchester City in 1904. He scored twice on his United debut against City but missed out on a second FA Cup-winner's medal in 1909, when United preferred Harold Halse.

CHARLES McGILLIVRAY, who won honours for Scotland at schoolboy level and did well at Ayr in 1930. He joined Celtic two years later and United in 1933 but failed to shine at either of the giants.

LEE MARTIN, who won the FA Cup for United in 1990. The first match against Crystal Palace had ended 3–3, but Lee scored the only goal in the replay. The 59th-minute goal from the left-back was a shock – Lee had not scored all season and had been substituted in normal time in the first match. The goal came after a pass from Neil Webb found Lee racing into the penalty area. His blast of a shot left keeper Nigel Martyn with no chance.

Lee left Old Trafford for a brief spell with Celtic and then played for Bristol Rovers and Huddersfield before moving to semi-professional League of Wales team Bangor City.

THOMAS MORRISON, who played for Celtic in 1895 and United seven years later. Equally at home on the right wing and at inside-right, he was an Irish international.

MICK MARTIN, who was a journeyman midfielder at United from 1973 to 1975 and, Celtic fans would probably agree, not much more memorable as a coach at Celtic Park from 1990 to 1992. Having said that, he did win 51 caps for the Republic of Ireland.

Ditto ASHLEY GRIMES . . . another Irishman who played for United for six years from 1977 and was a coach at Celtic in 1993–94. He was capped 17 times by the Republic of Ireland.

JIM HOLTON – personally one of my favourite players for his passion and battling spirit – who would arrive in the big-time at United in a dream move and died a tragic death. 'Six foot two, eyes of blue' was the terrace chant from the Stretford End I loved to join in as a young lad. The defender was born in Lesmahagow in 1951 and was initially on the groundstaff at Celtic. He played at West Brom and Shrewsbury before joining United for £85,000 from the Shrews in 1973. Signed by Tommy Docherty, he was the epitome of the Doc's new Trafford revolution. Big Jim was young, fresh and blew away the cobwebs of the desperate McGuinness and O'Farrell eras.

He was a dominating centre-half, and the ideal foil at United, and for the Scottish national team alongside the classy Martin Buchan, but a successful career at United was destroyed when he broke the same leg twice. Attempts to rebuild his career at Sunderland and Coventry were relatively unsuccessful and although he later signed for Sheffield Wednesday, he never played for the club because of injury. Jim retired in 1982 to become a publican in Coventry but died in 1993 of a suspected heart attack at the tender age of 42 at the wheel of his car.

Jim played in all three of Scotland's World Cup matches in 1974, making fifteen appearances in all for his country.

Before we close this chapter I think we should also mention the work of the Celtic Boys Club and a couple of lads it brought through to Celtic and United. Set up in 1966 as a feeder to Celtic FC, it has certainly proved its worth – providing Celtic with such glittering names as McStay, Aitken, Boyd, Burns and Collins.

Celtic manager at the time, Jock Stein, gave his full backing to the idea of a feeder youth club to bring boys through 'the Celtic way' – and the club was given full facilities at Barrowfield. In 1970, Frank Cairney was appointed general manager, with a brief to develop and recruit players for Celtic FC – his signing was a coup, as he had been on the brink of being made assistant manager at Hamilton. The lure of Celtic FC was such that a top pro would turn down a league team to take charge of the Hoops boys . . .

Of course, some starlets would escape the net – PAT NEVIN immediately springs to mind. He grew up supporting Celtic and scored 180 goals in a season for the boys but was ultimately rejected by the senior side for being 'too small'. It was a bad blunder: in a fine career, he would star for Chelsea and Everton and make twenty-eight appearances for Scotland, scoring eight goals. Weighed against that, the boys club unearthed more diamonds, such as Charlie Nicholas and George McCluskey.

Two others who would slip the net ended up at Old Trafford. The first was that old rascal ALAN BRAZIL, now a presenter on radio channel talkSPORT; the other, not such a big name, was SCOTT McGARVEY. The latter became a pro at Old Trafford on his 17th birthday in 1980, one year after coming down to Manchester from Celtic Boys Club. He appeared in twenty-five league games for the Red Devils, scoring three goals, and in 1983–84 made thirteen appearances for Wolves on loan.

The feeling at United was that he did not live up to expectations: that he should have been a star forward. In the end, he was transferred from United to Portsmouth for £85,000 at the start of the 1984–85 season.

Great things were also expected of Brazil, who, ironically, arrived at Old Trafford as McGarvey was walking through the 'out' door. Born in Glasgow in 1959, he had the attributes to be a legend, but it was not to be. A powerful, bustling forward, Brazil had been at the Celtic Boys Club in 1975 but slipped through the net, signing amateur forms at Ipswich Town a year later.

Brazil was an idol at Portman Road, becoming a full-time pro in 1977 and making 200 competitive appearances, scoring 80 goals and helping the club to win the UEFA Cup in 1981. In March 1983, he moved to Tottenham for £500,000 – playing in 38 games and hitting 13 goals – before United came calling in 1984, securing his signature for £700,000.

At Old Trafford, things never really worked out for Brazil – who also won 13 caps for Scotland. In two seasons, he played forty-four times, scoring twelve goals, but could not win a regular place in the side. It is no little wonder, as he was up against Mark Hughes, Frank Stapleton and Norman Whiteside . . .

By 1986, Brazil had been sent to Coventry for £300,000, then went on to play for Queens Park Rangers and Bury. Nowadays, he is a name in the media, with his *Alan Brazil Sports Breakfast Show*. A renowned lover of life and a drink, Brazil will, apart from his days at the Celtic Boys Club and Man United, be renowned for one of the biggest clangers on live radio. In 2004, while talking to fellow media star Gary Bushell, who was at a Bob Monkhouse tribute dinner, Brazil asked: 'So, er, Gary. How is Bob's health these days?' Confused by the question, Bushell replied, 'Well, Alan, he died. That's what the tribute dinner is for.' An embarrassed Brazil tried to wriggle out of it by saying, 'Well, I, er, heard two versions.'

Indeed you did, Alan. Indeed you did. He is a fully paid-up, if madly eccentric, member of the exclusive Celtic United history book . . .

13

··

THE DOC AND MACARI: BLOCKBUSTERS

Many's the time I've had an excellent bag of chips at
Lou Macari's on the way to a United match at Old
Trafford.

> *– My brother, Bob Worrall, talking about the legendary*
> *Lou Macari chip shop on Sir Matt Busby Way*

To get paid for something I loved doing. Playing
for my country, captain of my country and, later on,
managing my country. You don't get anything better
than that.

> *– Tommy Docherty, 2006*

THESE TWO bubbly characters will always have their say,
whatever anyone might think about them or their (usually
controversial) views. They are two men forever linked with
Manchester United FC and Celtic FC, Docherty as a player
with Celtic, then manager at United; Macari as a player for
Celtic, then United, then back at Parkhead as manager. The two
men shaped my belief in football while they were at United in
the '70s: they taught me here was a game that could be played

in such an entertaining, exciting way that you would be left wanting more, eager for the next match.

They were two blockbusters, as the song by the pop group Sweet would have it at that moment in time. The single hit No. 1 in January 1973, days after Docherty had taken over at Old Trafford. Its lyrics spoke of not looking into its protagonist's eyes – he would take you by surprise. Well, that was exactly what the Doc did at the slumbering, slipping and sliding United. He would bravely sort out the wreckage of the post-Busby era and lead United forward with fabulous attacking football. Before, perhaps inevitably, given the combustible nature of the man, it would all end in tears.

The Doc earned the right to manage at the very top of the tree after a tough, varied apprenticeship as both player and manager. He remains the only man to have captained and managed the Scottish national side. He once famously remarked that he had had more clubs than Jack Nicklaus. It wasn't that far off the truth: during his playing career, he did stints at Celtic, Preston and Arsenal; as a manager, he worked at Chelsea, Rotherham, QPR, Derby County, Oporto, Wolves and Aston Villa. Yet he remains steadfast about the highlights of a colourful career. I once asked him what they were and he instantly replied, 'Playing for Celtic and managing Man United. No doubt about it.'

He was United's blockbuster at a time when the club was in danger of losing it big time. True, he took United down to make them great again, but the way he stepped in and magnificently bucked that downward trend (which could have been much worse had another 'mouse' like Wilf McGuinness or Frank O'Farrell been appointed) earned him the eternal gratitude of Manchester United's supporters.

The Doc was a big man; he was never afraid to take big decisions as he gradually navigated the supertanker that was United back to glory. He would bring in Lou Macari, a mouthy little man, a mini blockbuster, from Celtic in controversial circumstances in 1973 and together they would be part of a magnificent revival at Old Trafford. They would blow away the cobwebs of apathy, lethargy and, latterly, failure that had so bedevilled the club after the European Cup triumph of 1968.

Doc's era at United – from December 1972 until July 1977 – was undoubtedly one of the most exciting times ever to be a fan of the club; a vibrant, youthful period as Docherty got rid of some of the deadwood from the Busby, McGuinness and O'Farrell eras and moulded a young team of hungry wannabe winners – with Macari at the forefront of the colourful revolution. The little man would end up owing much to Docherty after the aggressive Glaswegian transformed him into a United idol by astutely realising he could achieve much more with a subtle change of position from striker to central midfield creator.

Macari would certainly make his mark within Old Trafford – but also outside the stadium, by setting up the Lou Macari chip shop near the ground. It was a popular takeaway for fans back in his heyday and remains so today, 30-odd years on. It is putting it mildly to say he is not as well loved at Celtic Park: this owes much to his walking out on the club to join United for more money and his disappointing stint there as a manager.

His mentor, Thomas Henderson Docherty, was born in the Gorbals in Glasgow on 24 August 1928. His was a tough upbringing in a tough neighbourhood, made none the easier by the fact that his father, Thomas senior, died when young Tom was just nine. Up until his death, the whole family – father, son, his mother Georgina and sister Margaret – would share the same bed in their tenement-block flat. Money was tight, and it did not help that his father, an iron-foundry worker, was a drinker. His mother worked also, as a charlady, to bring in some much-needed money for food.

Yet even through that hard-edged childhood young Tommy

had hope in his life: inevitably, this hope was football and it was Celtic FC. The tenement block in Parkhead was not far from Celtic Park and Tommy would sneak into their matches 20 minutes from the end when the exit gates were opened.

Brought up a Catholic, he showed early promise as a footballer, turning out for his school team, St Mark's, and then, when he was 12, making a name for himself with a youth team, St Paul's Boys' Guild, which was run by a local priest. By the age of 14, the Doc had quit school and promptly got a job as a window cleaner. That was a rather short-lived enterprise: on the third day, he found he suffered from vertigo. Five jobs in as many months followed before he was signed for non-league Shettleston Juniors, earning a £3 signing-on fee and expenses of £1 a week. The young Doc was on his way – until national service and a spell in the Highland Infantry intervened.

While completing his national service, Docherty represented the British Army at football. On demobilisation in 1948, he was offered a contract with his beloved Celtic FC. They were not the only club knocking at his mother's front door. When he returned to Shettleston, she told him there were four men sitting in the lounge, each from a different outfit. Harry Potts from Burnley, Cliff Britton from Everton, a Manchester United scout and Celtic's secretary-manager Jimmy McGrory were all waiting patiently to put forward their cases for his signature.

The lure of Celtic was too big – even though they offered him only a part-time pro deal that consisted of £10 a week wages in the winter, decreasing to £8 a week in the close season. Doc found it hard to break into the first team, although there was some compensation to be had playing in front of 20,000 supporters for the reserves – such was the pull and magnetism of Celtic FC as the 1950s approached. They were big-time – arguably the biggest club in Britain bar none. Docherty could not have had a bigger first-team debut had he scripted it himself: at home to

Rangers in front of 50,000 fans. Unfortunately, he would end up on the losing side, as the Ibrox outfit triumphed 1–0.

He would play a total of nine first-team matches in the 1948–49 season and two in the Glasgow Charity Cup, scoring three goals. His best position was right-half, but that gave him and boss McGrory a problem – the slot at Parkhead belonged to the brilliant Bobby Evans. It meant the Doc was effectively his understudy and was banished to a life in the reserves. It was no good for a young hopeful with a fighting spirit like Docherty's: it was inevitable he would have to leave Celtic to achieve his ambition of regular first-team football.

So it proved: in November 1949, the Doc walked out of Celtic Park and into Deepdale, home of Preston North End, for a transfer fee of £4,000. It had been 11 years since Celtic had last won the Scottish league and 12 since they had lifted the Scottish Cup and it would later emerge that McGrory had been under pressure to sell squad players to raise funds for new first-teamers. In that sense, Docherty was a victim, but he did not mope. No, that was not his way.

He quickly got down to business at Deepdale, putting in the hard work on the training ground, and he would later admit it 'was a great move for me', although initially he would be paid £10 a week, the same rate Celtic had been providing him with for the part-time pro role.

Docherty made his debut for Preston on Christmas Eve 1949 in similar circumstances to his Celtic bow. For the Hoops, he had started as an outside-right and for his new club he would open his account at outside-left at Leeds. Never the conventional one was our Doc . . . and as that Celtic opener ended in a 1–0 loss to Rangers, so his Preston debut finished with a 3–1 defeat at Elland Road.

The following season was memorable for Docherty, as he lined up in the same team as the man he considers the greatest he would ever play alongside, the legendary Tom Finney. With Finney's dazzling skills and inspirational qualities, Preston and the Doc would storm to the Division Two championship that season. The next year they would finish a creditable seventh in Division One. The Doc would enjoy a further eight seasons before quitting the club in 1958 for Arsenal, where he was viewed as the successor to Joe Mercer.

A parting of the ways had become inevitable after he defied Preston and travelled to the World Cup finals in Sweden that year with Scotland. Docherty explained the fallout in this way: 'I was transferred from Preston on 14 August 1958, and signed in the Preston manager's office for Arsenal. I had been at odds with manager Cliff Britton because they didn't want me to go to Sweden to play for Scotland in the World Cup finals that summer because they had a club tour to South Africa. That was to last for about seven weeks and I could have gone for four of them, which I was quite happy to do. But Britton told me, "No, you either come for the lot or you don't come at all." The annoying thing about it was they took a young full-back called John O'Neill who had never played for the club – and I'd done ten seasons with them.'

The Doc enjoyed the most successful period of his playing career at Deepdale, making over 300 league appearances and appearing in an FA Cup final in 1954 – although North End would lose 3–2 to West Bromwich Albion at Wembley. At Preston, the Doc also received the first of his 25 full Scotland international caps.

Interestingly, he almost ended up at Manchester United as a player before Arsenal swooped with £28,000 readies. Matt Busby had made it clear he was interested and the Doc let it be known that he felt he could do a decent job at Old Trafford.

The Doc would buck the trend of defeat on his club debut with the Gunners: he took the number 6 shirt in their 3–0 win over Burnley and even scored a goal, the only one he would ever notch in his Arsenal career. 'It must have been from 12 yards because that was the nearest I ever came to scoring!' the Doc said.

His career at Arsenal would see him become respected as a top-class player; the *Sunday People* would sum him up like this in 1959 after the Gunners won 1–0 at Bolton early in that season: 'Docherty had another fine game, as befits a player who is now the complete wing-half.'

Despite his media image as a hothead and sometimes a buffoon who blundered in without thinking, Docherty was another much misunderstood man. He was much more of a muse than people imagine, a deep thinker who would spend hours pondering a problem or a new avenue in his life. That was the case even in his Arsenal days. Even before injury took away his playing career in 1961 the Doc was thinking ahead, planning for an uncertain future and trying to ensure it would be a future within the game he loved. That was why he took his FA coaching qualifications while still a player and why in 1960 he jumped at the chance of coaching non-league Barnet.

Two nights every week he would travel to the then Athenian League outfit's training ground – while still training as a player with the Gunners. The efforts paid off – and swiftly. In January 1961, he was offered the job of player-coach at Chelsea, a quite remarkable promotion given he was still a novice who had not worked in management outside the Football League. In his autobiography, Docherty tells how he bristled through the interview with his usual front. When chairman Joe Mears told him the board was also considering the merits of Vic Buckingham, the former West Brom player, Doc quipped: 'If you appoint him, it'll not be a coach you'll be needing, it'll be a hearse.'

When asked what he thought of the current Chelsea back four, Doc said he believed a jellyfish had more shape. And when asked if there was anything he was not good at, the Doc replied without thinking, 'Failure.' Later that night, Mears rang him to offer him the job – the Doc legend as coach/manager was truly born.

At the same time, a broken ankle was pushing him to consider calling it a day as a player. As he would later admit, he also no longer had the enthusiasm for the playing side; he had definitely caught the bug to manage. Now he would learn the hard way about the machinations of the board and the politics he would need to play to survive. His first 'enemy' was the manager, the rather dour Ted Drake. Drake's first words to him were, 'I didn't want you here. You weren't my choice. I wanted Vic Buckingham.' Docherty would weather the apathy Drake showered on him; indeed, within 12 months he would replace him as manager. Drake was shown the door with the club facing relegation. Docherty was likewise unable to keep the club in the top flight and Chelsea were relegated at the end of the 1961–62 season.

The Doc's answer was to enforce a major clear-out and put his faith in younger players – it would all bear an uncanny resemblance to his arrival at United just over ten years later. At Old Trafford, he would again be unable to save the club from the ignominy of the big drop, but he would rebuild with youth.

During his first year in charge at Stamford Bridge, he replaced many of the club's older players with talented youngsters such as Terry Venables, Bobby Tambling, Peter Bonetti and Barry Bridges. The team achieved promotion back to Division One at the first attempt, rounding off their campaign with a marvellous 7–0 win over Portsmouth. Docherty's Chelsea went into the history books as having the youngest average age of any team to have won promotion.

The following season, they finished fifth in Division One and Docherty sent out more new gems, including Marvin Hinton and John Hollins. In 1964–65, Chelsea were on course for a treble of the league title, FA Cup and League Cup. They won the League Cup in April with a 3–2 aggregate win over Leicester City but were beaten 2–0 by Liverpool in the FA Cup semi-finals. So emphatic was the nature of the Liverpool loss that Doc, with his typical wryness, exclaimed, 'And we were lucky to get nil!'

In the league, his team finished third behind Manchester United and Leeds. It was in this competition that Docherty faced his first taste of real player problems as a manager. His relationship with some of his players, especially his captain, Venables, was deteriorating. It all came to a head when eight of them broke a curfew before a crucial match at Burnley – at a time when they were just two points behind league leaders Manchester United. Doc acted quickly, sending home Venables and seven other players. It was a brave move given the enormity of the match and the possible consequences of defeat. But it marked Docherty down as a hard man, a manager who would take no messing. Those credentials would serve him well when Manchester United started their search for a tough guy to sort out their mess in 1972.

The Chelsea team that took the field at Burnley contained eight reserves hastily summoned up the M6 from London. They crashed 6–2 at Turf Moor and their title dream was over.

Still, the League Cup win had been the club's first trophy since winning the championship ten years previously and was a sign that Docherty was not only cut out for management but had what it took to make brave decisions – particularly his belief in giving youth its head. It would prove to be a good sounding board for the much bigger job that lay ahead. The win also ensured the Blues a coveted place in European competition and the next season Docherty would lead Chelsea to the FA and Fairs cups semi-finals. A year later, 1967, they reached the FA Cup final – only for the Doc to end up on the losing side for the second time in his career.

Docherty's time at the Bridge was almost up. In the October of that year, he resigned and the following month became manager of Rotherham United. He left the Yorkshire club the following year and was appointed manager at Queens Park Rangers FC, though he lasted just 29 days.

The Doc then became Doug Ellis's first manager at Aston Villa in December 1968, surviving for 13 months. On 19 January 1970, with Villa lodged at the bottom of Division Two, he was sacked. From there, he went to FC Porto and lasted four months.

By now it was July 1971 and the wanderer was hitching up at Hull City as assistant manager to Terry Neill. Just over two months later, on 12 September, it seemed as if the Doc had found his spiritual home and the constant moves were finally at an end. He was appointed as caretaker manager of Scotland, with the position becoming permanent in the November.

But fate had other ideas. Fast-forward 17 months. Two hundred miles down the road in Manchester the fans and board were unhappy with how things were going at Old Trafford. Frank O'Farrell had been appointed manager of Manchester United in June 1971, the former Leicester City boss bringing in his Foxes assistant manager Malcolm Musgrove with him as chief coach. Under the new managerial team, United had begun the 1971–72 season well and by Christmas 1971 O'Farrell's team had opened up a five-point lead at the top of the table. But United fell apart as the festive decorations came down and finished the season in a disappointing eighth.

When the 1972–73 season opened with three successive defeats to Ipswich, Liverpool and Everton, the writing was on the wall for O'Farrell and Musgrove. By December, United had played twenty-two matches, winning five, drawing six and losing eleven. On Tuesday, 19 December 1972, the inevitable happened: O'Farrell and Musgrove were sacked.

The spectre of Matt Busby had haunted the duo, and indeed their predecessor, one of Busby's former Babes, the hapless Wilf McGuinness.

Wilf had been forced to retire aged just 22 following a bad break in his leg. Fair due to the man, he quickly found a niche on the coaching side and by 1969 had been promoted from assistant trainer to chief coach at Manchester United. His progress was remarkable and in August 1970, at the age of 31, he was granted the title of manager of Manchester United.

It all turned sour as he struggled to make his decisions count; Busby was still pulling the strings at the club as general manager. When George Best went AWOL, for instance, Busby would reverse the punishment meted out by McGuinness. In December 1970, he was demoted to reserve-team coach, with Busby back as boss for the remainder of the season.

What United needed was someone who would be willing to make his own decisions, deal with the likes of Best and other ageing superstars such as Bobby Charlton and, if necessary, stand up to Busby. They needed someone with a bit of guts, someone who would not be cowed by the great man, someone who would sweep through with a vigorous new broom, someone loud and flamboyant . . . someone like the Doc.

Thomas Docherty was undoubtedly the right man in the right place at the right time when he walked into Manchester United to take the manager's chair as Christmas loomed in 1972. At United, the Doc would savour his most successful spell as manager, taking the Division Two championship in 1975 and reaching the FA Cup final in 1976, winning the trophy the following year. The 1977 victory was also a return from the wilderness for United: it was their first major trophy since the European Cup in 1968.

The Doc did not just bring the FA Cup back to the club, he also had the fans turning up excitedly in their thousands with a brand of football that was fun, brilliant and entertaining. He turned around a club in turmoil, the famous Man United on skid row. He managed to keep them in Division One in 1972–73 but papering over the cracks of an ageing, struggling squad meant the inevitable: United were relegated to Division Two a year later. Docherty described the experience of being the man who took United down in this way: 'For the first and only time in my life I was to know what depression was.'

It did not take long for him to recover and his remedy to restore the sick patient to its former glorious health was a simple one. Docherty chose to do as he had done at Chelsea: he turned to dynamic youth, showing the exit door to legends such as Best.

Journalist Andy Bucklow makes a point often overlooked in any assessment of the Doc era at United – that he actually built his team from the back. Bucklow told me, 'His brand of devil-may-care football is fondly recalled by all of us who signed up to his five-year roller-coaster ride to Wembley and back via Division Two. But the Doc was nothing if not a pragmatist and it took him nearly a year and a half to shake off his self-imposed shackles.

'When he arrived as the new messiah in December 1972, on the back of a 5–0 thumping at Crystal Palace – which eventually did for the hapless Frank O'Farrell – Doc's first aim was to make United hard to beat, epitomised in two of his first signings, no-nonsense defenders Alex Forsyth from Partick Thistle and the player who more than anyone was the symbol of the early Doc era, "Big" Jim Holton, for £60,000 from Shrewsbury. Indeed for a considerable time it was Holton, rather than any of the forwards of that era, who became the big Stretford End favourite.

'After a debut 1–1 draw with the then imperious Leeds at Old Trafford, the Doc slowly but surely managed to grind out enough results to steer United away from relegation – and most of it wasn't pretty. However, even the young Reds fans like myself saw the sense in needs-must. After all, apart from the brief Frank O'Farrell honeymoon period, which effectively proved to be George Best's last hurrah, the Reds had hardly been spraying the ball around the park anyway.

'At the start of the 1973–74 season, the Doc persevered with the functional football which had dragged him out of the deep stuff months before. But now it wasn't even doing that. I must be one of only a handful who still remembers a dire game at home to Stoke City, the second game following a 3–0 thumping by Arsenal on the opening day.

'With Bobby Charlton gone, United were skippered by George Graham and we won 1–0. But it was dreadful fare, which was followed by another lucky home win over QPR, this time 2–1. But it was clear that even after two wins in three, United were in trouble. By Easter, when relegation loomed through the awfulness of it all, Doc finally went for broke. Throwing off the shackles and introducing kids led by Brian Greenhoff, the Reds began a six-match unbeaten run with a 3–1 win at Chelsea, a 3–3 draw with Burnley and we also stuck three past Everton at Old Trafford. It proved too little too late and the season ended in three 1–0 reverses, including the infamous Denis Law goal for City that "sent United down". Actually, it didn't – we'd have gone down anyway on a 0–0 after Birmingham won their game to secure safety, but why let the facts spoil City's best moment of the past trophyless 33 years?

'At the dying embers of that relegation season, the template was set for the real Doc era to begin and it took Division Two football to perfect it.'

Good point, Andy – and true. I also stood on the Stretford End for every match of the 1974–75 season as a bullish Docherty led a revitalised, youthful United team back to the top flight. It was an exciting, wonderful time to follow United, as a team immersed in innocence but hungry for honours perfected the brand of attacking football Docherty had always dreamed of as he worked his way up the managerial ladder.

The names of the stars of the Doc era remain vivid in the old memory, as do the mental images of Gordon Hill and Stevie Coppell running down the wings, providing inch-perfect passes for the likes of Stuart Pearson. But my favourite of the lot was Macari, the battling wee man brought in from Celtic on 8 January 1973 for a fee of £200,000 – then a record for a Scottish league player. Luigi made his debut in the 2–2 draw against West Ham at Old Trafford 12 days later, scoring United's second goal after Bobby Charlton had grabbed the opener. He would give 12 seasons of fine service to the club, leaving for Swindon Town in 1984, having turned out 400 times for United, scoring 97 goals.

In the promotion season of 1974–75, Macari would grab a vital 18 goals and follow it up with another 15 in Division One in the following campaign. He was loved by the fans because of his all-action style, enviable work rate and commitment to the United cause.

He also earned several Brownie points because he had chosen the Red Devils over Liverpool when it became inevitable he would move from Scotland. Macari had been the target of Anfield boss Bill Shankly also. Shanks even wined and dined him as a guest of Liverpool when they played Burnley in an FA Cup tie. Luckily, for United at least, Old Trafford assistant manager Pat Crerand, who was sitting near Macari in the stands, learned of Liverpool's intentions and persuaded Macari to have talks with United instead. Five days later, Lou moved to Old Trafford and Shankly, in that typically mischievous way of his, tried to pour water on United's joy by saying that the striker would only have been a substitute at Anfield anyway.

In six years with Celtic, Macari had won two league championships and two Scottish Cups and played in three

League Cup finals. He did not leave Parkhead a hero: he was seen as one of the first footballing mercenaries. He had first requested a transfer from Celtic in 1971. The Hoops fans – similar to those at United – did not appreciate that a player had shown allegiance to himself rather than the badge. It goes some way towards explaining the antipathy to his appointment as manager at Celtic Park in October 1993, a stint generously best summarised as brief and unsuccessful.

It is often said Macari's head had been turned by the tales of big money at United he'd heard when he trained with the Scottish national team, and it is true that he asked Jock Stein for a signing-on fee in the event he stayed at Celtic – but laughed off the offer of an extra £5 a week, a 10 per cent pay rise, to stay at Parkhead. So, was he greedy and disloyal? You would probably see it that way if you were a Celtic fan, but there is another side to it – the club had been earning big chunks of income from their success at home and abroad and, in Macari's eyes, should have shown greater loyalty to men like himself who had helped them achieve it.

Undoubtedly, his PR skills left much to be desired. After signing for United, he criticised Stein as a control freak, once saying, 'He couldn't have really trusted players, because he never treated us like anything other than children.'

Docherty was not interested in any of that: his main concern was to get the player and get United back to the top of the pile. He celebrated when Macari signed, but after the initial euphoria, when the little man scored on his debut, there followed a period of doubt, when both men questioned the wisdom of the move to England.

Docherty knew Macari was not playing to his potential and dropped him in October 1973 before the home match against Derby County. Macari stormed off in a strop, but the decision would be the turning point in his career and their relationship.

'It was at that point I realised I was not playing him in the right position,' Docherty said. 'I had asked him to lead the line but that was not his preferred position. So I decided that instead of making him a target man, I would play him deeper. He became a different player, making runs into the penalty box.'

That is the Macari I and most United fans will remember best. The midfield dynamo who could not be thwarted, who would not be thwarted. The man who made the new United tick.

Macari's United career nosedived when Ron Atkinson replaced Dave Sexton in 1982. The Scot spent the majority of the next two seasons on the United bench and left in July 1984 to turn his hand to management. Macari's first role was as player-manager of Swindon Town, which preceded spells at West Ham United, Birmingham City, Stoke City (twice) and Celtic. He also worked as a scout for the Republic of Ireland. He is now, like his old mate Crerand, a regular pundit on MUTV.

I was up at Old Trafford recently and found that a fondness still exists for the little man. Many fans consider him a Red legend because of his exploits in the Docherty era. At the Lou Macari fish and chip shop on Chester Road, near the ground, Barbara, one of the girls behind the counter, said, 'Lou? Yeah, we still see him up here now and again. He still owns the building but not the business, although it still carries his name. He's a good lad; he always has a laugh and a joke with us. And he always says our chips are the best in town!' She was not far off the truth there – at 80p for a large portion compared with three quid in London.

Both Docherty's and Macari's career highlight was the 1977 FA Cup win over Liverpool. 'Mighty Liverpool', as they were back then. Most pundits believed the Scousers only had to turn up to take the cup back to Merseyside – this was the team on the brink of a first European Cup win, after all. They were a force to be reckoned with, while United were a brilliant but not yet finished article.

Docherty's men bravely tore up the form book and left an indelible mark on the history of the FA Cup, seeing off the challenge of the golden boys from the Mersey in a forever memorable 2–1 triumph. The win would also clear the way for Sir Alex Ferguson's men to lift the first treble 22 years later; had Liverpool triumphed at Wembley in 1977, they rather than United in 1999 would have gone down in the record books as the first English team to achieve the treble of the league, FA Cup and European Cup.

As was noted in an article in the *Daily Mail* at the time: 'Other sides have lost a game, a chance, a bonus; Liverpool have lost their place in history. One day some side may do this impossible treble, maybe even a side from Liverpool. But not these men.'

The victory also made up for the previous season, when United had lost 1–0 to Southampton in the same competition's final at Wembley. Then, the trip back north had been tear-stained and depressing after a Bobby Stokes goal killed off the dream of Doc's young turks. Now Docherty would shake off that defeat and dance around the famous old stadium with his team.

The goals had come thick and fast – three in a five-minute period. Stuart Pearson had put United ahead on 50 minutes, hammering the ball past Ray Clemence after being set up by Jimmy Greenhoff. Two minutes later United fans feared the worst when Jimmy Case equalised – but on 55 minutes United again took the lead, and this time they would not be caught napping.

Macari was involved, repaying Docherty's faith in him and writing his name forever in the United book of legends. Jimmy Greenhoff pounced on a mistake by Tommy Smith and fumbled the ball away. A shot by Macari was then deflected off Greenhoff's chest. The cup was on its way to Old Trafford.

Andy Bucklow remembers Doc's biggest day in this way: 'I was lucky enough to be there, ticket in sweaty hand, bedecked with United badges. There was only one slight problem. The ticket was at the Liverpool end, where my badge collection would be less than appreciated. I turned the jacket inside out, ran around the inner perimeter and threw myself on the mercy of a steward at the United end.

"'I've got a ticket for the wrong end and I'm being kicked and spat upon by the Scousers," I pleaded dismally. The steward glanced across the vast empty pitch to the vast empty terraces opposite. It was barely 1 p.m. and I was one of the first in the stadium. "Are you sure you're being kicked and spat on?" "Well, I will be in an hour or so." "Come back then." I mooched around at the bottom of the steps, not letting the man out of sight, until, luckily, right on the hour, he took pity and let me pass through with the United fans.

'It was worth the effort: three goals in five second-half minutes, the third of which, the winner, looped off Greenhoff's chest over a stunned Clemence.'

It appeared that the wilderness years were over at United.

But it was not to be. Just two months after the glory day out at Wembley, Docherty, the man who had led United out of the dark into the light, was unceremoniously shown the door. Even now I am certain he should never have been allowed to leave United. Under his leadership, the club had been turned around and, with a little more financial backing and a stronger squad, I believe he would have mounted a serious championship campaign. Instead, he was sacked, as he would remark, 'for falling in love' – with Mary, the wife of United physio Laurie Brown.

Thirty years on, there is still little doubt that the dismissal was a smokescreen. Some elements of the board wanted rid of the Doc and used the love affair 'scandal' as a front. In hindsight, it was a tragedy for both the man and the club. United had under his tenure re-emerged from the gloom of the post-Busby era and were an exciting team. They had won the FA Cup and were gearing up for the next two stages: the championship and Europe.

He would personally never again hit the heights as a manager and United would return to a level of mediocrity under Dave Sexton and indiscipline under Ron Atkinson. After the FA Cup win over Liverpool in 1977, Docherty was planning a realistic assault on the title, but that would all fall apart and it was another 16 years before that dream became reality, under the leadership of Alex Ferguson.

14

....

BLOOD, SWEAT, TEARS AND CHEERS (1977–2003)

THE QUARTER century from 1977 to 2003 was one of decay, renewal and ultimate triumph for Celtic and United. As we have seen on numerous occasions, the fortunes of each club seemed to mirror one another as each came to grips with the demands of different eras. These 26 years would be no different . . . they would start with the exit of Tommy Docherty from United and Jock Stein from Celtic, and see both clubs experience managerial and boardroom turmoil, but would end with a period of glory.

In 1999, under Sir Alex Ferguson, United would lift the treble of Premiership, FA Cup and European Cup; just two years later, Martin O'Neill would lead Celtic to their first domestic treble since 1969 and in 2003 take them to their first European final in thirty-three years.

There was no indication of the testing times that would follow at Celtic Park when Big Jock walked out of the club for the last time in May 1978; indeed, there was some celebration amid the gloom of Stein's departure. The man brought in to replace him at the helm was no Wilf McGuinness. No, Celtic had turned to Billy McNeill, a popular choice and probably the correct one, in the eyes of the fans and the press. He was a giant of a man, like Stein, and had been Jock's skipper during the glory years.

McNeill arrived at a time when he would be judged not by Stein's triumphs but the position in which he had left the club: fifth in the league, out of the European Cup in the second round and the Scottish Cup in the fourth round. McNeill, who had of course lifted the European Cup as captain 11 years previously, cut his teeth in the managerial trade with a year at Aberdeen. He was Stein through and through and in later life would stress his debt to the big man by dedicating his autobiography not only to his wife Liz but also, of course, to Jock, 'for making my dreams come true'.

Big Billy was also loved by and had a close relationship with the fans at Celtic Park. He once acknowledged the debt he and Celtic's glittering Lions owed to them in Lisbon that glorious day back in 1967, admitting that they had swept him and his teammates to glory with their non-stop support on the terraces. He would call them the team's 'twelfth man' and describe them as 'incredible'. Billy could identify with them – their battles, their hopes, their dreams.

His Scottish denomination was down to his Lithuanian grandparents, who arrived in Leith after believing they were on a ship to New York. Billy was born in March 1940 in that footballing stronghold of Bellshill, the same place that had begat, among others, Matt Busby. His father Jimmy served in the army and he spent the first six years of his life living with his parents in his grandparents' little mining cottage in the town. It was hardly a silver-spoon existence. After the war, he and his parents moved into a prefab.

When he was nine, his father's job took them south to Hereford for a two-year stretch – stretch not being far from the correct word. For Billy, it was a prison of sorts: until they returned to Lanarkshire, he was forced to play rugby union instead of his already beloved football and he missed Celtic FC terribly.

His first association with the club that would become the

backbone of his life came when his aunt Grace took him to see the Hoops play in October 1949. Even then, they were winners, demolishing Aberdeen 4–2, much to the delight of the young Billy boy. His favourite player was the marvellously talented Charlie Tully, whom McNeill would go on to describe as 'the Henrik Larsson of his generation'.

At the age of 17, he made his first appearance at Hampden – for his school team, Our Lady's High, Motherwell, in the Scottish Schools' Cup final, unfortunately scoring an own goal in the 1–1 draw. Then came his big break: in 1957, he played in the Scotland schoolboys side that battered England 3–0. Stein, who was present, quickly told Celtic chairman Robert Kelly that he had found a boy with massive potential. In May of that year, McNeill signed provisional forms with the club.

Initially, he was loaned to Blantyre Vics and continued his education while training two days a week at Celtic Park, but he would make his debut in the League Cup against Clyde on 23 August 1958, as the Bhoys strolled to a 2–0 win. Billy would remain a part-time player for the next three years, while also working for an insurance firm, but after Bobby Evans left for Chelsea in May 1960 the door opened for him to establish himself as the club's first-choice centre-half. Which he did – with style, grace and power for the next 15 years. McNeill would also win 29 caps for Scotland.

The year 1960 would also be the one in which he earned the nickname that would stay with him throughout his playing days: Cesar. It derived from the actor Cesar Romero, who played the getaway driver in the (original) *Ocean's Eleven* film. In those austere times in Scotland, McNeill was the only Celtic player to own a car . . .

As captain of the Bhoys, he won nine Scottish league championships, seven Scottish Cups and six Scottish League Cups, and of course he was the first British footballer to hold aloft the European Cup. Billy made 486 appearances for Celtic, but he could have left the club before he had really got going if the board had had its way. When he was 23, Spurs came in for him. The Celtic directors were happy for him to go, rubbing their hands at the prospect of a big transfer fee from the club who were the top dogs of England at the time. But Billy could not bear the thought of quitting Celtic – even though Spurs boss Bill Nicholson had promised that his weekly wages would soar from £28 to £100.

He admits that two years later his head might have been turned had Matt Busby followed up his interest in him. By 1965, McNeill had become disillusioned at Celtic Park, sensing a lack of direction and motivation at the club. He wanted a new challenge and had decided that he would move if the right club came in. In his autobiography, he admits, 'I might have found it much more difficult to reject their overtures had Manchester United followed up their initial interest with a firm offer of employment.' Busby knew Billy's parents – having been born and bred in Bellshill, having been a pupil at the same Lanarkshire school and having got to know his father in wartime. He could easily have made contact if he had wanted to test the water with McNeill.

It would certainly be Celtic's gain.

McNeill went on to win nine Scottish league titles, seven Scottish Cups, six Scottish League Cups and one European Cup as a player. Plus there was the small matter of five Scottish league titles, three Scottish Cups and one Scottish League Cup as a manager. Not a bad haul of silverware for a man the board was willing to let walk away back in '63. He also holds the distinction of playing in a record 12 Scottish Cup finals, winning the Scottish FWA Footballer of the Year award in 1974 and that year also being awarded the MBE.

Busby was searching for a replacement for the ageing Bill

Foulkes and Billy recalls it all in this affectionate way: 'Apart from Sir Matt, there were several other Scots at Old Trafford. My former Celtic teammate, Paddy Crerand, had established himself . . . and, of course, Denis Law was a hero with the Stretford End. Would I have fitted in? I think so. Playing alongside the likes of George Best and Bobby Charlton could only have made me a better player.' But fate would intervene and bring into McNeill's life the man who would steer and shape his career. The great Jock Stein knew McNeill and the other Celtic protégés from his time as coach. As manager from 1965, he would take them to greatness.

Little could McNeill have guessed that he would take over from Stein in similar circumstances 13 years later. Billy began his management career at Clyde in April 1977, staying just two months before moving to Aberdeen, then to Celtic the following year. His five years in charge in his first stint would see the Hoops win three league championships, one Scottish Cup and one League Cup. He should have stayed at the club to build up a dynasty like Maley and Stein, but in 1983, disillusioned with life at Celtic Park, he moved on.

Stein was the man who had chosen McNeill as his successor at Parkhead four years earlier. He approached him at Aberdeen and Billy took no persuading to move south to Glasgow. McNeill would win the title in his first season back at the club in 1979, with new signings Davie Provan and Murdo MacLeod playing a key role, their passion taking the team up a vital gear. Pace and inspiration were urgently needed after Bobby Lennox had finally hung up his goalscoring boots at the grand old age of 37 in the March before Billy returned. Celtic's greatest post-war goalscorer, with 273 in 589 appearances, he had joined the club in 1961 and, along with McNeill, had been a major contributor to the great Lisbon Lions side. He would leave with nine league championship medals, six Scottish Cup medals, four Scottish League Cup medals and that European Cup gong.

The first title win as a manager had been particularly sweet for McNeill, coming as it did on the back of a resounding 4–2 win over Rangers. Before kick-off, the scenario could not have been more clear-cut: a win would take the crown to Celtic Park.

The following year saw Aberdeen pinch the crown off Celtic, although the Hoops did have the consolation of lifting the Scottish Cup. They beat Rangers 1–0 with a goal from George McCluskey, but the game was marred by a riot on the terraces as the two sets of supporters got to grips with each other. BBC pundit Dougie Donnelly recalls it in this way: 'My worst cup final experience was the Old Firm riot in 1980. I was the after-match reporter and charged on to the park at the final whistle with a camera behind me. Then the hordes spilled on from either end and I turned round and ran. It was horrific.'

In an interview with the BBC, Murdo MacLeod remembered it in fonder terms. 'The 1980 game will always have a special place in my heart because it was my first Scottish Cup final,' he said. 'Having spent my early years with Dumbarton, the step-up was colossal, but I think I adapted to life at Celtic quickly and I always enjoyed the big occasion. I had had a taste of the Old Firm clashes and loved the tension during the build-up and the colour and passion on the day. I had been lucky enough to play in the league championship decider with Rangers the year before and scored in what was a wonderful game.

'The cup final was not a classic. It was a very tight affair, with not too many efforts on goal, which was unusual for an Old Firm game. Rangers were the more experienced side, packed full of good players, but we had a great bunch of young lads and we were all full of confidence. Eight of our side won their first cup-winner's medals that day.

'We didn't find out about the trouble that had erupted after the game until later that night when we got back to the hotel. We were told we couldn't take the cup back on to the pitch, but I didn't really think about it and when we left the stadium everything had quietened down.' On a sidenote, the fighting – which saw 210 people arrested – would bring about the ban on the sale of alcohol at Scottish football grounds.

McNeill grabbed the league title back in 1981, thanks in no small part to his brave decision to set up a new young and lively strike partnership, the 18-year-old Charlie Nicholas linking with Frank McGarvey, signed for £250,000 from Liverpool. Billy had stamped his image on the new side: it was fast, aggressive and winning. The team that would retain the title in 1982 also contained names such as Danny McGrain, Roy Aitken and Tommy Burns.

It was a side that was sure to go places – or at least it seemed that way on paper. Within a year, the dream had turned sour. Nicholas and McNeill were both gone. Nicholas, who netted 46 goals for the club, helped McNeill to his fifth trophy in five seasons, scoring once in the 2–1 League Cup win over Rangers. Charlie would also win both Scottish Player of the Year awards before heading south to join Arsenal in a £625,000 deal. He would rejoin Celtic in 1990 for a new spell of six years but could never recapture the glory of his younger days, eventually packing his leather trousers for the final time in '96 with a move to Clyde.

McNeill would also return to the club, but first he was heading to Manchester, only not to United as he had once dreamed. Billy had been unhappy for some time: he was frequently falling out with chairman Desmond White over transfer money and his own salary (reportedly not even in the top two in Scotland at the time), and when White demanded he sack his assistant, John Clark, he decided it was time to make an exit: Manchester City providing a reasonable escape route.

In hindsight, the loss of McNeill can be seen as the start of a troubled period for the club. After Stein's departure, he had brought with him the chance of long-term stability and success at Parkhead. He was lost too cheaply and Celtic would pay over the following years – arguably up until the appointment of Martin O'Neill in 2000 – as they struggled to find a settled backroom and consistent glory.

David Hay, who had also played for the club, would follow McNeill. His previous post was as a boss but not of a football club . . . he had been managing his own pub. He had led Motherwell to promotion in 1982 but by the time Celtic came calling had quit football to run a bar in Paisley. McNeill had left him a fine welcoming gift in the form of Brian McClair, who would end up as the club's top scorer in Hay's first season, with 31 goals. Hay would last four years, and to give him his credit he did win the Scottish Cup (1985) and the league title (1986). In his tenure, he had the misfortune of coming up against an Aberdeen inspired by a feisty and talented young manager called Alex Ferguson.

When Celtic finished the 1986–87 season without a trophy, Hay was out. McNeill returned after a troublesome spell in England: he had become one of the few to manage two relegated teams in the same season. He started the campaign in charge of Manchester City but quit in September 1986 to take charge of fellow strugglers Aston Villa. When Villa were relegated after finishing bottom of the First Division in May 1987, McNeill stood down to make way for Graham Taylor, and returned to Celtic.

The magic touch that appeared to have deserted him in England was evident again when he was reunited with his first love. Celtic won the double of league championship and Scottish Cup – it was all the sweeter coming in the club's centenary year. It was also their first double since 1977. He won the Scottish

Cup the following season as well but quit in 1991. McNeill, who would also serve as an interim manager of Hibernian, had earned his place in the ranks of eternal affection among the faithful at Celtic Park.

It would be another ten years (after the win in '88) before Celtic once again paraded the league title. Rangers, under the guidance of Graeme Souness and Walter Smith, and with cash aplenty to splash on big-money signings, would take control of the limelight. From 1989 to 1997, the Ibrox outfit matched Celtic's record nine title wins.

When McNeill left for the second time, the fans began to voice their discontent. They saw Rangers on the ascendancy, from the big-money signings to the refurbishment of Ibrox. They wanted change. They quite rightly wanted Celtic to match their biggest rivals on and off the pitch.

Liam Brady took over from McNeill in the summer of 1991. He was the first manager of Celtic FC to have not played for the club. Despite his credentials as a player with Arsenal and Juventus, the Irishman could not cut it as a big-time manager. Amazingly, this was his first experience in such a post. He would fail to bring any success to the club, although he did bring poor signings.

One of the most conspicuous defeats came early in Brady's reign, as they crashed 5–1 away to Swiss minnows Neuchâtel Xamax in the UEFA Cup in October 1991. Two years later, almost to the day, he was gone.

But the nightmare was not yet over: Lou Macari would replace Brady at the club he had served as a player. It was to prove another unfortunate signing, as the barren years continued apace. In retrospect, Macari was never given a chance. His tenure would be a short one as a new saviour appeared on the horizon.

It is remarkable how many times Celtic and United have been saved by the timely intervention of a forward-thinking businessman during their respective histories: John Glass in the early days at Celtic, John H. Davies and James Gibson rescuing United as they rocked from side to side in the first half of the twentieth century. In 1994, expatriate businessman and Celtic supporter Fergus McCann would help steady the good ship Celtic after a long period of boardroom inadequacy. McCann stepped in eight minutes before the club would have been declared bankrupt on Friday, 4 March, ousting the board of directors. It was the end of the road for the Whites and the Kellys, the families who had lost their direction at the helm.

McCann replaced the hapless Macari three months later with another ex-Celt, Tommy Burns. Burns vowed he would rejuvenate the team on the pitch, while McCann outlined how he planned to transform Celtic Park into the best ground in Scotland. One of McCann's first moves, under what he termed his 'Five-Year Plan', was to turn the club into a public limited company to raise cash and cut debts. Around 10,000 people took up the offer of investing a minimum of £620 and the share issue netted £14 million towards the refinancing of the club, which saw the redevelopment of Celtic Park into a 60,830 all-seater stadium to rival the best in Europe.

Celtic would play home fixtures at Hampden Park during the 1994–95 season as work progressed at Celtic Park. But it was still hardly the stuff of wine and roses. Under Burns's leadership, the side won the Scottish Cup in 1995 but failed to end Rangers' dominance in the Scottish Premier League. Burns did make some commendable moves, such as setting up a scouting network for young players and signing Pierre van Hooijdonk and Andreas Thom. It was Dutchman van Hooijdonk who won the club their first trophy for six years in 1995 when he headed home the only goal of the game in the cup final against Airdrie. It was Celtic's 30th triumph in the competition.

But when Celtic finished trophyless in 1997 – and, just as

painfully, if not more, Rangers equalled their nine-in-a-row league wins – Burns was shown the door, along with his coaching staff.

McCann wanted to change the way the club operated and so he brought in two men to replace Burns: Jock Brown as general manager and Wim Jansen as head coach. The Dutchman had, of course, played against Celtic for Feyenoord when they won the European Cup final in 1970 and he became their first foreign coach.

Again there is a feeling that had Jansen been given the time, encouragement and full backing to do the job – just like during Billy McNeill's first spell as Celtic boss – he could have embarked on a Stein-like era. Jansen enjoyed three special successes that season. The first was persuading the great Henrik Larsson to join him for a bargain £650,000 fee from Feyenoord. Then he guided Celtic to the first League Cup final victory in 15 years in a 3–0 defeat of Dundee United at Ibrox, the competition then being sponsored by Coca-Cola. Jansen saved the best until last: winning the Scottish Premier League in 1998, the first time Celtic had lifted the trophy in ten years. They also stopped Rangers notching up what would have been a record ten in a row.

Yet two days after the triumph, Jansen was gone following a row over transfer funds for the next campaign. It was surely a tragedy for Celtic FC and its fans that the man who had promised so much – and delivered so much in such a short space of time – should be allowed to leave so cheaply. General manager Jock Brown would follow him out the door shortly afterwards.

The Jock Stein Stand opened for the new 1998–99 season, completing the four-year stadium development plan initiated by McCann. The fans would continue to see exciting football but under the sixth manager in a decade. Enter Dr Jo, otherwise known as Dr Jozef Venglos, who had made his name as manager of Czechoslovakia. As that nation's overlord from 1978 to 1982, Venglos had led his side to the final of the 1980 European Championship, where they lost to West Germany.

His reputation had been somewhat sullied by a season in charge of Aston Villa. The first foreign manager to take charge of a top-flight club in England, he would leave in 1991 after the club finished just two places above the Division One relegation zone. Following spells in Turkey, his native Slovakia and Oman, the 61-year-old Venglos finally surfaced at Celtic Park on 17 July 1998. Rangers would complete another double in his one season in command, but he would quickly be moved sideways into a scouting/ambassadorial role. His achievements were threefold: his style of football was entertaining, he brought fellow Slovak Lubo Moravcik to the club and he led the Bhoys to a 5–1 win over Rangers in the league in November 1998 – at the same time getting one over on their continental coach, Dick Advocaat.

Fergus McCann's time was also up at the club: his five years now done and dusted, he passed control over to Allan MacDonald. He quickly appointed his pal and golfing partner Kenny Dalglish in what had been Brown's role as general manager and Dalglish brought in the man who is by many fans remembered as the biggest disappointment in Celtic FC's proud managerial history. Enter John Barnes . . . former Liverpool and England winger, lately of Charlton Athletic, but at the time managerial virgin and simply not cut out for the job of head coach. His appointment would also leave a stain on Dalglish's reputation with the bhoys of the Jungle.

Barnes lasted until February 2000, his dismissal following the catastrophic Scottish Cup defeat to First Division Inverness Caledonian Thistle, the 3–1 loss resulting in the now legendary headline in *The Sun*: 'Super Caley Go Ballistic, Celtic Are Atrocious'. Dalglish stepped in as head coach until the end of the season, with Celtic finishing as runners-up to Rangers in the league but 21 points behind. The only consolation was a 2–0 victory over Aberdeen in the League Cup final.

But after the darkness would come the light – at the gleaming new Celtic Park – in the shape of the brilliant, effusive, unpredictable Martin O'Neill. The comparison with the rookie Barnes could not have been more stark or severe: here was a man finally with top credentials, marked out as a possible future manager of Manchester United and a man who, six years later, should undoubtedly have been competing for the job of England head coach alongside former Middlesbrough boss Steve McClaren.

The Irishman took the reins in June 2000 on a three-year deal worth £1 million a year. Born in Coleraine, Northern Ireland, on 1 March 1952, Martin Hugh Michael O'Neill began his career at Derry City before Brian Clough took him to Nottingham Forest. O'Neill would play for Forest from 1971 to 1981 as part of the magnificent side built by Clough that won the league in 1978 and the European Cup in 1979 and 1980. O'Neill then had relatively short stints at Norwich, Manchester City, Notts County, Chesterfield and Fulham.

Equally at home on the right side of midfield or in his preferred central role, O'Neill won 64 international caps for Northern Ireland and played for his country in the 1982 World Cup finals in Spain.

On retiring from football, he headed for a career in management, with the estimable aim of reaching the top by starting at the very bottom – the exact opposite of John Barnes. Martin O'Neill began his managerial career at Grantham Town in 1987. After a brief spell at the helm of Shepshed Charterhouse, he moved to Wycombe Wanderers. Success at Wanderers marked him out as a man to be watched; in 1993 as Conference champions, Wycombe earned a place in the

Football League and followed that with a second successive promotion into Division Two.

In 1995, O'Neill moved to Norwich but resigned after just six months following clashes with chairman Robert Chase over funds for team building. Here was a man blessed with integrity and principles: characteristics that would serve Martin O'Neill supremely well as he moved steadily up the managerial ladder. He was appointed as the new manager of Leicester, guiding them into the Premiership via the play-offs at the first attempt before winning the League Cup the following season.

The giants of football started to circle but, a man of loyalty, Martin O'Neill stayed at Leicester. His loyalty earned him great respect, but when Celtic came knocking at his door in the summer of 2000, it was an offer too far: one simply too big and too good to resist.

It would be a marriage made in heaven. Under his leadership, Celtic won three Premier League championships out of five and in his first season in charge the team also won the domestic treble. He had worked wonders at Leicester – but only after a testing start. At Celtic, he would get off to an absolute flyer, with four victories in their first four league matches. Next up was his first Old Firm derby. Martin again delivered the goods in style, thrashing Rangers 6–2 at Celtic Park. It was all the sweeter for the Jungle Bhoys as their team had not beaten Rangers in the previous seven encounters. Employing his favoured 3-5-2 line-up, O'Neill turned the team around in super-quick time – the signing of £6 million striker Chris Sutton appearing a particular stroke of genius. The former Chelsea man grabbed a brace against Rangers and linked up superbly with Larsson over the following campaign as Celtic romped home in the title race, winning it with a record 97 points, 15 clear of their Ibrox rivals, who finished runners-up.

To complete a sensational first season at Celtic Park, O'Neill's men would also win the League Cup, with a 3–0 victory over Kilmarnock, Larsson's hat-trick presenting Martin with his first trophy as Celtic manager, and the Scottish Cup in a 3–0 win over Hibs, tying up a remarkable treble triumph, the club's first since 1969. The win over Hibs would prompt a telling compliment from Sir Alex Ferguson: 'Martin is a no-nonsense manager who is strong and has a personality – these qualities are important at a big club . . . Any recognition and praise that Martin gets is deserved. For him to go to Celtic and change it all around in one season is remarkable.'

O'Neill signed fellow Northern Irishman Neil Lennon in December 2000 for £5.75 million. The former Leicester player would become the man he could rely on in the trenches and, along with Larsson, the key player of his reign.

Lennon was born in County Armagh in 1971 and started his football career as an apprentice at Manchester City in 1989, going on to play for Crewe before arriving at the Foxes. Initially viewed as not much more than a battling journeyman in his time in England, he would come into his own at Celtic Park, his passion and inspiration central to the type of team O'Neill wanted to create. His game developed and he became a fine holding midfielder. He and O'Neill would make a very good team.

Lennon played his final game for Celtic on 26 May 2007, when he captained the club to a Scottish Cup-final victory over Dunfermline Athletic, the 1–0 win clinching the league and cup double. When it was announced he would be leaving, Lennon, almost in tears, said, 'I would like to thank the Celtic fans for their support. I have enjoyed a good relationship with supporters and sincerely appreciate the backing which they have given me over a number of years. This season has been particularly pleasing, having won the championship, making the Scottish Cup final and obviously getting to the last 16 in the Champions League.

'It was a boyhood dream to play for the club I loved – I

am very proud to have achieved this and played for Celtic for so many years and, clearly, when [current Celtic manager] Gordon Strachan made me captain of the club I was, of course, extremely honoured.'

Lennon's time in the east end of Glasgow also earned front-page headlines. Capped 40 times by Northern Ireland, whom he also captained, he quit international football after being the target of a death threat before a home game against Cyprus. He was also assaulted near his home by two Glasgow University students, one studying medicine, the other law, who had kicked his car when it stopped at a pedestrian crossing. Neil would reveal that he had struggled for many years with clinical depression and took anti-depressant drugs.

Strachan admitted that Lennon's decision to quit in 2007 left a void at Celtic Park similar to that left at Old Trafford when Roy Keane had left two years earlier; he would, in fact, alter the Hoops' style of play the following season. 'Neil leaving is like Roy Keane moving on from Manchester United,' Strachan said. 'You don't just try to replace that one player, you have to alter your team a little bit. There's nobody out there who can replace him as a person and a player. So what you have to do is make sure the team shape is right for the players that we have there.'

Strachan paid this farewell tribute to Lennon by saying, 'Neil was mentally strong and he made himself physically strong. His skill and passing was better than anything I've seen for a long time and, despite what some people say, there is a skill in passing to your teammates all the time. His first touch is fantastic and I don't think that has ever really been appreciated.

'There is no doubt about it, he has helped the players, and me and the coaching staff especially, to win two titles and I will always be thankful for that. And on top of that, I think I have a good friend now as well. I could spend two hours talking about

Neil Lennon, but all I'll say is that I'm thankful he has stayed for the last two years.'

Rolling back the clock, Celtic would retain the title in O'Neill's second season – for the first time in 20 years – and the deep-thinking manager began to adapt his team's game to European competition. On three occasions, his side qualified for the Group stage of the Champions League and in the only one for which they failed to qualify, they would go on to reach the final of the UEFA Cup. Under O'Neill's leadership, teams such as Juventus, Porto, Valencia and Barcelona visited Glasgow to face Celtic and returned home defeated. Celtic also notched up an unbeaten run of 77 home matches spanning from 2001 to 2004, and a Premier League record for the most consecutive wins in a single season.

The 2002–03 season had ended trophyless – but the 80,000 Hoops fans who enjoyed their break in the Seville sun were hardly complaining. Reaching the UEFA Cup final was a major achievement although defeat to Porto was hard to stomach. O'Neill would face disciplinary action following his outburst over the standard of refereeing.

Celtic won the Scottish Premier League for a third time under O'Neill on 18 April 2004. That year Martin was also named the Scottish Football Writers' Manager of the Year, and was awarded the OBE.

In May 2005, the end was in sight for Celtic's most successful and charismatic manager since the era of Jock Stein. Martin, as always a man of honour and principle, decided he needed time out to care for his seriously ill wife, Geraldine. In his final season at Parkhead, the club failed to win the title, but he ended his spell as boss on a high by beating Dundee United 1–0 to lift the Scottish Cup. Martin, whose wife was receiving treatment for cancer, said, 'I am leaving Celtic purely for personal reasons and I am extremely sorry to be departing in such circumstances.' The great man would stay out of the game for 15 months, eventually returning to manage English sleeping giants Aston Villa in August 2006.

The search for his successor at Celtic Park did not take long. On 25 June 2005, it was announced that Gordon Strachan would be the new man at the helm. The decision by the board was hardly met with unadulterated joy by many Celtic fans, but more of that later.

Now let's turn our focus to a similar set of trials and tribulations experienced by Manchester United from 1977 until the advent of the current glory era under Sir Alex Ferguson. After Tommy Docherty was ousted in the summer of 1977 over 'the Mary Brown affair', Dave Sexton stepped into his shoes. It was a prospect that chilled United's army of supporters. Sexton, who would become known as 'Dull Dave' or 'Dour Dave' on the terraces during his four years in charge, had seen history repeat itself at a different club – he had also taken Docherty's job at Chelsea in October 1967. Sexton would win nothing with United, although he would take them to an FA Cup final and sign some players of genuine class and stature.

In June 2007 while looking at an Internet discussion site about the possibility of Mourinho succeeding Ferguson at United, I noticed what I think is a fairly adept commentary on the Sexton era. The writer had this to say: 'Mourinho is the most technical of tacticians whose mantra is "keep it solid". Lord Ferg is an artist whose mantra is for players to "express themselves". If Mourinho became boss at United, it would be a bit like the Dave Sexton era – solid, progressive in terms of results, but boring and most definitely not United.'

And I think that just about sums up Sexton's time at Old Trafford. After his spell at Chelsea, where he won the FA Cup and then the Cup-Winners' Cup, he joined QPR in 1976–77. They would finish just a point behind league champions Liverpool.

That second-place position still remains the club's highest league placing, a sign of the good work Sexton had done.

On the back of his achievements at Stamford Bridge and Loftus Road, he became United's 13th manager. Looking at it on paper, you would have to say the appointment seemed a sound one. Here was a man with solid achievements and respect within the game; indeed, after United he would eventually be appointed manager of the England Under-21 team and they would win the UEFA championship twice with him in charge. In 1984, he would also become the first technical director of the FA National School at Lilleshall.

So he was sound, but he just wasn't a Manchester United manager because the playing system he advocated was essentially dull and defensive: it was not the adventurous, exciting brand United fans had been reared on under Busby and Docherty. Sexton would last four years at Old Trafford. During that time he broke the club's transfer record four times, signing Joe Jordan from Leeds United for £388,888; Gordon McQueen, also from Leeds United, for £495,000; Ray Wilkins for £825,000; and Garry Birtles for £1.25 million. Jordan was a fierce, determined centre-forward; McQueen was a fine, classy centre-back and Wilkins a similarly classy midfielder.

I know Birtles did not cut it at Old Trafford, but back then even he seemed a fair gamble given the goals he had scored at Forest. Let's not forget that when he arrived at United in October 1980 he had won two European Cup-winner's medals and had played three times for England. Under the guiding hand of Brian Clough he had also scored more than 50 goals in 130 appearances for Forest. But at United he fell foul of what would become known as 'strikers' graveyard' syndrome. Others who suffered from the weight of expectation in front of massive crowds included another Forest stalwart Peter Davenport, as well as Ted MacDougall, Terry Gibson and Alan

Brazil. Birtles would take 26 games to grab his first league goal for the Red Devils, but at least he would not suffer like Brazil: the former Ipswich striker would be spat at by fans on occasions as he struggled to bed in.

Birtles would be grateful to Sexton when the United boss allowed him to return to Forest just under two years later for £250,000, a fraction of the price United had paid. He had played just 64 times for United, scoring a miserly 12 goals.

Ray Wilkins was another who, on paper at least, looked a great buy, an investment for the future. Sexton knew he had to turn United into a title-chasing team: that was why he was investing in undoubted quality. But, like Sexton himself, Wilkins would suffer from a lack of panache, a lack of glitter and colour. Don't get me wrong, Ray Wilkins was a quality midfielder but, again like Sexton, 'Butch' was not a natural United man: he lacked the attacking skills needed to win over the crowd. He was not a risk taker and lacked that which epitomised United's love of entertaining football.

Apart from Butch, his other nickname was 'The Crab', because of his love of moving the game sideways with safe passes rather than forwards into attack. Yet it would not stop him captaining United and England on occasions and winning eighty-four caps for his country in a ten-year spell from 1976.

Wilkins moved to Old Trafford from Chelsea in August 1979. He had been a schoolboy prodigy at the Bridge, where he replaced veteran Ron Harris as captain at the age of 18, their youngest ever skipper. He scored 30 goals in 179 games for the Blues before rejoining his former Chelsea boss Sexton at United. He gave United five seasons of consistent performances, making 194 appearances and scoring ten goals, before leaving to play in Italy for AC Milan. He was made a CBE for services to football in 1993 and is now a pundit on Sky Sports, where he is respected for his measured points of view.

The two highlights of Sexton's United career were the FA Cup final in 1979 and a second-place finish in Division One in 1980, two points behind eventual champions Liverpool. The 1979 final has, of course, gone down in the annals of football history as one of the greatest ever finals at Wembley ... although not in the United history books. The bare bones of the story are that for the best part of 85 minutes they were outplayed by a Liam Brady-inspired Arsenal, but they came back from the dead in true 1999 European Cup-final fashion, grabbing two late goals. Brady set up goals for Brian Talbot and Frank Stapleton to give the Gunners a 2–0 lead by half-time, but late goals from Gordon McQueen and Sammy McIlroy gave United hope when they had none.

But that is where the similarities with 1999 end. With seconds to go, chief tormentor Brady set up the goal that would crush United and their fans, flying down the left wing and crossing to the far post. He found Alan Sunderland, who slid in the winner to cap what many pundits believe is the most remarkable finish ever seen in an FA Cup final: 3–2 to Arsenal.

United fan Rob Daniel remembered the occasion as a roller coaster of emotions and, I am sure, his sentiments are shared by many who travelled to Wembley that sunny May day in 1979. 'My first FA Cup final, the build-up, the crowd, the game, everything lived up to my expectations,' he said. 'Arsenal outplayed United until those last few minutes. I remember Sammy Mac's run, it seemed to last forever, and finally the ball rolled over the line. Cue the celebrations: it went wild in the United end. I ended up on the floor with many others, and as I recovered and got back on my feet there it was running towards us: the biggest perm in football had just scored the winner for Arsenal. I didn't see the goal, just Alan Sunderland running down the pitch celebrating. Heartbreaking, but I always remember the United fans singing right to the end and after the final whistle. That memory will always stay with me.'

The following season, 1980–81, saw United slip down the table to eighth position and crash out of the FA Cup in the fourth round, the UEFA Cup in the first round and the League Cup in the second round. Consolation would come as United won their last seven games of the campaign, but it was too late for Dull Dave and he was sacked by the United board.

Just as Celtic had searched for the right manager after the eras of Stein and McNeill, so United would continue their hunt for the rightful successor to Busby. After the mischief of Docherty and the grey days of Sexton, the board now plumped for Ron Atkinson. Like a schoolgirl lover on the rebound, they went for Mr Personality after the man some fans dubbed Mr Charisma By-Pass. 'Big Ron', as he liked to be known, could not have been more different from Sexton: with his jewellery, loud suits and even louder opinions, he was the very antithesis of the man he would replace.

He arrived at Old Trafford in June 1981 and would treat United fans to more than five years of glitter and bombast. He took United to the edge of the promised land but could not gain the visa that would have allowed unlimited access to the dream. Unlike Ferguson, he allowed things get out of hand when, with a little more of the boot camp and less of the holiday camp, he could maybe have won the league. But to be fair, he did achieve a lot. And let's not forget that Big Ron's reign coincided with the dominant years of Liverpool.

A Scouser himself, Atkinson worked on the Mars bar premise: if you worked hard, you deserved to play hard. But he failed to instil the third tenet of the manifesto into his players: that they also needed to rest hard and look after themselves. When Ferguson took over, he was stunned by the poor levels of fitness and the lack of respect some of them had for the manager and the club.

There's a saying often associated with Atkinson and his time at Old Trafford – and I think it is an apt one. The United fans loved him, until it all started to go wrong. Then they questioned whether he was tough enough to ever bring the really big honours (i.e. the league title and the European Cup) back to the club. It is a fair point. Atkinson, always a bon viveur, would, to his credit, answer back with the line, 'Well, it was bloody good while it lasted.' He would also point out that he won the FA Cup twice, in 1983 and 1985.

A journeyman wing-half as a player, he nonetheless was Oxford United's captain through their rise from the Southern League to Division Two, achieved in just seven seasons. He was also the first man to captain a club from the Southern League through three divisions of the Football League.

Atkinson opened his managerial career in 1972 when, at the age of 32, he took the reins at non-league Kettering Town. He won the Southern League First Division and Premier Division championships and took them to within one vote of gaining league status. In December 1974, he stepped up into league management with Cambridge United. In his second full season at Cambridge, Ron guided them to the old Division Four championship and later into Division Two.

By 1978, he had been appointed into the hot seat at West Bromwich Albion, taking them to the top reaches of the old Division One and twice into the UEFA Cup, in 1978–79 and 1979–80.

United's board decided Big Ron was the perfect antidote to the dreary years of Sexton and he rewarded them with the entertaining football the fans demanded. Along the way, he signed some quality players – men who would ensure the team continued to perform with bravado and gusto. Chief among them were Frank Stapleton, Gordon Strachan, Arnold Muhren and 'Captain Marvel' himself, Bryan Robson. The latter was his best buy and one of United's greatest ever purchases. A British record transfer of £1.5 million saw Robbo arrive at Old Trafford in October 1981 and he would be the man around whom Atkinson would build his team of musketeers.

Robson would certainly prove worthy of the fee: he would go on to become the top British midfielder of his generation and earn his place in the annals of United legend with his all-action displays and inspirational captaincy skills. In his 12 years at Old Trafford, the number 7 would make 437 appearances and score 74 goals for the club he grew to love. Famed for his superb tackling and driving runs, he would also captain his country, winning 90 caps and scoring 26 times in the process.

His years as United skipper also make him the club's longest-serving captain of all time. Robbo is still the only British captain to lead a side to three FA Cup wins (1983, 1985, 1990). He also won the Cup-Winners' Cup in 1991 and finally won the league championship in 1993 and '94. His number of appearances for club and country and his achievements are all the more remarkable given the injuries he suffered along the way (including three broken legs).

Robson would admit to enjoying his years under Atkinson more than he did his final ones at United under Ferguson. He liked the way Atkinson went about the game – and the way he would unwind with the players. Robbo's love of 'his pint' is almost as legendary as his playing prowess; indeed, at United he was, along with Paul McGrath and Norman Whiteside, known as one of the club's 'Three Musketeers'. It is a credit to his footballing dedication and application that out of the trio only he survived the cull under Ferguson's tougher regime. Atkinson was as famed for his love of champagne (United's performances under him were often described as 'champagne football').

In his second season, United lost the Milk Cup final to Liverpool. This was United's first-ever appearance in the League

Cup final and was a close encounter, with the game going to extra-time. A young Norman Whiteside had put United in front with a beauty of a goal, but Alan Kennedy made it 1–1. Bruce Grobbelaar should have been sent off for a terrible challenge on Gordon McQueen but only got a yellow card. In extra-time, Ronnie Whelan scored a fantastic curler, which gave Liverpool a 2–1 victory.

But in May 1983 they were back at Wembley to beat Brighton in the FA Cup in a replay. United had drawn the first match 2–2 but made no mistake in the second, thrashing the Seagulls (or as the Stretford End would call them, 'Seaweed') 4–0, with two goals from Robson and one apiece from Whiteside and Muhren.

United were also back in Europe and the Cup-Winners' Cup campaign of 1983–84 saw them into the semi-final against Juventus. It was a last-minute goal by Italian star Paolo Rossi that finally killed off the dream.

In both of the next two seasons, United made a bright start in the league only to fade away at the end. Once again, the FA Cup was their consolation prize in 1985, as they beat Everton 1–0. While the score was 0–0, United had Kevin Moran sent off – the first player to be dismissed in a cup final – but Norman Whiteside's marvellous goal from an acute angle took the cup back to Old Trafford once again.

The following season United started like a train, winning their first ten league matches, and stayed unbeaten for fifteen. But they ran out of steam and finished fourth, 14 points behind seeming perpetual champions Liverpool. Atkinson paid the price in the following season for a poor start when he was dismissed in November. The departure of Mark Hughes to Barcelona for £2.5 million and Ray Wilkins to AC Milan for £1.5 million had added to Big Ron's woes: it left a feeling around Old Trafford of futility and hopelessness . . . that they would never win the league. At any other English club, Atkinson's legacy – two FA Cup wins and league finishes of third, third, fourth, fourth and fourth – would probably have been seen as an acceptable return. Not so at United.

The days of easy, relaxed smiles – and the holiday camp atmosphere – were over. In their place came an altogether more serious, tougher regime, one designed to turn United from a successful cup-competition side to a successful side full stop. The days of Alexander Chapman Ferguson would bring to an end that agonising quest for the holy grail as United finally returned to the top of the pile by once again winning the top-flight title and the European Cup.

The abrasive Scot became United's eighth post-war manager on a cold, dreary day in November 1986. A man of the people, he walked into Old Trafford and quickly made it clear that, unlike Big Ron, he was no champagne Charlie. He would be at his office at 8 a.m. five days a week and would have as much time to talk to a lowly cleaner as he would one of the board of directors.

Brought in from the granite city of Aberdeen, this was the man who had at Pittodrie broken the Glasgow stranglehold on Scottish football with his exciting young side. Now his aim was to do a similar job in England by breaking the hold Liverpool had on the English top-flight title. He would turn the club upside down after surviving an uneasy initial three years and achieve his ambition of overwhelming Liverpool within seven years. By the time Martin O'Neill had taken Celtic back to the European big time in the UEFA Cup final in 2003, Ferguson had brought the European Cup back to Old Trafford for the first time since 1968, the triumph of 1999 made all the sweeter as United lifted their legendary treble.

Later I will look more closely at the Ferguson dynasty at Old Trafford, examine how Gordon Strachan is building on the solid foundations laid by Martin O'Neill and look at what the future holds for Celtic and United. But now, let's look at the effect on United and Celtic of arguably the key player of Fergie's reign at Old Trafford: the legendary Roy Keane.

15

ROY KEANE: SWEET SIXTEEN

I had to find out if Roy was interested. I told him
where I was going, he said he was up for it.
*– Celtic manager Gordon Strachan after signing
Roy Keane, December 2005*

Roy Keane has taken Sunderland from relegation
candidates to Premiership promotion contenders in
just five months. If he completes the journey, we might
just have a new Special One on our hands.
– Des Kelly, Daily Mail, *23 January 2007*

ASK ANY Manchester United fan who, if they could have
one dream choice, they would one day want to manage their
football team and the majority will say straight out, 'Roy Keane'.
Indeed, if you put the same question to the loyal fans at Celtic
Park, the outcome might not be that different. If one man in
the modern era represents the romantic ideals of both clubs, it
is Roy Keane.

Here was a footballer who would have died for either club
as he went into battle: a warrior who did not just want to play
for both clubs but felt it was his destiny, his right to do so. That
he achieved this is a credit both to himself and the men behind

the scenes who ensured he would be a Celtic United star before he hung up his boots. Sir Alex Ferguson was the man who splashed out a then British record transfer fee of £3.75 million to Nottingham Forest for the abrasive midfielder in 1993, while Dermot Desmond was the Celtic majority shareholder who ensured with determination and readies that the deal to bring Keane to Celtic Park in the twilight days of his playing career was always more than just a pipe dream. Ferguson would see off the persuasive Kenny Dalglish, then manager at Blackburn, to get his man; Desmond would go to great lengths to make Keane forget his dreams of Real Madrid to join the Hoops.

Not that it was too difficult once Keane had visited Celtic Park. Along with United, this was the team he had always loved, had supported as a fan and wanted to play for. But there was still a certain amount of legwork to be put in.

Celts manager Gordon Strachan can also take some credit for the signing of Keane in December 2005. In some quarters, he was unfairly lambasted as being the man who did not want Keane, the man who had him foisted upon from above, a helpless stooge in the sensational signing. I am informed Strachan actually played an important part in selling the idea to Keane, explaining to him where and how he wanted him to play and how he envisaged the team developing with Keane on board. Sure, there were a couple of fallouts in the months that followed – more of that to come – but nothing to tarnish the relationship and mutual respect that had been established between the two men before Keane quit playing for good in May 2006.

Roy Maurice Keane was the man who was born to be king of the Stretford End and the Jungle. A proud son of Cork, he was a man convinced of his destiny, with a conviction that he would one day complete his mission of starring at both Celtic Park and Old Trafford. This was a man who was also a loyal fan of both clubs – although his boyhood team was actually Spurs because of his love for the stylish play of Glenn Hoddle.

In May 2003, Keane travelled to Spain to support Celtic in the UEFA Cup final in Seville. He sat and mingled with the masses of Hoops fans in the Olympic Stadium, having a great time before, during and after the match – even though Porto would shatter Celtic's hopes of winning their first European trophy for 36 years.

An estimated 80,000 Celtic supporters created a party atmosphere in Seville, as the city was swelled by what UEFA described as the largest travelling support ever to have assembled for a single game – and Keane enjoyed the occasion as much as any of the loyal fans from Glasgow.

'I met a lot of Celtic fans when I was in Seville and I've always enjoyed that banter, as I did at my previous clubs,' Keane said. 'I think it's important you don't lose touch with reality because again that has crept into the game a touch. I think fans have lost touch with the players and I think players are guilty of that as well.

'Seville was brilliant. I think I lost two stone that night because of the heat, but I think it was a great occasion. Not the result, but it was great that Celtic were even there after beating teams like Liverpool and challenging for a European trophy.'

When Keane signed for Celtic, Phil Gordon, writing in *The Independent*, brilliantly summed up the elation of the moment and helped explain why it was so poignant an occasion for both player and club, which had beaten off the approaches of Real Madrid for the legendary number 16:

> Madrid may have seemed like the perfect curtain call for a performer who has spent the best years of his life at the Theatre of Dreams, yet Roy Keane's mind was really made up in another part of Spain over two years ago. On a hot suffocating evening in Seville the Irishman discovered he had some soul brothers.

Around 80,000 of them, in fact. That was the number of Celtic fans who turned up to watch their club's first European final in three decades.

Keane's love for Celtic was more of a slow burn than was his affection for United. In 2006, in my book *Roy Keane: Red Man Walking*, I made the point that Roy was a bit of a johnny-come-lately as far as Celtic was concerned. He was quick to point out that he had loved the club for 'many years', but I learned that his devotion was not truly formed during his childhood in Cork, or even his teens. No, Roy Keane became a true Hoops aficionado from his mid-20s. The first time he spoke of this new bond was after United won the treble in 1999, when he admitted, 'I can see myself one day finishing my career at Celtic.' In the following years, he would often travel up to Glasgow with some United teammates, incognito, wearing his trademark baseball cap, to watch Old Firm games. Witnessing Celtic fans fill Old Trafford in 2001 for Ryan Giggs's testimonial, which Martin O'Neill's side won 4–3, also gave him a massive buzz about one day turning out for the Bhoys.

The Roy Keane story begins on 10 August 1971 when he was born in Cork, the fourth of five children. He grew up on a sprawling council-house estate in Mayfield in the Northside area of the city with his parents Mossie and Marie, his three brothers, Denis, Pat and Johnson, and his sister, Hilary. From an early age, he was proud of his roots and one day would say, 'I am from Cork first, Ireland second' and 'Irish by birth: Cork by the grace of God'. A shy, diffident boy at school, he would not excel academically; indeed, he would later fail the Inter Cert exam, the Irish school-leaving certificate. He would, however, show massive promise early on in football and boxing.

Keane began his career at the age of eight. He chose to play for the renowned Rockmount FC in Cork rather than his local club, Mayfield, where all his schoolmates played. He was swayed by the fact that his brothers, Denis and Johnson, also played for Rockmount before they moved to Cobh Ramblers. At Rockmount, he was nicknamed 'The Boiler Man' (the fiery one who gets things heated up) and his battling skills were no doubt honed from his days as a promising fighter, with four knockouts from four fights for Dillon's Juniors in the Irish novice boxing league.

Keane was a late developer as a footballer and initially was not one of the boys singled out for potential stardom across the water by the major football scouts in the Republic. His shyness goes some way to explaining his delayed entry into the professional game. He always knew he was good enough but was held back by the fear of rejection; he never pushed himself when scouts were present in case they told him his best was not good enough.

There were also fears that he was not tall enough or big enough to make it, but he certainly enjoyed applying a solution to the problem: beefing himself up with stodgy food and a few pints of Guinness. Roy also took a job lifting beer barrels to build up his strength.

His persistence paid off. After several abortive attempts to get apprenticeships with any English league clubs, his big chance came in 1990 when, at the age of 18, manager Brian Clough took him to Nottingham Forest. Scout Noel McCabe is the man who brought Keane to the attention of the bombastic Forest boss and convinced him to sign the Irishman. Clough, inevitably, made his presence felt within minutes of meeting the nervy novice. 'He can play a bit, boss,' explained Ronnie Fenton, Clough's assistant, when the boss walked in while the deal was being brokered. He was told to wrap it all up quickly. Forest played Cobh the grand sum of £47,000 for the signature of the man who would one day become a legend at Old Trafford and Celtic Park. Keane, in turn, put pen to paper on a three-year deal that would earn him £250 a week.

A promising youngster with a fierce, even ruthless, competitive streak, by the end of his first full season Keane had played in the 1991 FA Cup final, collecting a runners-up medal. Clough was good to him, nurturing him in his own idiosyncratic way. Whenever he wanted Keane's attention, Clough would shout, 'Hey, Irishman,' and he initially had him running around doing errands for him. But 'Old Big Head' knew he had stumbled upon a gem and was quick to promote him into his first team and offer him these pearls of wisdom: 'You get [the ball], you pass it to another player in a red shirt.'

Keane had arrived at a time when Forest were very much a club and a team in transition. Clough had taken them to unexpected glories in an amazing run from 1978 – trophies won included the old First Division championship, the European Champions Cup (twice) and the European Super Cup, and four League Cups. It was a remarkable achievement by a remarkable manager at a club that had been viewed pre-Clough as existing in a distant footballing backwater and run on a shoestring.

Clough had arrived in 1975 to work his magic on the banks of the Trent, but by the time Keane joined him 15 years later the great glory days were effectively over. Forest had won the League Cup the previous summer, but the big prizes now seemed beyond them.

It meant Keane was joining a team in which his work ethic, as they came to battle relegation, would develop along with that confrontational style. It was a good grounding: this was no United of the late '90s or Celtic of 2006, where Keane could spray the ball around with style, confident that he had enough powerful artillery within the rest of the team to show his class. At Forest, it would be pure dogs-of-war stuff, as Keane and his teammates battled for top-flight survival.

Keane's debut for Forest was, inevitably, not a quiet shuffle into the spotlight at the likes of Coventry or Derby; no, our Roy was wheeled out at Anfield against Liverpool in front of a baying Kop on 28 August 1990. Keane had arrived at the City Ground that morning to learn that Steve Hodge and Stuart Pearce were unfit: he and striker Phil Starbuck were told to get on the coach destined for Anfield to make up the numbers.

Keane was in the dressing-room getting the kit ready when Clough pulled him to one side. 'Irishman,' he said, 'what you doing?'

'Helping get the kit ready, boss,' Keane replied.

Brian Laws, one of Roy's teammates that night, takes up the story in Daniel Taylor's fine book, *Deep into the Forest*:

> ... We started laughing, thinking Cloughie was taking the mickey out of this kid. Cloughie said, 'No, he's playing – Lawsy, look after him, he's playing right midfield.'
>
> But there was no fear in him. John Barnes was playing left-wing for Liverpool and Roy kicked seven bells out of him. Barnes turned to Roy and said, 'Who do you think you are?'
>
> 'F**k off,' said Keane.

Already the confrontational take-no-prisoners attitude of the Irishman that would eventually make him a hero at Old Trafford and Celtic Park was taking shape. And interestingly enough, sitting in the Anfield stands that debut night had been Manchester United scout Les Kershaw, who reported back to his boss, Alex Ferguson, that he had seen the future ... and that the future was Irish. Its name was Roy Keane.

From that moment, United were keeping weekly tabs on the man Ferguson hoped would continue to develop into a player who could one day lead his own team.

By 1991, Keane was a regular in the Forest side, taking the place of England midfielder Steve Hodge. He scored three goals during the run-up to that year's FA Cup final, which Forest would lose 2–1 to Tottenham. A year later Keane returned to Wembley with Forest for the League Cup final but again finished on the losing side, as Manchester United triumphed 1–0.

By now, Alex Ferguson was making plans for the young Irishman. In his autobiography, *Managing My Life*, he admitted he loved the fiery way in which Keane played and his win-at-all-costs mentality. Of one game between United and Forest involving Keane, the warrior, Ferguson writes:

> The game kicked off, the ball went back to Bryan Robson, and Roy absolutely creamed him. I thought: 'Bloody cheek of him – how dare he come to Old Trafford and tackle Robbo like that!' I made a mental note there and then that we had to get this boy to Old Trafford.

Brian Clough went out of his way to make sure the young Irishman was given every chance to develop under his control. He knew this was a boy who needed both reassurance and a certain freedom. While out on the pitch, Keane would be aggressive; off it, he was shy and unsure of himself.

One week early in their relationship, Clough affectionately admitted that getting his footballing message over to Keane was never a problem but making sense of his accent was: 'In his early days at the City Ground, we thought about bringing in an interpreter. His Irish brogue was so pronounced and rich that, for a second or two, I thought we'd landed someone from the Continent!'

Clough, himself a man who enjoyed the odd glass or two, would be concerned by Roy's 'nights out on the lash' and was often seen cajoling him to settle down and get wed. He managed to get Keane in digs and allowed him to return to Cork for frequent trips, understanding the boy's natural homesickness and not wanting to antagonise his prodigious talent. 'Brian Clough understood me and was very understanding of my needs at the time,' a grateful Keane would later admit.

In May 1991, Keane was spotted by Jack Charlton, manager of the Republic of Ireland national team, who gave him his first full international cap. Controversy would follow Keane throughout his career – and it did not take long for him to make his mark with the Irish squad. That year, a game against the US was followed by a night on the booze in Boston. A 7.30 a.m. departure the next day was delayed to 7.45, then 8 a.m., after everyone had been accounted for apart from Keane. By the time he turned up, Charlton was purple with anger and barked at him: 'Nineteen years old, your first trip, do you have any idea how long we have been waiting?' Even then, the self-assured Keane would take no bullshit – even from his national team boss. 'I didn't ask you to wait, did I?' he said with a shrug, before finding a seat.

Later in his career, when Keane was asked about life at Old Trafford, he said, 'My problem is I can never remember the players I'm not talking to. I have a go at so many people during games that I never know who's talking to me and who's not.'

In 1993, Nottingham Forest were relegated after finishing bottom of the newly formed Premiership and Brian Clough resigned. Keane, who had carried the team for most of the 1992–93 season, was sold to Manchester United for that record fee of £3.75 million. His spell at the City Ground had been a good bedding-in exercise, a useful learning period and he had been tutored by one of the game's greatest ever motivators and managers – now he was heading for a new, similarly top-class mentor, Alex Ferguson at Old Trafford.

Keane departed the City Ground with this wonderful tribute from Clough ringing in his ears: 'The Irishman has everything he needs to go all the way. He can tackle, he can pass, he can head the ball and he can score. And he can do it all with the impression he has plenty of time, which is always the indication of a top-class player. You didn't have to be a genius to see he had something going for him – even my wife could have spotted it. He is one of the best headers of the ball I have come across. Blow me, I've not seen anyone jump so well since Red Rum called it a day.'

Keane had certainly given Forest good service for the £47,000 they had paid for him. In his three years at the City Ground, he had played in a total of 154 games and scored 33 goals. Clough also acknowledged how he had put himself on the line for the club during that depressing final season, saying, 'Roy Keane shone like a beacon through all the gloom of that desolate season.'

It was July 1993 when the young Irishman finally walked through the doors at Old Trafford as their most expensive signing ever. He would admit that there was a certain poignancy as he stepped over the threshold that day – United had been the only English club he had not written to for a trial as a 16 year old back in Cork because he had thought himself not good enough.

The move to Old Trafford had been mired in controversy. Alex Ferguson had snatched Keane from the grasp of Kenny Dalglish, then boss at Blackburn Rovers. Dalglish, who of course had graced Celtic Park as a brilliant player from 1971 to 1977, was never a friend of Ferguson. The pair had regularly been at odds while Dalglish was managing Liverpool from the mid-'80s, their most memorable run-in probably one that occurred in 1988, when Fergie had walked down the tunnel at Anfield complaining to the referee about a penalty decision, while Dalglish was nearby, cradling his new baby in his arms. With a wry smile, he had told newsmen, 'You might as well talk to my baby daughter. You'll get more sense out of her!'

After joining the club in 1991, Dalglish had swiftly led Blackburn into the Premiership and turned them into title challengers with the help of club benefactor Jack Walker's millions. Alan Shearer had turned down United's overtures to join Dalglish in a £3.3 million transfer from Southampton in

July 1992 and, a year later, the Rovers boss was convinced he had sealed the signing of Keane to further stiffen and strengthen his Ewood Park revolution.

He was wrong . . . Ferguson secured Keane's signature at the 11th hour in what was a devastating blow for Dalglish's ambitions. Without Keane, he did not have the rock-solid base upon which to build his team.

Three months later, Dalglish would unveil the man who had been tasked to take on the Keane role: David Batty. The man signed from Leeds for a million less than Keane was a battler, but he was no Keane. He did not have the vision or the ultimate warrior sensibilities of the Irishman: it was like being promised a real diamond and instead receiving a flimsy imitation from Argos.

Keane had taken little persuading to move to Old Trafford and snub Dalglish. His family were all United fans and the club would always have been his No. 1 choice if he had only believed he was good enough. Some critics claim he was dishonest in double-crossing Dalglish after shaking hands on a deal with him, and it is not easy to argue against that accusation. But here is the rub – and for this book on United and Celtic it falls easily into place – this was the beginning of a love-in with United fans that would never be broken. Ever. In the eyes of those supporters, Keane had quickly shown how much playing for the Red Devils meant to him by doing the dirty on Dalglish. In the same way, 12 years later, he would turn down Real Madrid to be with the fans of the other club close to his heart – Celtic.

Roy Keane was a man who could hardly have been put together better by a computer identikit as the ideal footballer for Celtic and United. He had red and white and green blood running through his veins.

From being a big fish in a small pond, Keane was now very much the opposite. The United he joined had just won the league title for the first time in 26 years and his teammates included names such as Bryan Robson, Paul Ince, Mark Hughes and Ryan Giggs. Keane would begin his United adventure at right-back, but Ferguson knew Robson was on the last lap of a fine career and had already earmarked Keane for his marauding midfield role.

Keane's wages reflected his step up onto the big stage. From the initial £250-a-week deal at the City Ground, he was now on £8,000 a week basic. He explained why he had chosen United in this way: 'I signed for Manchester United because they have got the best stadium, the best team and the greatest supporters in the country. Blackburn Rovers made me a fabulous offer, but as soon as United declared an interest there was only one outcome. This is a career move. To come to a club of this size is good for my future.'

His United debut came on 7 August 1993 in a Charity Shield win over Arsenal at Wembley. The match had ended all-square at 1–1, but Keane won his first piece of silverware with the club after United triumphed on penalties. He played his first league game at Norwich on 15 August 1993, setting up Ryan Giggs for the opener in the 2–0 win, and was introduced to Old Trafford on Wednesday, 18 August 1993 as the Red Devils crushed Sheffield United 3–0 in the Premiership. Roy even grabbed two of the goals in his dream start in front of the fans he would grow to adore, in what would become a massive mutual appreciation society. Giggs returned the compliment from the Norwich match by setting Keane up for his first; the second came via Mark Hughes, who grabbed the third goal.

As Brian Clough had noted Keane's liking of a night out and the drink, so did Ferguson and he, like Clough, encouraged the boy to settle down. He was more successful than Clough in this area. Keane, still abrasive, shy and aggressively defensive off the pitch, started to date his first steady girlfriend, Theresa Doyle, who would later become his wife. He also bought a £600,000 home in the stockbroker belt of Bowden in Cheshire. The readies were rolling in from his wages and the £200,000 boot deal he had signed with Diadora.

Life was good, too, on the pitch with United. In his first season, he helped the club to the coveted league and FA Cup double. It was their second successive Premiership win and the icing on the cake was the 4–0 FA Cup final walkover against Chelsea.

The following season was a disappointment. Keane had at least finally cemented his place in the heart of the United midfield after Bryan Robson left to become player-manager at Middlesbrough, but the Red Devils ended the campaign trophyless, surrendering their league title to Blackburn and losing 1–0 to Everton in the FA Cup final.

Ferguson realised urgent changes were needed and he acted swiftly, selling off Paul Ince, Andrei Kanchelskis and Mark Hughes and bringing in his so-called 'fledglings' – youth-team stalwarts Paul Scholes, the Neville brothers and David Beckham. 'You'll never win anything with kids,' TV pundit Alan Hansen would carp on BBC's *Match of the Day* as United lost 3–1 at Aston Villa in the first match of the new season. He was left red-faced as the United boys proved him wrong, winning the league.

The Keane era had truly begun now, in tandem with that other footballing genius Eric Cantona. 'The King' would take the captain's armband until 1997, when he would pass it on to Roy, an honour of which the Irishman had always dreamed.

Keane and Cantona inspired United to another double in the 1995–96 season and Roy was particularly delighted to get one over on Liverpool in the FA Cup final – United running out 1–0 winners.

The triumph brought further rewards in the shape of an improved contract: a new four-year deal was signed on 20 August

1996, with his wages increasing from £8,000 to £20,000 a week, enabling him to buy his parents a new luxury home on the edge of Cork's Northside. The fact that he had signed the deal made the United fans take him even closer into their hearts, for he had turned down the advances – and the prospect of much more money – from the cash-rich clubs of Italy's Serie A, including Juventus and AC Milan. Here was a man who was loyal to the club and its supporters; the fans in turn idolised the man who would become their on-the-pitch representative and leader.

The 1996–97 season was one plagued by injury for Keane, first with a knee problem, then a leg injury. There were two consolations: United retained their league crown and, after Eric Cantona quit United in May 1997, boss Ferguson chose Keane to become his new captain.

Keane was 26 on 10 August 1997 and was looking forward to the biggest season of his career, one that would surely involve more glory with United. Yet the dream lasted just 48 days and the consequence of its collapse would have far-reaching repercussions for both his career and his reputation as an honest sportsman.

Disaster struck at Elland Road on 27 September, when he suffered a horrific cruciate ligament injury in a clash with the Tykes' Alf-Inge Haaland. Keane would never forget how the big Dane stood over him, hissing and shouting, claiming he was a cheat as he lay injured on the pitch. There had been suggestions that Keane had tried to trip Haaland and some claimed it was rough justice that he himself had ended up injured. Roy was none too happy with such a crude analysis, commenting, 'I don't think I deserved the injury because I nearly lost my career for trying to trip a bloke up. Obviously there were a few people who are happy to see me injured, but they just keep me going. Their attitude made me hungry to get better.'

They were defiant words, but, in the absence of Keane that season, United would lose their Premiership crown to Arsenal and end the campaign without a trophy. The only fillip was that by July 1998 Keane had successfully come through two friendly matches on United's pre-season tour of Scandinavia.

The dark night of the lost season for Roy Keane would soon be replaced by a bright dawn, as he and Manchester United embarked upon the most successful campaign in the club's history: the 1998–99 treble-winning season. Yet even in the euphoria, there was misery for Keane: it seemed that Roy's life often mirrored the two sides of his personality. The outgoing warrior on the pitch who loved and lived for his football and the surprisingly shy, introverted character who was not so sure of himself off the pitch – the light and the darkness that make up this complicated human being.

In the year of the treble, Keane would forever be haunted by the fact that he did not play in the European Champions Cup-final win over Bayern Munich in Barcelona. In his mind, it meant he did not deserve a winner's medal, that he was *not* a European champion. It was all nonsense, of course: he richly deserved it after virtually single-handedly dragging United into the final after they had looked down and out against Juventus in Turin.

Having drawn the first leg of the semi-final 1–1 at Old Trafford, Ferguson had told his troops to play it slowly and solidly and not concede any goals in the early part of the return leg in Turin. They did not heed his words; indeed, they were soon 2–0 down and looking for a miracle if they were to reach their first European Cup final since 1968. Juve were 3–1 up on aggregate when the miracle arrived in the shape of a wound-up Keane.

From a David Beckham corner on 25 minutes, the skipper rose superbly to head home for United. Disaster struck eight minutes later when Keane was booked for catching Zidane with a tackle: it was a booking that would rule him out of the final should United – still losing 3–2 on aggregate – get there. Keane did not let it get to him. Instead he selflessly drove his troops on, covering every blade of grass as he tried to urge them to an equaliser. It was the most magnificent display and it quickly reaped dividends as Dwight Yorke put United level on the night and ahead on the away goals ruling just two minutes later. Six minutes from time Andy Cole crowned one of United's greatest nights in Europe when he slotted home United's third.

The battling Keane visibly slumped as the final whistle went. Now it truly sank in: he would play no part in the final. But typical of the lion-heart of this man, he blamed only himself when he finally faced the waiting press. He said he would never forgive himself for picking up a booking for dissent in the previous round at home to Inter Milan, that it was not his booking in Turin that was to blame for his predicament. 'I don't mind so much getting booked for making a tackle but to get one for dissent or arguing is a bit of a nightmare,' Keane said. 'I am annoyed because what really cost me was the booking I got against Inter in the quarter-final.'

The tributes for his performance in Turin poured in, but none would mean more to him than the words from his manager, Ferguson, who would later write: 'The minute he was booked and out of the final, he seemed to redouble his efforts to get the team there. It was the most emphatic display of selflessness I have ever seen on a football field.'

And that doyen of sportswriters, the *Sunday Times*' Hugh McIlvanney, had this to say after the 3–2 triumph over adversity: 'Keane . . . is the most important player in the recent history of Manchester United.'

Yet even Roy's consolation prize – a place in United's FA Cup-winning team a few days before the European Cup final in Barcelona – would be tinged with regret. Again, the dark and the light shadows. He would last just eight minutes before bowing out to injury. If he looked at the glass half-full rather than half-empty, he would surely concede that he would never have made the European Cup final anyway – because he was injured. His regret at missing out is understandable but it is time to finally take the whip off his own back and accept he did not, after all, miss out because of those bookings and accept that he deserves the European Cup winner's medal for his efforts in Turin.

The last time Roy spoke on the situation, he said, 'Football is a very selfish game. No matter how many people tell me I deserve that Champions League medal, I know I don't.' And my understanding is that Roy has still not looked at the medal. I am sure United and Celtic fans would agree that enough is enough of this self-inflicted pain and that it is time to finally dig it out.

Looking at the Celtic United link again, United's triumph in Spain again mirrored that of the Hoops, this time 32 years earlier. The United win meant they had become only the fourth side in history to secure their domestic league and cup competitions and Europe's premier club tournament in the same season. Only Celtic in 1967 – the first ever to do so – Ajax Amsterdam (1972) and PSV Eindhoven (1988) had ever done it before.

Roy Keane would not win the Footballer of the Year awards presented by the Professional Footballers' Association (PFA) and the Football Writers' Association in 1999, despite having led United to the treble; both bodies honoured the dilettante talents of Tottenham winger David Ginola. But the following season Keane would get his fair dues when he would take both gongs from the Frenchman's custody. He also signed a new four-year deal at Old Trafford worth £52,000 a week, after the board had initially appeared reluctant to tie their best player into a new long-term commitment. By May 2000, Keane had rewarded them by leading United to their sixth Premiership title in eight years, at the same time scoring, by his standards, a record-breaking twelve goals. He repaid them again the following season, securing the Red Devils' seventh Premiership title, their third in a row, which put them in the illustrious company of the record breakers from Arsenal, Huddersfield and Liverpool.

In April 2002, Keane's – and Ferguson's – obsession with winning the European Cup reared its ugly head once again; this time both men would be devastated as United crashed out in the semi-finals to the distinctly unremarkable German outfit Bayer Leverkusen. The first leg at Old Trafford ended 2–2 and United could only manage a 1–1 draw in Germany a fortnight later, going out of the competition on the away goals ruling. Ferguson's dream of recapturing the cup at Hampden Park in his native Glasgow was dead – and Keane's long sulk over his failure to play in a European Cup final would continue. It was a devastating blow for both men and would only fuel Keane's resentment towards life at United. Within three and a half years, he would be gone, but for now he was talking about the loss as 'a disaster' and criticising his teammates.

He had already spoken sarcastically about some of the players being only interested in Rolex watches and big cars, now he said of their performance in Germany, 'It is very hard to win the European Cup if you give away goals like we did in the semi-finals. This club deserves to win European Cup finals and we blew it . . . It was probably not the standard we expected over the two games.'

The following month his rage flared again when United lost 1–0 at home to Arsenal. He attacked the efforts of his teammates, but as Ferguson was the man responsible for buying them and picking them, Keane was indirectly criticising the work of his manager. Their previously rock-solid bond was beginning to weaken. 'There are a lot of cover-ups sometimes and players need to stand up and be counted,' Keane said. 'I am not sure that happens a lot at this club.'

At the end of the next season, United regained their Premiership crown from the Gunners, but Keane's holy grail would again elude him as United exited the Champions League at the quarter-final stage to a rampant Real Madrid. Keane was left feeling bitter, resentful and ultimately unfulfilled. In the 2003–04 season, United won the FA Cup, but Keane saw that as small change. He was 32 years old and his body was creaking from the injuries he had sustained: a ruptured cruciate ligament; the hamstring strains (recurring); the hip problems (career-threatening); the hernias (recurring); the knee ligaments (career-threatening) and the back injuries (recurring and also career-threatening). He remained an isolated, restless and unhappy soul: in short, he was burnt out, a casualty of his own inner drive for perfection and that unattainable European Cup win. He continued to criticise his teammates and had even fallen out with some of the United fans who helped pay his wages by dubbing them 'the prawn sandwich brigade'.

What he really needed was a break from the game to recharge his batteries and to find his love for football again. But being the man he is, that was never going to be on the agenda. He was heading towards his inevitable final bust-up at Old Trafford.

Keane suffered from his own excesses: on the pitch, with the particularly damning incident involving Alf-Inge Haaland in 2001, which besmirched his reputation more than any other; and off it, in his fallout with Irish team coach Mick McCarthy over training facilities at their Saipan base in preparation for the World Cup in 2002.

It is still difficult to find any words in Roy's defence regarding the Haaland stamping disgrace. Keane had finally taken his revenge on the big Norwegian in the Manchester derby at Old Trafford in April 2001. A crude stamp on the City player's knee had left Haaland badly injured and Keane red-carded. Keane admitted in his autobiography:

> I waited until five minutes before the end. I hit him hard . . . Take that, you c**t. And don't ever stand over me again sneering about fake injuries. And tell your pal [David] Wetherall there's some for him as well. I didn't wait for Mr Elleray to show the red card. I turned and walked to the dressing-room. Even in the dressing-room afterwards I had no remorse. My attitude was 'What goes around comes around'. He got his just rewards. My attitude is an eye for an eye.

It was a horrific crime and as much as I admire Roy for his other attributes it was indefensible. The tackle did not end Haaland's career, however, as is usually thought, and a few days after the stamp he played in an international for Norway. The injury that would end his career affected his left knee – Keane had crashed into his right one.

As for his being thrown out of the World Cup in May 2002, I believe, in this instance, Roy certainly had a case for our compassion. Keane had complained about training facilities at the Irish camp and, as skipper, did he not surely have the right to do so? McCarthy called a team meeting in which he asked if anyone had any grievances. He then produced a copy of the *Irish Times* in which Roy had complained of the rock-hard surface upon which the players had to train and the attitude of the Irish team who he felt seemed only to be there for the craic.

Teammate Niall Quinn gave his side of the story to the press at the time:

> Words used include spineless, useless, stupid, gutless. Every grievance is ordered and filed neatly with an appropriate insult attached . . . Roy shouts as he gets to the door. 'I'll not go to the f***ing World Cup. Now you have your excuse. It's all Roy's fault. See you later, lads.' And he's gone.

The more I look back on the affair, the more I see it as the result of a long-term clash of personalities. Now both men would suffer. McCarthy's actions had deprived him of his key player. Keane would miss out on the World Cup, just as he had missed out on playing in the European Cup final. These were two key disappointments that he would forever regret and brood on.

It was a mighty shame for the man who would bow out on a proud Irish international career with sixty-six caps, spanning fourteen years and three managers. He had also been named Ireland's player of the tournament at the 1994 World Cup in the USA, when Ireland famously beat tournament favourites and eventual finalists Italy 1–0, before losing to Holland in the second round.

By 2005, Keane's era at Old Trafford had also come to a sad end. United had been replaced by Chelsea as the team to beat in England and Keane could no longer tolerate being part of a team that seemed to be going nowhere: a team of losers, as he saw it. He would leave United on 18 November 2005 after a long spell on the sidelines due to injury. His final competitive game for the club was the 0–0 draw at Liverpool in September that year in which he suffered a broken foot after a challenge with Luis Garcia.

In total, he had led United to 13 major honours, making him the most successful captain in the club's history. Keane's trophy haul with United included seven Premiership titles (1994, 1996, 1997, 1999, 2000, 2001, 2003), four FA Cups (1994, 1996, 1999, 2004), a European Cup (1999) and an Intercontinental Cup (1999). He was inducted into the English Football Hall of Fame in 2004 and was picked for the FIFA 100, a list of the 100 greatest living footballers, selected by the great Pele.

His achievements were magnificent, his commitment to United undeniable – he had literally shed blood for the cause

– so why did it all go so wrong? My information is this: Keane and Ferguson's assistant, Carlos Queiroz, did not get on that well at times – and ultimately Fergie chose the Portuguese as last man standing.

There was a suggestion that Keane did not gel with Queiroz, the man who had returned to Old Trafford on 1 July 2004 after a failed spell as head coach at Real Madrid, the job for which he had quit United a year earlier. I am told Keane didn't rate him as highly as some of United's previous coaches – particularly current England manager and former United number 2, Steve McLaren – and that Keane felt left out as Queiroz and Ferguson became close.

Keane had been convinced that Ferguson was grooming him to take over the manager's role when he eventually retired, but with Queiroz's return that all seemed to change. Suddenly, the Portuguese was the man who was taking training and being tipped by Ferguson as his replacement. Keane initially fell out with Queiroz over his choice of a pre-season training camp in Portugal. Roy did not agree with the training or the time off that Queiroz allowed the players, deeming it unprofessional. He also felt the facilities were not good enough for Manchester United; I am reliably informed he moaned at Queiroz after one of his children complained the outdoor pool was too cold.

Ferguson was not happy at Keane's attitude during the summer of 2005 and made it clear that Queiroz, in his eyes at least, should be afforded much more respect. At one stage in the 2005–06 season, the manager even allowed Queiroz to take charge of the team and the way they played. The No. 2 believed in a more disciplined 4-5-1 system, which did not go down well with Keane or United's massive support, which was raised on attacking football.

United were playing badly and after a dismal 4–1 loss at Middlesbrough on 29 October 2005 Keane blew a fuse. He went on to the club's television channel, MUTV, and I am told he verbally attacked seven of his teammates and the tactics of Queiroz. Keane's most stinging vitriol was allegedly reserved for Ferguson's record signing, Rio Ferdinand. 'Just because you are paid £120,000 a week and play well for 20 minutes against Tottenham, you think you are a superstar,' Keane is alleged to have said. 'The younger players have been let down by some of the more experienced players. They are just not leading. There is a shortage of characters in this team. It seems to be in this club that you have to play badly to be rewarded. Maybe that is what I should do when I come back. Play badly.' Not surprisingly, the video, originally scheduled as part of the 'Roy Keane Plays the Pundit' slot on the club's channel, was pulled at the insistence of Ferguson.

It was all heading towards an inevitable showdown. Ferguson insisted comments like these should be kept strictly in the dressing-room. It only served to emphasise the gulf that had now opened between the manager and his captain. Previously he had been more than happy for Keane to sound off in public as his mouthpiece about poor performances by the players; indeed, he had encouraged him to do so. Now, it seemed, Keane was breaking the rules. But, and here's the rub, wasn't Roy Keane actually correct in his assessment of the playing strengths at United at the time? Of course, he was.

His ultimate legacy to the club was that soon after he left Ferguson reined Queiroz in and reverted to 4-4-2 and a much more attacking philosophy. The reborn, adventurous United of 2006–07 was a direct result of Keane's sledgehammer attack on the club's 'stars' on the MUTV tape that had been banned by Ferguson.

By 18 November 2005, Keane was gone. I am told he was devastated and had to be helped into the back seat of his car by his agent, Michael Kennedy.

He had never wanted it to come to that. Ferguson had chosen Queiroz over a man who lived and breathed Manchester United. True, Ferguson had made his choice out of loyalty, but in my opinion it was misplaced loyalty. For many United fans, it was seen as a disgraceful, shameful way to treat a man who had done so much for the club. Shareholders' United chairman Sean Bones succinctly summed it all up when he said, 'As supporters, we have to thank Roy Keane for the wonderful service he gave to Manchester United. He was without doubt the best midfielder of his generation . . . and he is part of the fabric of the club.'

Lou Macari, another Celtic United legend, also chipped into the inevitable debate about Keane's undignified exit with these incisive words: 'I've always thought of Roy Keane as a major part of Manchester United . . . Trying to replace Roy Keane is almost impossible . . . [He] will be gutted that he is no longer a Manchester United player.'

Keane had gone the same way as Jaap Stam and David Beckham – and the way Ruud van Nistelrooy would also go. Out swiftly, as if they never existed: there could only be one man with an opinion at Old Trafford – even if it frequently appeared to be wrong in the three years from the summer of 2003 to 2006.

I am not saying Keane still deserved an automatic place in the team; after all, his time as a top-class player at United was almost up. But surely there is an argument that Ferguson could have tried to find a middle ground. There seemed to be no grey areas for the United manager.

He and Keane could have sat down like adults and Ferguson could have offered him a player-coach role as a reward for all he had done for the club. This was no Eric Djemba-Djemba we were talking about here; Keane was the man who walked shoulder to shoulder with Ferguson during the most exciting, successful period in Manchester United's history.

The people who mattered – the fans of United – made it clear who they backed in the great debate and it wasn't the man who remained at the club. A banner at the first United match at Old Trafford after Keane's exit told the story: '12 YEARS – THANKS FOR EVERYTHING ROY'. Chants of 'Keano, Keano' rang around the stadium from every corner that day.

Eleven days before Christmas, Roy Keane received a fabulous present when his dream of becoming a player for Celtic became a reality. United's loss would be the Glasgow club's gain. They signed the man who is surely the greatest player ever to turn out for both clubs and the epitome of all that you would ever associate with the words Celtic United. Two football clubs, one shared passion. In Keane, they had a shared player who typified everything the fans of both clubs loved in their football stars: aggression; commitment; allegiance to the cause; undiluted, wonderful talent.

Celtic fans would not see Keane at his peak; those years had passed – he was 34 and choosing his battles more carefully now. But they would always be able to tell their grandchildren they had witnessed at first hand the man who was the greatest midfielder of his generation, that they had seen a legend, not only in the flesh but also in their club shirt. For United fans, the thrill would have been the same if Maradona had played for the club in the twilight of his career.

And the fans at Celtic Park quickly took the hard man from Cork to their hearts. They adored him from day one; he was one of them, one of theirs, an idol worth paying to see; a man who would never just take the money and take it easy. The back page of the *Mail on Sunday* of 11 December 2005 led with the splash headline, 'Keane Signs for Madrid'. It was that close ... yet Roy had ultimately gone with his heart and moved to his second home, Celtic Park.

Keane explained his decision in this way: 'Having spoken to

the Celtic manager and having been offered the contract, I knew this was the club for me. I made the right decision. I feel this is the place where I belong.'

I am reliably informed by sources in Madrid that Real president Florentino Perez had offered Keane £70,000 a week; he joined the Hoops for £30k a week less, such was his desire to play for Celtic. This figure was based on a basic wage of £18,000 with the rest being found apparently by Dermot Desmond. He would not comment on this projected breakdown of the readies but did admit, 'In fairness to Roy Keane, he left a lot of money on lots of tables because of his love for Celtic.'

There were immediate doubts about how Keane would fit into the team – and how he would deal with not being skipper. Neil Lennon, a fine pro for the Hoops, occupied both Keane's natural position in the team and the role of captain. In both areas, without meaning to be disrespectful to a fine servant, he was not in Roy Keane's league.

Keane quickly tried to allay fears that his stay at Celtic Park would be one littered with bust-ups with players and the manager, Gordon Strachan. He said he respected Lennon and his new teammates and that he also had a lot of time for Strachan. I am told that the two had met in London prior to a deal being set up and that Roy was impressed with Strachan's hunger to win and his footballing vision: to win, but with entertaining, attacking football. To a student of Clough and Ferguson, with the basic instinct of Manchester United throughout the years, this was joy to Roy's ears. On the day he signed at Celtic Park, thousands of fans turned up to greet him, like the returning hero he was, and he made time to sign autographs and chat to as many as he could.

Then Roy the Bhoy tried to clear up a few misconceptions about himself: 'I have been misrepresented, without a doubt. I probably don't tiptoe around people at this level, but generally, as a professional for 15 or 16 years, 99 out of 100 players that

I've played with either like me or have enjoyed playing with me. The players at Celtic have done very well, so I am under no illusions that I will walk into the team. I aim to try hard and give the manager a problem.'

I am told by my sources that the idea that Strachan was against the signing of Keane is nonsense. Indeed it was his enthusiasm when he jetted down to London to talk to Roy that had helped usher him into Celtic Park. Plus there was another intriguing angle: Strachan had urged Keane to join him to prove Ferguson wrong in letting him go. The little Scotsman had also left Old Trafford under a cloud after Ferguson told him he was no longer needed in March 1989. Strachan went to Leeds and won a championship medal at the expense of his old boss, and he urged Keane to prove a point to Ferguson.

Jim Divers, secretary of the Celtic Supporters Association, summed up the momentous nature of Keane's signing at the time, saying, 'We know we are getting someone exceptional in British football. Everyone here in Glasgow – and fans around the world – is excited at the prospect of seeing Roy Keane in green-and-white hoops.'

There was a notable, perhaps inevitable, dissenter to the Keane transfer – Jack Charlton. The former Republic boss had obviously had numerous run-ins with Keane on international duty and could not allow the big move to pass without putting the verbal boot in for old time's sake, at the same time denigrating Celtic and Scottish football. 'Let's be honest,' Charlton sneered, 'Roy is past his best. He's made the right decision, as the SPL will not be as demanding as the Premiership or a move to Real Madrid. It won't be as hectic in Scotland and Roy will find it easier to push forward from midfield. I'm convinced Keane would never have been allowed to leave United if the manager felt he could still make a contribution to bringing back the glory days.'

Keane had signed an eighteen-month deal with the Hoops but would be gone within six, taking with him a Scottish championship medal and a League Cup-winner's medal. Not bad for the final chapter of a magnificent career. Of course, Keane being Keane, there were ups and down during that six-month stay. His career at Celtic began in ignominious fashion with the Glasgow giants crashing in a 2–1 defeat to lowly Clyde in the Scottish Cup third round on 8 January 2006. Just a day later, his mentor Alex Ferguson was also suffering as United struggled to a 0–0 draw away at non-league Burton in the English FA Cup. It's ironic that their fortunes continued to intertwine, despite their falling out.

A month later, Keane scored his first Celtic goal in the 2–1 SPL victory over Falkirk. In between, he had made his home debut playing at centre-half in a 4–2 win over Kilmarnock. He had always complained when Ferguson had asked him to play in the centre of defence for United, now he just got on with the job. It was a good sign for all those who feared he would combust at Celtic. Roy was clearly moved by the reception the Celtic fans had afforded him and left the pitch with a clenched fist.

Injury then sidelined him for an away match at Motherwell and my sources tell me that the first inkling of friction between him and Strachan came when Celtic entertained Dundee United at Parkhead. It appears Keane had expected to be back in the team for the match, but instead Strachan started with him on the bench. The official line was that Strachan would bring him on late in the game to tighten things up, but the alleged sequence of events that occurred is nothing short of bizarre.

It goes like this: Celtic were leading 3–1 and Keane wandered off to the toilet. When he returned, the visitors had made it 3–2 and Strachan decided not to use him after all. Why would the manager not send Keane on to bolster a clearly leaky defence? The match ended 3–3, and apparently Keane had got peed off rather than gone for a pee. I can't see how a consummate pro like Roy would have been caught short in a match. It had certainly never happened before. I am informed that Keane had gone down the tunnel in a huff only for Strachan to apparently smooth things over.

Keane's mood was not lifted eight days later when Lennon put him down in a newspaper interview. The skipper told the *Daily Telegraph* that Keane had never been signed as an automatic shoo-in for the team but as a back-up to him and Petrov. 'Gordon Strachan told Stiliyan Petrov and me at the start of the season and again when Roy was coming in that we would be his first choices,' Lennon said.

By April 2006, I was being told by sources in Manchester and Glasgow that Keane would not see out his 18-month deal but rather would quit at the end of his first season. His final match would be a testimonial at Old Trafford between United and Celtic in which he would play one half for each team. Those predictions proved to be both absolutely correct, yet in public at least the suggestion was that Roy had quit because of ongoing injury problems. On 12 June 2006, he said, 'Having received medical advice from my surgeon and the Celtic club doctor, I feel my only option is to retire.' No one is denying his hip injury was real and painful, but I am told Roy had also lost the will to play football: he had reached the point of no return both mentally and emotionally. He loved the fans at Celtic, but rather than just take the money and con them he decided, in his typically forthright and honest way, to get out. That summed up the real Roy Keane: the man who loved and was loved by Celtic United, but the man whose heart was no longer in playing football.

Roy had played a total of 13 matches for the Hoops, his final 'official' match being the 2–0 win over Kilmarnock at Celtic Park on 3 May 2006. It would be his testimonial at Old Trafford, however, six days later, that I will forever remember. More than 30,000 Celtic fans travelled down for the celebration and mingled contentedly with United supporters. I took my sons, Frankie, eight, and Jude, five, to the match – it was Jude's first live United game and one he will also never forget.

Supporters from both teams were wearing scarves with the colours and emblems of both teams; it was a great occasion, a true Celtic United affair. We were in the Stretford End in the Family Stand and the many Celtic fans also there were greeted with smiles, not vicious grimaces. That was probably the moment when I came to fully realise the empathy between the two clubs; the fondness and respect the fans, the players and the suits had for each other.

It was Keane's night in front of a crowd of 69,591. It was also the third testimonial between the clubs I had witnessed (the others being for Bobby Charlton and Lou Macari), but it was easily the best. For the record, United won 1–0, with a goal from Cristiano Ronaldo, and there was also a slight tightening of Roy's shoulders when Ferguson tried to muscle in on the proceedings. I am told he wanted to address the crowd, but Roy refused to sanction it, a typical move. He wasn't going to put on a false front just to please the photographers and placate Ferguson himself. Roy Keane did not forgive and forget easily.

Roy said afterwards: 'This is something I'll remember for the rest of my life. I'm grateful to both clubs, the players and of course the supporters.' And with that, a final lap of honour and a wave, Roy Keane, Celtic United legend, was off to what would be a new role as manager of Sunderland, well away from Old Trafford and Celtic Park. The king was in exile, for the time being at least. Although having won the championship for Sunderland in his first season after taking over when they were third from bottom, he was swiftly being mooted as one of the favourites for the United job when Ferguson finally quits.

In June 2007, David Beckham commented on the new managerial 'Special One' and his words provide a fitting end to our chapter on Keano: 'People always ask me what Roy Keane was like and was he horrible, and yes, he was horrible at times but that was the reason we won so much – because of his mentality and his passion for the team.'

16

HENRIK LARSSON: SWEDE DREAMS

It rains all the time – take your scuba gear with you.
> – *Feyenoord players to Larsson when he*
> *quit for Glasgow in 1997*

Henrik was my idol.
> – *Ronaldinho in 2006*

Michael Owen is the poor man's Henrik Larsson.
> – *Former Scotland boss Craig Brown in 2007*

SOME CELTIC fans told me that if there had been no Jinky, Henrik Larsson would have been their all-time favourite player at Parkhead. And if the Swedish superstar had signed for Manchester United rather than the Hoops in 1997, replacing the great Eric Cantona, some United fans tell me they think Larsson could have been as much of a king as Eric was. He could have been one of their greatest players of all time, too.

As fate would have it, this was not to be the sequence of events. Jinky would dazzle and in 2002 was voted Celtic's greatest player ever. Henrik would dazzle at Parkhead from 1997 – and earned a major accolade when Hoops fans voted him the only foreign player in their greatest-ever Celtic team. In his own way, Larsson was Celtic's Eric Cantona: just as the Frenchman swept United to new peaks, so the Swede galvanised the Hoops with his undiluted brilliance.

As far as United fans were concerned, the loan of Larsson in 2007 was similar to Roy Keane's move to Celtic a year earlier: it was a welcome addition, a chance to see a superstar in action, but, at the end of the day, it only served to remind them of what might have been had either man signed for the other club earlier in his career.

Journalist Andy Bucklow summed this up – and gave a perceptive overview of Larsson's career – when asked how things may have panned out had the Swede plumped for United instead of Celtic ten years earlier. 'Unlike other Celts who eloped to Old Trafford, Henrik Larsson turned up for what was the football equivalent of a one-night stand – and in his case one last stand.

'Larsson had been very happily married to Celtic – too happily married for Fergie's liking, as he had even rejected the chance of an earlier move to Manchester United. Indeed, the Swedish star had planned to retire at Celtic, but when he was eventually enticed by a far-off admirer he settled for the Camp Nou rather than Old Trafford and signed off his brilliant career with a telling late contribution as a super sub in Barcelona's Champions League final victory over Arsenal.

'When his brief on-loan spell as a United hero ended in March 2007, it left the club regretting what they had missed as much as appreciating the impact he had made as a thirty-five year old in just ten weeks. For there is no doubt that Larsson was an archetypal Manchester United player who would have flourished under Ferguson in the Premiership and provided the missing link in Europe had he been secured in his prime from Celtic Park five or so years earlier. He would have been, like Eric Cantona before him, unfazed by the challenge.

'He had all the skills backed up by a self-assurance and a quiet arrogance. In short, he had the bottle. Had Larsson been positioned alongside first Ruud van Nistelrooy, then Wayne Rooney during the Arsenal/Chelski championship years, who knows how things could have turned out. Had he been there, would the Reds have ever tumbled out of Europe at the first Group stage in 2005, or failed to make the quarter-finals in the previous three seasons?

'I think that, above all, having Larsson in the team would have provided that vital ingredient for United at the time when outgoing captain Roy Keane was questioning the desire and direction of United's young, disparate talents – *belief*. When Larsson did arrive, his record of three goals in thirteen games seemed unremarkable. But to witness his exquisite movement off the ball and his immediate influence on the likes of Rooney and Ronaldo, already world class in their own right, was a taster, albeit bittersweet, of the feast United missed. If only it had been a taster of things to come.

'One other attribute he shared with Eric Cantona, and even more pertinently Teddy Sheringham, was his consummate professionalism. He had looked after himself, which meant that he could play at the highest level long after others were forced into lower leagues or retirement. When Larsson left Old Trafford to return to Helsingborgs in his home country, he said, "I'm almost 36 now, and I have to say I'm going to keep playing as long as I can, even though playing in Sweden isn't as high a level as Spain or the Premiership."

'Two more years doing a Teddy in the Premiership as an impact player or super sub would have suited United very nicely. And what would the club pay now to turn back the clock to grab the 26-year-old version who signed for Celtic in 1997 – just as one Eric Cantona was stunning Reds fans by announcing *his* retirement from football ...'

Henrik Edward Larsson, MBE was born in Helsingborg in the Skåne region of Sweden, its southernmost province, on 20 September 1971. His mother, Eva Larsson, was a factory worker and his father, Francisco Rocha, was a sailor from the Cape Verde islands off Senegal on the west coast of Africa. He has an elder stepbrother, Kim, and a younger brother, Robert. He was named after his uncle Henrique, but it was agreed that he would use the Swedish version, Henrik, and that he would take his mother's surname to help him fit in. His Christian name was soon abbreviated further to Henke by his childhood friends.

Larsson admits he owes a debt to his father for becoming a top-flight footballer. He told Douglas Alexander of the *Sunday Times* that his father had shown him a video of Pele and that this had stirred a desire within him to follow his lead as a goalscorer. 'We had this programme in Sweden where they showed English games every Saturday. I used to sit up with him and watch European Cups, World Cups, European Championships, the Swedish national team. We watched it all. He loves football. Brazil was his favourite team and we always used to go for them when it was a World Cup.'

His father showed him a video of Pele, which Henrik would watch again and again. 'If you look at Pele, he could score goals, but he could also set up a goal. He has always been my idol,' Larsson said.

Henrik started his football career at the age of six as a youth player at Högaborgs BK, progressing through the ranks into the first team. At 13, he thought about giving the game up because he was too small and lightweight, but fortunately he had second thoughts.

In 1992, Larsson turned pro for his home-town team, Helsingborgs IF. He made 56 appearances for his new club, racking up a remarkable 50 goals, before leaving for Holland for a £295,000 fee a year later.

His next stop was Celtic bogey team Feyenoord, the Hoops' conquerors in the disappointing 1970 European Cup final. Ironic, then, that it would be from Feyenoord that arguably the greatest Celtic player of the modern era would come forth.

In four years at the Dutch club, the Swede grabbed twenty-six goals in 101 appearances. When Larsson's initial mentor and coach at Feyenoord, Wim Jansen, quit and was replaced by Arie Haan, the writing was on the wall for Henrik. Haan did not rate him in the same way as Jansen; he would play him out of position in midfield or not use him at all. But the best – by a mile – was yet to come; indeed, Larsson would admit he was glad to see the back of Feyenoord as he was not being played often enough.

Dreadlocked and handsome, he arrived at Celtic Park on 28 July 1997 for just £650,000. In another twist linking back to that European Cup final, the man who brought him to Scotland was Jansen, then Hoops manager. The Dutchman had played against Celtic in Milan in 1970, helping Feyenoord to their surprise win.

Jansen had been appointed Celtic head coach on 3 July 1997 and bringing Larsson to the club was one of his first, and arguably finest, decisions. The Swede admitted Wim's role at the club, along with Celtic's fine history, played a key part in persuading him to move to Parkhead. 'There wasn't a moment's hesitation on my part,' he said. 'I knew a bit about Celtic. I knew they were a big club with a rich history and I had learned all about their defeat to Feyenoord in the 1970 European Cup final. On top of that, of course, I knew Wim Jansen very well and I was pretty sure he wouldn't have taken the job if he hadn't been confident it was a club that was going places.'

But Larsson's debut was a disaster: at Easter Road against Hibernian, he gifted the ball to Chic Charnley in the box and Celtic lost 2–1. He apologised to his teammates, only to hear the reassuring refrain, 'Nae bother.' Larsson knew he had finally come home; here were players and a coach who would patiently nurture him until he settled in and then look after him.

Jansen had been brought in to replace Tommy Burns and he swiftly guided Celtic to their first League Cup-final victory in 15 years, as they swept aside Dundee United 3–0. He then steered the club to their first Scottish league championship in a decade, just as importantly stopping Rangers from surpassing Celtic's nine-in-a-row record, with Larsson contributing 16 goals. Yet Jansen would be gone from the club a couple of days after the title was secured with a 2–0 home win over St Johnstone, the result of a personality clash with general manager Jock Brown and a dispute over transfer funds. Much to the relief of the fans, Larsson would stay put under the new reign of Dr Jozef Venglos, the former manager of Czechoslovakia.

The first season under 'the Doctor' would provide no tonic for Larsson. He scored 39 goals, including 29 in the league, and won the Players' Player of the Year award and the FWA Footballer of the Year gong – yet he admitted he would have swapped them all for silverware, as Celtic lost their league crown and were also beaten in the final of the Scottish Cup.

The 1999–2000 season was Larsson's *annus horribilis*. He was sidelined for almost a year after breaking his leg in two places while playing against Lyon in a UEFA Cup match in France on 22 October 1999. The Swede was stretchered off in agony in the 12th minute of the game after he attempted to challenge Serge Blanc. His left leg was limp at the base; after the match, it was revealed to be a double fracture, reminiscent of the career-ending injury suffered by Coventry's David Busst in 1996.

Yet he would return the following season and win the Golden Boot, as Europe's top goalscorer, netting 53 in total, including 35 in 37 SPL matches for Celtic. He would also return without his golden dreadlocks, instead re-emerging with a shaven head. He has not grown the dreadlocks back since.

Manchester United won the treble of European Cup, league championship and FA Cup in 1999. In the following season, Larsson's Golden Boot goals would spearhead Celtic towards their own treble, albeit a domestic one of league title, Scottish Cup and League Cup. He scored his 100th goal for the club – in just 135 games – on 2 January 2001 in the 53rd minute of the 6–0 home win over Kilmarnock. Being Larsson, he did it in true style, grabbing another three before the game had ended.

In March of that year, Celtic won their first silverware of the season, retaining the League Cup after a 3–0 victory, with poor Killie again the victims. Larsson was inevitably the hat-trick hero as the Bhoys lifted the cup at Hampden. By the end of the campaign, they had also regained the league championship with five games to spare and won the Scottish Cup, walloping Hibs 3–0 in the final, Larsson grabbing a brace.

By 2002, Larsson had set another record: he became the highest-scoring Celt at the World Cup finals after notching up three goals in Sweden's run to the second round. He was by then also the highest-paid player at Celtic Park, on a reputed £45,000 a week.

Larsson would go on to collect a total of ninety-three caps for Sweden, rewarding them with thirty-six goals – including one in the 4–1 win over Bulgaria which clinched third place for his country in the 1994 World Cup. Let's not forget that for many of those 93 matches he played in midfield or as a winger, which makes his haul of goals all the more impressive.

He was certainly a big-game player for his country, also hitting the back of the net at three World Cup finals (1994, 2002, 2006) and two European Championships (2000, 2004). He shocked his countrymen by retiring from the international scene in 2002. A national outcry followed, with fans and celebrities –

even the UEFA President Lennart Johansson and the Swedish prime minister – pleading with him to return. Eventually he did, but only apparently after his son had also asked him to do so. A quintessential family man – five years later he would refuse similar pleas from Sir Alex Ferguson to stay on at Manchester United because he had promised his family he would return to Sweden at a pre-ordained date – Henrik Larsson is also very much a man of dignity and principle. Once he has made a decision, he usually keeps to it.

Larsson also featured well at the 2006 World Cup in Germany. He scored in the final minute of the match against England to earn his country a 2–2 draw in their final game in the Group stages, also becoming only the sixth player to score in World Cup finals 12 years apart from one another. The goal also sealed Sweden's qualification for the second round of the tournament.

But in Sweden's last-16 clash against the German hosts the fairy tale came to an abrupt end when he blasted a penalty over the bar. If he had scored, it could have given his team a lifeline after having trailed 2–0 for most of the match. But this would be his endgame. He retired from international football at the age of 34, for the second time, on 17 July 2006, saying, 'It is time to quit now. It feels right. I'm done with the national team.'

Back in 2003, he had again shown his world-class abilities as Celtic stormed to the final of the UEFA Cup under Martin O'Neill. Henrik grabbed two superb goals in the final, even though the brave Hoops side would go down 3–2 to Jose Mourinho's Porto in Seville.

O'Neill's side had twice equalised through Larsson, only for the sending off of Bobo Balde in extra-time to turn the match in Porto's favour. O'Neill would comment: 'We came roaring back every time they scored a goal and, when we had 11 against 11 in extra-time, I think we were the more mentally strong. But it was not to be with Bobo getting sent off. It was a massive blow.'

Mourinho would hardly endear himself to Celtic with his analysis of the match. 'I'd prefer to ask whether the behaviour of the Celtic players was normal in your country,' he said. 'What Balde did to Deco in front of me could have ended his career. The referee didn't affect the result, in that there were no doubtful decisions, but I think Balde could have had a direct red for his foul and Thompson could also have seen a second yellow card on two occasions.

'The referee wanted to end the game with 11 against 11 and I think maybe he was a bit afraid to send anyone off. There was a lot of commitment in Celtic's game, commitment, toughness and aggression. I'm tempted to use another word – but I won't.'

The following season would be Henrik's final one at Parkhead. A record-breaking run of consecutive victories in the league helped the club win the title again – and qualify for the Champions League outright.

Another double was also achieved, as the Celts, with Larsson at his majestic best, grabbing a brace, swept aside Dunfermline in the Scottish Cup final. It would be his final day of glory in a Hoops shirt before leaving for Barcelona. His time at Celtic Park had seen him score 242 goals in 315 appearances, making him Celtic's third all-time highest goalscorer (in all competitions). This statistic is all the more remarkable when you take into account the fact that he lost almost a year due to his leg injury. Larsson's reign at Parkhead also helped the team to win four SPL titles, two Scottish Cups and three League Cups, while he himself won a host of personal awards from football writers and fellow professionals.

Tom Shields, writing in the *Sunday Herald*, summed up Larsson's contribution in this amusing way:

> What has Henrik Larsson ever done for Celtic? Apart
> from scoring hundreds of goals. Apart from selling
> millions of pounds worth of merchandising. Apart

from being Celtic's leading light when the club has won four league championships out of seven, all during his career in the Hoops.

And apart from scoring the decisive goal in a UEFA Cup semi-final and two in the final itself, what has Henrik Larsson ever done for Celtic? Quite a lot, actually . . .

The Swede allowed himself a few moments of nostalgia before leaving Glasgow for good. 'Once I move away, I am going to realise what I am going to miss here the most,' he admitted. 'It's a big part of my career; this is the club where I made my name. I will never forget it.'

But he would also concede nothing could make him change his mind. 'I am very stubborn. Very, very stubborn. I think it's a quality to have, but you always have to know when you have to compromise as well – and the older I get, the more I compromise. But I am still very stubborn.'

Indeed he was. At the end of the 2003–04 season, Larsson signed a one-year contract with Barcelona with an option for a second year. He moved to the Camp Nou with high hopes for an Indian summer to his career, but his first campaign did not match the glory days he had learned to take for granted at Celtic. He was plagued by injury and played only a nominal part in Barca's La Liga win. He made just six appearances, scoring three goals – although one was against Celtic in Barcelona's 3–1 Champions League victory at Parkhead.

His return to Glasgow in a Barca shirt came just 111 days after he had left Celtic. His goal came after a poor header back towards his own goal by Alan Thompson. Larsson intercepted it and two touches later the ball was in the back of the net. There was no celebration from the Swede but plenty from his teammates. After the game, he readily admitted, 'It was very difficult for me to celebrate my goal because I had so many great times here.'

Even Barca boss Frank Rijkaard recognised the feelings Larsson's goal must have aroused. 'Henrik had a great impact on the game and made a huge contribution. He gave the team confidence at a difficult time and the way he didn't celebrate his goal showed you what Celtic has meant to him,' Rijkaard said.

In terms of the Celtic United link, the Larsson goal – and the player's obvious heartache at scoring against his old beloved club – brought to mind memories of the goal Denis Law would rather forget. That, of course, occurred in 1974, when Law scored a late winner at Old Trafford for Manchester City in the last game of the season. As one critic pointed out, 'it was like a son turning off his father's life-support machine'. Law, dubbed 'the King' by adoring United fans after hitting 236 goals in 11 years with the club, killed off any hope his beloved former team had of avoiding relegation from the First Division by backheeling Francis Lee's cross past goalkeeper Alex Stepney.

At Celtic Park some 30 years later, Henrik Larsson suffered a similar gut-wrenching feeling to the man with whom many pundits have compared him over the years. Both were brilliant free-scoring centre-forwards of pace, tenacity and pure physical strength.

Two months after the win over his old teammates, Larsson would suffer more despair when, after 72 minutes in the league match against Real Madrid, his studs caught in the grass and he fell badly. At first it did not seem so serious, but a scan revealed three injuries to cartilage and ligaments in his left knee. He missed the rest of the 2004–05 season, but Barcelona took the option to extend Henrik's contract.

While recovering from his injury, Henrik admitted he missed Celtic and the way of life in Scotland. 'During seven years in Scotland we got to know the neighbours, we made friends and we built up a social circle,' he said. 'That takes time and we have not had time to start socialising yet. The weather is fantastic [in

Barcelona], the tempo is slower and it fits me perfectly – that way I can stay in bed a little bit longer. We haven't got used to dining late, though. My wife and I have been out to eat a couple of times and when we get to a restaurant at 9 p.m. we are always the only ones there.

'But we usually have dinner earlier so we can have some time together after the kids have gone to bed. Playing matches at 10 p.m. is also new to me.'

In 2005–06, Larsson scored ten goals in fourteen matches as Barcelona won La Liga for a second consecutive year. Being his own man, in January 2006 Henrik announced that at the end of his contract in July he would leave Barcelona and return to Sweden to end his career. Club president Joan Laporta asked him to stay on, but Henrik would not be swayed.

His swansong could not have been more glorious, winning a European champions medal in the 2–1 Champions League-final triumph over Arsenal. Not only that – it was Larsson's skill and imagination that turned the game Barca's way.

Before the final even the great Ronaldinho had expressed his affection and admiration for the Swede. 'With Henrik leaving us, this club is losing a great scorer, no question,' the Brazilian superstar had said. 'But I am also losing a great friend. Henrik was my idol and now that I am playing next to him it is fantastic . . . I just want to enjoy the remaining time he has with us rather than dwell on what we will be missing when he's gone. I haven't tried to convince Henrik to stay at Barcelona. I respect him so much that I can't try to influence his decision. It's something he has thought about for a long time. I'm not happy he's leaving, but I'm not going to pressure him at all. At Henrik's age, many players announce their retirement from international football, but no one I know his age is at the great physical level Henrik is at right now. He could play at the highest level for a long time.'

It was a fine tribute and the comment at the back end of it

about Henrik being good enough to play at the highest level was one that Sir Alex Ferguson would pick up on – and act on 18 months later.

Larsson would come on as a 61st-minute substitute in the Champions League final and play a part in both of Barcelona's goals. Sol Campbell's thumping header had given Arsenal a first-half lead after goalkeeper Jens Lehmann had been sent off for bringing down Samuel Eto'o. But Barca scored twice in the last 14 minutes to beat their ten-man rivals to the trophy in Paris – thanks to Larsson. Eto'o fired home with 14 minutes left after being cut free by a delightful pass from Henrik, who then set up fellow substitute Juliano Belletti four minutes later with a fine cross from the right-wing, much to the joy of his Barca teammates, their fans and thousands of Celtic Larsson admirers throughout the world.

Afterwards a demoralised but gracious Thierry Henry paid tribute to Larsson's contribution, saying, 'People always talk about Ronaldinho and everything, but I didn't see him today – I saw Henrik Larsson. He came on and changed the game; that is what killed the game. Sometimes you talk about Ronaldinho and Eto'o and people like that, you need to talk about the proper footballer who made the difference and that was Henrik Larsson tonight.'

Larsson himself was typically modest about the endeavours that had won the biggest trophy in European club football, saying, 'My job was to come on and try and move and open up the defence.' The striker was once again adamant he would not sign a new deal at the Camp Nou and that he would instead take up the 18-month deal he had been offered with his home-town club, Helsingborgs.

'It was an unbelievable way for me to finish my career at Barcelona,' he said. 'I have had a fantastic experience here in my two years, with two league titles and now this. It's amazing.

But I'm almost 35 years old. I've got kids and they need to understand how we live in Sweden. My house there is finished and we need to go back there. I want to play football. I feel I haven't played as much as I would love to because of the great players we have at Barcelona. I maybe have one or two more years playing at a decent level and I want to do that playing for ninety minutes.'

More tributes poured in for Larsson before he headed for semi-retirement back in Sweden. The *New York Times* purred, 'Larsson had only just come on the field as a replacement, but he knew exactly what he was doing. He has vision. He is 34 and he has been in the game for the whole of his adult life . . . Larsson again showed the ability to find the pass that destroys defences.'

As planned, Larsson walked off into the sunset and again joined Helsingborgs, making his second debut for his home-town club against Hammarby in the Swedish Cup on 6 July 2006. He would make fifteen appearances, scoring eight goals, before a call came out of the blue as the Christmas of that year loomed . . . from Sir Alex Ferguson and Manchester United.

Soon it was revealed that the former Celtic hero would spend the final ten weeks of his big-time career in Manchester – on loan from his Swedish club from January 2007, returning on 12 March in time for the start of the Swedish season. It was an audacious surprise, a brilliant capture by United boss Ferguson, who was suffering a striker crisis with Ole Gunnar Solskjaer injured and Alan Smith still seeking full fitness.

Louis Saha would soon join them on the treatment table and the Larsson loan turned out to be a godsend as United tried to keep Chelsea at bay in the battle for the Premiership. 'United have been after me before,' the Swede said, 'after the first or second season with Celtic. It feels good to come and play for such a big club. I may not start every match, but it feels like a fun thing.'

He was wrong about not playing many games: he would, in fact, feature in thirteen altogether, scoring three goals. But he was right about Ferguson having wanted him all along. The United manager admitted, 'I have always admired Larsson. I made a move for him when he was at Celtic, but then they managed to persuade him to stay. He is a great player. It is a terrific bit of business for us. We are bringing someone in who can change a game. We won't be going for any other strikers. We have exhausted all avenues and this, without doubt, is the best option.'

United and Norway forward Solskjaer also paid tribute to Larsson upon his arrival at Old Trafford, saying, 'He must be the best Scandinavian outfield player since [Denmark's] Michael Laudrup. You won't find many better players around Europe. He's been fantastic for the last 15 years and he showed at Celtic and Barcelona that he can handle the pressure of being at a top club with expectations. I think he'll have a good influence on us, and he'll relish the opportunity at his age.'

Cometh the hour, cometh the man: Larsson almost inevitably, in true *Roy of the Rovers* style, scored on his United debut in an FA Cup third-round 2–1 win over Aston Villa at Old Trafford. And there was a further link, in Villa's outstanding new manager: yes, the great Martin O'Neill – the man who led them out against the player with whom he had forged such a brilliant alliance at Celtic Park.

His last competitive match for United was also in the FA Cup, on Saturday, 10 March, in a quarter-final at Middlesbrough, which ended 2–2. It was not the ending the Swede was hoping for – he was booked just before the interval for diving. Still, Larsson was happy with his contribution over the ten weeks; a contribution that I am told cost United £1.2 million, with half going to the player and half to his Swedish club.

'I'm pleased with my time here,' Larsson said of his spell at

Manchester United. 'I don't have anything to complain about really. A little bit more luck and maybe I'd have scored more goals, but that's the way it goes; sometimes you put everything away, others you don't put anything away.'

The Swede found time to salute the United fans and thank them for their support during his brief time at Old Trafford, saying, 'They've been absolutely brilliant since day one for me. It's always better to have the fans on your side than not, and I'm really pleased and it's been a pleasure for me playing here.'

My personal favourite memory of Henrik's spell at Old Trafford is of the superb header which took United into the last eight of the Champions League. Leading 1–0 from the first leg in France against Lille, United had to wait for 72 minutes to confirm their place in the quarter-finals. That was the moment Larsson latched on to a cross from Cristiano Ronaldo and powered the ball home. The technique behind the header was simply fabulous: Henrik soared high, pulled his head backwards and then dived forwards, giving the keeper no chance.

It was his first Champions League goal for United and would prove to be his last, as his loan spell ran out five days later. Two minutes after his goal, he was substituted and as he walked off this consummate showman would pause at the edge of the pitch to salute the crowd, having sealed United's passage into the last eight and his own place in the club's illustrious history.

Three days later he would tie up his loan move with that final showing at the Riverside – and then explain what playing for United had meant to him: 'My last match was a little bit sad because it's always difficult to leave guys that have become friends and who you've enjoyed working with. I knew it was coming and I knew from the start that if United got through the FA Cup rounds that my last game would be on 10 March, so I was prepared for it.

'Having said that, it was difficult because they are a great bunch of lads and everything about my time at the club was fantastic. The club itself, the players, the fans and the gaffer have all gone beyond what I could have hoped for. I was only there for ten weeks, but I felt I developed a good relationship with the fans. They have been supportive of the team and me, and you can't ask for more than that.

'I'm really happy that the United fans understood my game and what I tried to do for the team. I know that I might not always be as exciting to watch as some players who have all the skills and trickery, because I don't have that in my locker. I'll never be like a Ronaldinho or Cristiano Ronaldo, who can do amazing things with the ball. But I like to think that I can offer something else to the team in terms of making the right runs, offering options and bringing other players into the game. My movement off the ball is quite decent and I will always give 100 per cent for the team. I might not always achieve everything I set out to do in a match, but my effort will always be there.

'I will take away a lot of things from my time at United and one of them will be the impression of a club that is so well organised that nothing is left to chance. Nothing is taken for granted and the club will help the players with absolutely anything. You are made to feel part of the most professional set-up. The training facilities are second to none.

'There are a lot of great players at United and it would be wrong to single out individuals who I particularly enjoyed playing alongside. The fact is that I enjoyed playing with all of them, because they are a great bunch of lads and they are all great footballers. I have been in a few dressing-rooms in my career and I can say that the atmosphere at United is as good as any I've known. There is a fantastic spirit and great banter. That is probably what I will miss the most simply because I've enjoyed being a part of that family of players.'

United would miss him, too: his inspiration, influence and

steady head had helped propel them towards glory in the Premiership and the Champions League and, for a while, they would struggle without him. That was the true mark of Henrik Larsson's short but sweet cameo at Old Trafford. Many at the club would say the same thing: 'If only we had had him earlier in his career.' The only consolation was that he had starred back then at Celtic, the club United and their fans have most affection for away from Old Trafford.

There were suggestions that United might try to tempt Henrik to stay until the end of the season, but Ferguson knew that was a no-go given the principles of the man he had managed for ten weeks. 'It is difficult, but Helsingborgs have been good to us with this deal and we have to be fair with them,' he added. Larsson would return as a guest of United for the 2007 FA Cup final at the new Wembley, but that would be it.

The footballing traveller was on his way again . . . but what are the chances that this Celtic United legend will one day return to Britain? Well, just a fortnight after leaving United for the last time he was quoted as saying he would love to one day go back to Celtic Park as part of the management set-up. 'I am always telling Paul Lambert that he should coach Celtic and then I could come and be his assistant,' Larsson said in an interview on BBC Radio Scotland. Lambert spent eight years at Celtic, seven of them alongside Larsson; at the time of Larsson's comments, he was cutting his managerial teeth at Wycombe Wanderers.

A few days later, back in Sweden, Henrik added to the intrigue by admitting, 'Football is what I can do and it is possible that I continue being involved in football in the future. We have to see if I can find something interesting.'

Celtic fans will no doubt be hoping that he finds that 'something interesting' at Parkhead. There will always be a warm welcome if the wandering hero decides to one day return to his spiritual home.

···

STRACHAN, FERGUSON AND THE FUTURE

My greatest challenge was knocking Liverpool right
off their f***ing perch . . . and you can print that.
                                        – *Sir Alex Ferguson*

Reporter: 'Can I have a quick word, Gordon?'
Strachan: 'Velocity.'

AS WITH many other characters in the history of Celtic and
Manchester United, the fates and fortunes of the two men who
manage the clubs as this book goes to print at the back end of
2007 appear inextricably intertwined.

Gordon Strachan and Sir Alex Ferguson certainly have what
the Americans call a 'history' with each other, their association
taking root back in the 1980s when one managed and the other
played a vital role on the pitch in the famous Aberdeen side that
broke the stranglehold of the Old Firm in Scotland.

Strachan would again play for Ferguson in England at
United, but this time the fairy tale did not have a happy ending.
The two fell out and in 1989 Ferguson jettisoned the man who
many felt would have helped him break a similar stranglehold
in England: Liverpool's in Division One. Within three years of

taking command at Old Trafford, Ferguson allowed Strachan to leave for Leeds, believing his best footballing days were behind him. It was a mistake that would rebound mightily as a revved-up Gordon, motivated by Ferguson's dismissal of his talents, took the Whites to an unexpected title at the expense of the Red Devils in 1992.

Strachan had also been voted the FWA Footballer of the Year for the previous campaign – one in which he had helped Leeds to fourth in the top flight just a year after inspiring them to promotion from Division Two. It was a remarkable retort to the man who had let him go: Strachan had proved he had lots of good football left in him. In some ways, the decision by Ferguson had mirrored that of Matt Busby in 1963 when he had allowed Johnny Giles to go to Leeds. Giles would also prove instrumental in that club's success under Don Revie and would show what a great player he was while at Elland Road – undoubtedly motivated by Busby's verdict that he was not good enough for Manchester United.

The desire to prove Ferguson wrong would be a constant motivation for Strachan, and when he became a manager – first at Coventry, then Southampton, and finally Celtic – the two men would clash again. This time they would compete over their skills as motivators of men and, again, Strachan would not be found wanting. Although at an obvious disadvantage given United's massive spending power, he would send out his teams with a tactical nous that allowed them to fight on a more even playing field than might have been expected.

I will admit right now that when Strachan was made manager of Celtic after Martin O'Neill, my initial reaction was one of surprise. What had he done as a manager to earn such a top job? He had taken Coventry down from the top flight for the first time in 34 years and then had only managed in the footballing backwater of Southampton. Also he hardly had any obvious affiliation with Celtic, did he? Quite the opposite, in fact – he was one of the most disliked players among the Bhoys in the Jungle during his time at Aberdeen. Also he appeared, on the surface at least, a rather unpleasant piece of work – someone who always had to be a smart arse at press conferences, with answers that were incomprehensible and defensively snappy.

Celtic diehard Stevie Murray summed up the general feeling at Parkhead at the time of Strachan's arrival when he said: 'Yes, when the news of Strachan's appointment filtered through I was staggered. It seemed like another desperate, wrong move. What had he ever done? He had only failed as a manager and many of us couldn't stand him. He used to be a right pain in the arse when he played for Aberdeen against us – constantly winding up our players; he was a niggler of the first degree. It was a kick in the teeth when he was made manager. I felt low: after the great years of Martin O'Neill, it now looked as if we were returning to the bad times.'

I know what Stevie is saying. It was only after sitting back and looking at the man Celtic fans now call WGS – Wee Gordon Strachan – that I began to see a different picture. As Bill Campbell, Mainstream Publishing supremo, once pointed out to me: this was a man with a fine track record in terms of his tactical skills. Bill was right: WGS could see the way things would pan out on a football pitch like few others. He could set up his side to get the maximum out of his players, and when I examined his managerial record without bias I found he had done a sterling bit of work in keeping Coventry in the English top flight from 1996 to 2001, and then had taken Southampton to eighth, their highest-ever league position, and an FA Cup final in the 2002–03 campaign.

When he took a year out from football in the spring of 2004, Strachan continued to impress. His punditry on *Match of the Day 2* showed he had a lighter side and his weekly column in *The Guardian* emphasised his in-depth tactical know-how. This was a man with much more to him when you looked beneath the surface and since his arrival at Celtic on 1 June 2005 this has only been highlighted. He has reshaped the squad and earned the respect – albeit in some cases grudging – of the fans. He has consolidated the domestic success every Hoops fan takes as their natural right and took Celtic FC to a new level by reaching the knockout stages of the Champions League, leading them to victory over United in the Group stages en route.

More of that later, but let's first take a closer look at the careers of the two men who are charged with taking the legend of Celtic and Manchester United to a new platform.

Sir Alex Ferguson would never be a favourite of the Jungle Bhoys, although they would no doubt admit respect for the man who came from a tough background and battled his way to the very top of the footballing pile. When Ferguson arrived at Old Trafford in November 1986, he was largely unknown to fans of English football. That was remarkable given the way he had turned the Scottish game on its head by transforming Aberdeen into the country's No. 1 side at the expense of Celtic and Rangers.

Born on 31 December 1941 in Glasgow's Govan district to a Protestant working-class family, his leadership skills first came to the fore as a shop steward in the Clyde shipyards when Ferguson led an unofficial walk-out over a pay dispute. He began his career as a player with Queen's Park in 1958, staying two years before moving to St Johnstone. A bustling centre-forward, he would spend four years at Muirton Park, the club's ground at the time, before finally turning professional and joining Dunfermline in 1964. It would be almost ten years in total before he finally made the big time, signing for Rangers in 1967 for a fee of £65,000, at the time a record between Scottish clubs.

What should have been a joyful peak as a player ended with an acrimonious split after he was fingered for his team's 4–0 thrashing by Celtic in the 1969 Scottish Cup final. He was blamed for one of the goals and was forced to play for the club's junior side instead of the first team. According to his brother, Ferguson was so upset by the experience that he threw his losers' medal away. There were claims that he left Ibrox over discrimination because he married Cathy, a Catholic, but in his autobiography, Ferguson stresses this was not the case. He explains that the club knew of his wife's religion when he joined and that he quit Ibrox because of the bitterness over the cup final.

The following October, Nottingham Forest wanted to sign Ferguson, but Cathy was not keen on a move to England at the time so he went to Falkirk. He was promoted to player-coach there, but when John Prentice became manager he removed Ferguson's coaching responsibilities. Ferguson responded by requesting a transfer and moved to Ayr United, where he finished his playing career.

As a manager, Ferguson started out as part-time boss of East Stirling in 1974, at the age of 32. He was paid the grand total of 40 quid a week but quickly earned the respect of his players with his disciplinarian attitude. It was at his next club, St Mirren, that the famous 'frightening bastard' quote originates. Striker Bobby McCulley once said of Ferguson: 'He terrified us. I'd never been afraid of anyone before, but he was such a frightening bastard from the start. Everything was focused towards his goals. Time didn't matter to him; he never wore a watch. If he wanted something done, he'd stay as late as it took or come in early. He always joined in with us in training and would have us playing in the dark until his five-a-side team won. He was ferocious, elbowing and kicking.'

Tony Fitzpatrick, the then St Mirren captain, would add

many years later: 'He made me captain at just 17 and was always fantastic with me. I've heard all about his reputation now, but he never threw teacups at me or anyone else – but he had a very young team and it wasn't necessary. He is one of those people with an aura about him; you could just feel it. I think he's one of those great figures we see running through history. He's definitely got the gift of leadership.'

His qualities as a leader among men would also be taken up when he quit Love Street for Aberdeen in 1978. In the granite city, a similarly rock-hard approach was a winner. Ferguson won three championships, four Scottish Cups and the European Cup-Winners' Cup in six years at Pittodrie. It was an incredible haul given the traditional gulf in resources between the Dons and Celtic and Rangers.

His centre-half at Pittodrie was Alex McLeish. He would comment: 'Alex is a leader of men. That's what he does best and it wouldn't have mattered where or when he managed a club like United, he would have been successful. He just gave players so much belief, and even when we played Real Madrid in that Cup-Winners' Cup final he wasn't fazed at all and made sure we weren't either. His enormous mental strength is unquestionable.'

Before becoming manager of United, Ferguson would also briefly manage the Scotland national team after the tragic death of Jock Stein. His tenure as Scottish boss started on 16 October 1985 and ended on 13 June 1986, taking in that year's World Cup in Mexico. Of his ten matches in charge, he won three, lost three and drew four, the side scoring eight goals and conceding five.

The World Cup campaign was hardly a success. Ferguson got it off to a controversial start by ignoring the requests of one Alan Hansen for inclusion in the squad. Scotland then lost their first game 1–0 against Denmark, their second 2–1 against West Germany (Strachan ironically giving Ferguson hope with a consolation goal) and drew their third and final game 0–0 against the Uruguayans.

When he returned to Aberdeen, he found he was much in demand. He was approached by Barcelona, Arsenal, Rangers, Tottenham and Manchester United. The Spurs job appealed to him and he was tempted, but when United entered the fray there was only one destination for the much-travelled Scot. His journey was over. He became United boss on 7 November 1986. His first match was the following day: a 2–0 defeat to Oxford United in the old First Division.

In 1987, Ferguson attempted to turn the club upside down, signing Steve Bruce, Viv Anderson, Brian McClair and Jim Leighton. Yet they still finished runners-up to Liverpool by nine points. It would be 1990 before United would lift their first trophy in Ferguson's reign: it was once again the FA Cup, the competition they had last won five years earlier under Atkinson. The final against Crystal Palace ended in a 3–3 draw, but United won the replay 1–0, with a goal from Lee Martin. Bryan Robson became the first player to lift the FA Cup three times at Wembley as captain.

The Ferguson era was truly under way – yet there were clear signs that the board was losing patience and may have sacked him if he had not won a trophy that season. Ferguson had certainly been under immense pressure from fans and the press as he entered the Christmas of 1989 – a 5–1 Division One defeat at Manchester City the previous August hardly helping his cause.

Ferguson confidently approached what would go down as one of the defining games of his reign on 7 January 1990. The pundits were contending a defeat to Nottingham Forest in the third round of the FA Cup that month would spell the end of the Scot. Ferguson survived, thanks to the game's only goal from reserve striker Mark Robins.

The following season United won the European Cup-Winners' Cup, beating Barcelona 2–1 in Rotterdam with a magnificent brace from Mark Hughes. Then at the back end of 1992, Ferguson made one of the most significant signing of his 20-year-plus reign by bringing in the brilliant but enigmatic Eric Cantona for a bargain basement fee of £1.2 million from Leeds. Cantona was the spark that ended 26 years of misery in 1993 when the Red Devils lifted the league title for the first time since 1967.

The buying and selling of players has always been the key plank of Ferguson's reign. There have been a fair few duds (the expensive £28-million misfit Juan Sebastian Veron is probably the biggest), but there have been more gems like Cantona. Ferguson has also never been afraid to show men the door if they have what he perceives is an attitude problem. Norman Whiteside and Paul McGrath, brilliant but boozers, were sent packing early in the Fergie years. Keeper Jim Leighton, an Aberdeen old boy, was shown no sentiment when he was axed from the 1990 cup replay in favour of Les Sealey following his nightmare first game.

And there are various other players he arguably allowed to leave too early, perhaps because he could not handle it when they told him the truth about certain things. Step forward Jaap Stam, one of the greatest defenders ever to grace Old Trafford; Roy Keane, who saw how Fergie had allowed standards to slip between 2003 and his departure in 2005; and Ruud van Nistelrooy, who was shunned because of a training-pitch dispute with Carlos Queiroz and Cristiano Ronaldo. Ferguson would flog the Dutchman to Real Madrid for £10.2 million and saw him win La Liga for them with his goals in his first season. He scored almost two of every five Madrid goals last season, ending with twenty-six, as he and David Beckham wrapped up the league crown by the middle of June 2007.

Back in 1994, following their first title triumph in 26 years, Ferguson's new United would win the double of the league and FA Cup. They won the title with ten points to spare and crushed Chelsea 4–0 in the FA Cup final. The following season would be an empty one, with no silverware on the table after Cantona's crazed kung-fu kick on a Crystal Palace fan destabilised the team. But he and they would be back with a vengeance for the next year's campaign . . . the one that saw the advent of the Fergie babes.

Ferguson and his boys – the Neville brothers, Paul Scholes, David Beckham and Ryan Giggs – appeared to take up the gauntlet throughout the season. Backed by the inspiration and wordly wise focus of Cantona, they swept to another magnificent double. Cantona would ice the cake as far as United fans were concerned by scoring the only goal in the 1–0 FA Cup-final win over Liverpool at Wembley. The Frenchman, by now captain, lifted the cup to the acclaim of the United hordes. In their eyes, he had now paid back the debt he owed after rocking the club with his act of violence the previous season.

In May 1997, Eric walked out on the club, and football, in a dispute over image rights, claiming he had fallen out of love with the game. It was totally unexpected, but given the enigmatic wonderment of the man perhaps not that much of a shock. He was, after all, a man you could hardly imagine leaving in a conventional way, with a gold carriage clock and a pat on the back.

There were those who had argued that Eric could not cut it in Europe – and there is substance to that point of view. He never proved himself on the Continent with United or on the world stage for France. Ferguson seemed to accept this failing in his star man for no sooner had Cantona walked out the door than the manager brought in Teddy Sheringham. I am told this was no off-the-cuff rebound move but one designed to bring that very success on the Continent that Eric, for all his wonderful talent, had not managed to deliver. It would not take long for the £3 million splashed out on Teddy to pay a beautiful dividend. Along with the £23 million captures of Jaap Stam and Dwight Yorke, Ferguson transformed his team from European also-rans into the champions in 1999.

First up was the league title, as United beat Spurs 2–1 at Old Trafford on the final day of the season. Then a week later, they overwhelmed Newcastle 2–0 in the FA Cup final to complete the second leg and their third double in five years. Finally, it was on to Barcelona and the holy grail. For 90 minutes, United were outfought and outclassed and 1–0 down to the Germans of Bayern Munich. Then came the greatest, most dramatic comeback in European Cup-final history, as injury-time goals from Sheringham and Ole Gunnar Solskjaer, both set up by dipping corners from David Beckham, took the Champions Cup back to Manchester for the first time since 1968, movingly on the day that would have been Sir Matt Busby's 90th birthday.

The long soul search was over for Manchester United FC and Alex Ferguson. Soon after he would be made a knight of the realm and United would go on the next season to play some fabulous attacking football, lifting yet another Premiership title in 2000, the Scot also winning his fifth Manager of the Year award in eight years. They won it again in 2000–01, the third on the trot. Ferguson was the first manager to achieve such a feat in English football and the 2001 triumph also elevated him above the great Bob Paisley of Liverpool as the most successful manager ever in the English game – his 14 major trophies finally overtaking Paisley's 13.

Yet there was unease within the ranks; unbelievably, really, given the level of success achieved. It stemmed from the very top of the club, from Ferguson and Roy Keane, and it revolved around the European Cup. By now, winning the Premiership seemed to bring merely a shrug of the shoulders: in itself it did not satisfy the massive hunger of ambition within the hearts of both men. Ferguson had joined Busby by becoming only the second United manager to win the European Cup; Keane felt a great deal of unease within himself after his non-playing role in Barcelona. While Ferguson seemed to have no more summits to climb, Keane was becoming impatient that he was still, in his own eyes at least, at the base camp. He wanted United in the European Cup final every year.

For Keane, it would lead to a gnawing resentment; a feeling of failure and anger that those around him had not pushed harder to win the trophy again. For Ferguson, it would lead to the incredible events of the 2001–02 season, when he would initially say he was retiring only to U-turn during the campaign itself. The decision and the uncertainty affected United's form that season. It also seemed to have the effect of Ferguson losing his Midas touch; from the summer of 2001 to 2006 some of his transfer and tactical decisions were baffling, to say the least.

This was a five-year spell that had United rocking precariously and one that many pundits, including myself, thought was the end of the glory reign of the manager. He would prove us all wrong; in May 2007, we would all end up eating humble pie, as United once again won the league title. Ferguson emerged laughing, but some of his moves in those previous years were still questionable.

In what he had heralded as his retirement season, he signed Juan Sebastian Veron for £28 million and Van Nistelrooy for £19 million. Van was the man for the next few seasons, scoring goals at a rate unknown since the days of Denis Law. But Veron was a flop and Ferguson's attempts to justify his inclusion in the side at the expense of David Beckham, for example, sounded simply ridiculous. Similarly, the sale of the best defender of his whole reign – Jaap Stam to Lazio – and the introduction of Laurent Blanc on a free transfer as his replacement defied belief.

In February 2002, Ferguson completed his U-turn, signing a new three-year deal at Old Trafford. I am told he did not like the idea of Sven-Göran Eriksson swanning into United and taking over, and also he must have remembered Bill Shankly and the way he had been treated after he retired prematurely at Liverpool. Images of the great Shanks, unwelcome at Liverpool's training ground and sitting aimlessly on the front at Blackpool, staring out forlornly over the Irish Sea, may have played vividly in Ferguson's imagination. It was reported that his wife Cathy had also told him she could not stand the idea of him hanging around all day with nothing to motivate him. No, Ferguson was like his mentor, the great Jock Stein: he had lived his life in the addictive world of football and would probably die in it, too.

That season was a write-off for United. The players and Ferguson were distracted and it was Arsène Wenger's side who stole the glory, lifting their own double of league title and FA Cup, as they had done in 1998.

Yet in the following campaign United would regain the crown – their eighth Premiership title in 11 remarkable years and, given the fact Ferguson appeared to be losing his grip, perhaps their best yet. It was a season in which Roy Keane went public with his claim that United's 'stars' were too happy to live off former glories; Ferguson spent £29 million on the hard-to-like Rio Ferdinand; and in which the manager accidentally kicked a boot into the eye of one of his greatest ever servants, David Beckham.

Then it all seemed to fall apart as the critics had imagined it would 12 months earlier. Beckham left for Real Madrid and Ferguson's transfer policy went haywire, with journeymen like Eric Djemba-Djemba, Liam Miller, Jose Kleberson and Tim Howard being brought in. To be fair, he would also sign two boys with massive potential – Cristiano Ronaldo and later Wayne Rooney – but he could not seem to solve the problem positions of goalkeeper and central midfield.

In January 2004, Ferdinand was suspended for the rest of the season for missing a drugs test and Ferguson's own judgement and credibility were called into question as he took on a legal battle against, of all people, two men who had a majority shareholding in Manchester United. Without Ferdinand, United struggled at the back and there were concerns that the manager was taking his eye off the (foot)ball by taking on the so-called 'Coolmore Mafia' of John Magnier and J.P. McManus over the ownership rights to the racehorse Rock of Gibraltar.

Ferguson part-owned the horse with Magnier's wife, Susan, and had watched it win a record seven Group One races as a three year old. But the Scot's name was dropped from the list of owners when the colt went to stud. Ferguson contested the decision, and Magnier and McManus criticised the United manager's behaviour, particularly over transfer deals, in a letter to the club's board. It appeared Ferguson's United days could again be numbered, as rumours began of Coolmore forcing him out of Old Trafford. In the end, Ferguson settled out of court.

The affair certainly imploded upon the club. Consolation would come with the winning of the FA Cup, a comfortable 3–0 triumph over Millwall in Cardiff in which Ronaldo starred, giving a definite glimpse of what he would offer further down the road. Hopes were further raised with the arrival of Rooney signed from Everton the following August.

But the wiser sages among the press pack warned that all was not hunky-dory. That season Arsenal had taken the league title back, with United trailing in third behind Chelsea. It was a warning sign: the shape of English football at the very top was changing and for the Red Devils it appeared to be for the worse.

Roman Abramovich had taken over at Stamford Bridge and was willing to spend as much as would be necessary to achieve the title. (He did not have to wait long; he would win it the next season, in fact.) At United, there was only pessimism: while Chelsea were being bankrolled by the Russian's roubles, United were being loaded with debt as the American Glazer family took over the club, much to the ire of thousands of United loyalists. They foresaw a dark future in which United would no longer sit at the top table of English football, the Americans having pumped the club dry to service the enormous loans they had taken out to buy the club.

By May 2005, the warnings of the doom-mongers took on new credence, as United finished third in the Premiership yet again, this time trailing 18 points behind runaway champions Chelsea. They lost in the FA Cup final to Arsenal on penalties. It was scant consolation that they should have won the cup after dominating the north Londoners in Cardiff.

By the end of 2005, it appeared the Ferguson era was over. He had been booed by his own fans after a series of insipid displays by the team, and Roy Keane left the club in November after falling out with him. A month later United would exit the Champions League at the first stage for the first time in a decade. The writing was on the wall . . . Yet digging deeper than he had done since the bad old days of 1987 and '88, Ferguson somehow managed to rewrite the script. From a man who was seemingly losing it, after what many agreed were a series of poor decisions, Ferguson enacted one of the most remarkable personal resurrections this side of Christ.

In February 2006, he and United won the League Cup for only the second time, thanks to a 4–0 thrashing of Wigan in which Rooney and Ronaldo were outstanding. They then finished a place higher in the Premiership than in the previous campaign, runners-up to Chelsea, and cut the points gap from eighteen to eight. The following November, Ferguson celebrated 20 years in charge at Old Trafford with the team on course for a remarkable regaining of the Premiership crown.

It was arguably the most brilliant of Ferguson's achievements at the club given the strength, quality and financial power of Chelsea under Mourinho and Abramovich. It was achieved thanks to a coming together all at once of several potent forces in a volatile mix. Rooney and Ronaldo turned magical potential into regular outstanding performances; old-timers such as Giggs and Scholes suddenly found a new lease of life after previously looking at the end of the road; and the defence was well marshalled and solid, with Nemanja Vidic's Jaap Stam-like ruggedness providing the perfect foil to the more flexible skills of Ferdinand. Edwin van der Sar was getting on in goal but, for the first time since the great Peter Schmeichel, United had a keeper they knew would generally be a reliable last line of defence. Michael Carrick also brought a trusting hand to what had been a wobbly, inconsequential midfield and made some of us critics eat our words. At a cost of £18 million, I myself had argued he was overvalued by at least £10 million (and still have my doubts about his pace and concentration levels), but he would prove a reliable Steady Eddie – and, as even my little boy, Frankie, points out, 'He is a good passer.' They would all play their part in United's first title for four seasons – and probably one of their least expected ever.

But credit where credit is certainly due: Ferguson was the mastermind. Here was the man who had reshaped the club – nay, rebuilt it – from top to bottom in a 20-year dynasty. The Old Trafford youth set-up, overhauled to once again become the bedrock of the club, had seen talent roll off its production line Busby-style. The likes of Giggs, Sharpe, Beckham, the Nevilles and Scholes saw Ferguson like a patient surrogate father. He put the hairdryer away and let them develop, quietly at first, then with a resounding drum roll when he knew they were finally ready to be let free. On the whole, his transfer buys were excellent, too: Denis Irwin, Schmeichel and Cantona were all bought in for amounts that Abramovich would regard as a satisfactory tip in a restaurant and the big-money youngsters, like Rooney and Ronaldo, lived up to their price tags.

United won the league in 2006–07, finishing on eighty-nine points – six ahead of runners-up Chelsea and a massive twenty-one ahead of third-placed Liverpool – and in the close season Ferguson threw down the gauntlet to his rivals by snapping up England's midfield enforcer Owen Hargreaves for £17 million and the dynamite potential of Brazilian Anderson and Portugal's Nani, again for similar fees. It was astute business. Hargreaves would add further weight to central midfield, while Nani and Anderson would one day be ready-made replacements for Ryan Giggs and Paul Scholes respectively. As Ferguson approached the 2007–08 season as manager of Manchester United, his haul of trophies at the club read like this: a European Cup, a European Cup-Winners' Cup, nine Premiership titles, four FA Cups, a League Cup and an Intercontinental Cup.

The only let-downs for him in the 2006–07 campaign had, of course, been the Champions League semi-final defeat in Milan and the FA Cup final loss to Chelsea. In both matches, United had seemed fatigued and at the new Wembley Mourinho's suffocating tactics had proved a bridge too far for tired legs.

Despite those failings, the Scot declared himself more than happy with the results of the campaign and revealed a little more about Alex Ferguson, the man away from the game. It emerged that he had a life too, as he told of his passion for cooking Chinese food, studying American history and listening to Scottish music on his iPod. Always an impressive name-dropper, the United manager also let it be known that he was a good friend of current Prime Minister Gordon Brown.

Ferguson, a Labour supporter, said Brown shared his interest in the history of the United States, particularly the assassination of John F. Kennedy. 'Gordon sent me 35 CDs on it, which was brilliant of him,' he said. 'I've got about seven books by the side of my bed and I have JFK's autopsy report. I also have a brand new copy of the Warren Report signed by [former US president] Gerald Ford, which is the only one he signed, so it's one of a kind.'

The United manager had opened up during an interview aired on Manchester radio station Key 103. Movingly, he admitted that he wished his father, who died in 1979, had been around to share his success. 'He'd be very proud of me,' he said. 'One of the sad things of my life is that he never saw me win anything. I went to Aberdeen and he didn't see any of it, which is unfortunate because he was football mad.'

Despite the success Ferguson delivered against the odds in 2007, there remained grumbles among the fans – primarily about the behind-the-scenes manoeuvrings of the Glazers. Ferguson had said in public that he was happy with the new regime under the Americans; they were easy-going and did not interfere, preferring to stay in the background, and it was easier to get transfer funds without the rigmarole of going through red-tape procedures as had been the case while a plc.

Still the fans were unhappy. They didn't like the way the Glazers dealt with ticketing nor what they saw as smokescreens to lever more money out of them. I could certainly sympathise with them. I knew three season-ticket holders who were similarly discontent. They told me that the Glazers had turned their coveted tickets into 'league match ticket books' (LMTBs) by what they felt was 'a sleight of hand'. One put it this way: 'Ticket prices have risen by double-figure percentage points for the third time in a row and the average Manchester United season ticket for all 19 home league games is now 44 per cent more expensive than it was before the Glazers' takeover. All season-ticket holders are now required to join the automatic cup scheme and so commit themselves to buying tickets for all three cup competitions, whether they want them or not. If we play just three games in each of these cup competitions, then the real price of a season ticket that cost around £400 in 2004–2005 jumps to well over £1,000.

'Season tickets used to guarantee a seat at cup semi-finals and finals. Now all they give is the chance to enter a draw.'

For the 2007 FA Cup final against Chelsea, I am told United also made what friends called a 'despicable decision' in asking those season-ticket holders whose names had been entered into a ballot to ring a phoneline to learn whether they had been successful. The phoneline was an 0870 number.

Back on the field of play, it was in Europe that Ferguson again came face to face with Gordon Strachan – which brings us to an ideal bridge over which to travel to assess the man who has slowly but surely started to build his reputation at Celtic Park, gradually convincing the fans of his worth.

Gordon David Strachan was born on 9 February 1957 in Edinburgh's Muirhouse to father Jim, a scaffolder, and mother Catherine. He was a contemporary of the author Irvine Welsh. In his autobiography, Gordon, a big fan of Hibernian as a boy, recalled how tough it was being brought up in such a socially deprived area of Edinburgh and admitted that it was 'a struggle for [his parents] to buy enough food to last us the entire week comfortably'.

Celtic striker Derek Riordan, brought into the club from Hibs by Strachan, was also born in Muirhouse and confirms his boss is in no any way exaggerating. 'It is not the easiest place to grow up – Drylaw, Muirhouse, Pilton. That's where I spent my time as a kid and it's a pretty rough area, no getting away from it. The one thing your upbringing there makes you, though, is streetwise. It makes you try your hardest to get better things in life.'

That last sentence could be Strachan's epitaph: a prickly man, who most people seem to either love or loathe, he has always tried to better himself.

As a promising schoolboy talent at Craigroyston School in Edinburgh, he was scouted by Rangers but eventually ended up joining Dundee in 1971, becoming an apprentice pro a year later. He had the chance to join Manchester United back then but decided against it because he had given Dundee his word. He made rapid progress at Dens Park, debuting in the first team at 16. Within three years, he was a regular in the side and had become their youngest-ever captain at nineteen. A clever right-sided attacking midfielder, he was also twice voted Player of the Year at Dundee and scored 15 goals in 87 appearances. Given his fiery commitment and ginger hair, it was perhaps inevitable that some of the Edinburgh press would big him up as the new Billy Bremner.

Aberdeen would come for him in November 1977 for a fee of £50,000, but for a few months before his transfer he mingled with two Celtic greats at Dens Park. Tommy Gemmell had been brought in as manager and Jinky Johnstone had arrived from Sheffield United. Fate had brought along a third legend from Parkhead to secure his move to Aberdeen: Billy McNeill, then embarking on his first managerial role at Pittodrie. An ankle injury would limit Strachan's appearances and impact in the one season McNeill stayed in the granite city.

Strachan feared he also might be a five-minute wonder at Aberdeen, but that worry was unfounded and premature. The next season McNeill departed to be replaced by the upcoming young manager Alex Ferguson. It was the start of a relationship that would bind Ferguson and Strachan emotionally to the present day: through thick and thin, love and (if we're being truthful) probably hate, to the present gentlemanly truce that appears to have been brokered between the two men, built of similarly fierce aspirations to be the No. 1 in whatever they do in life.

In Ferguson's first season, Aberdeen finished fourth in the top flight and reached the semi-finals of the Scottish Cup and the final of the League Cup (both times being beaten by Rangers). Strachan was an immediate regular under the new manager and together they quickly beat a path into the annals of the Scottish game for their legendary achievements at the club.

In 1980, Aberdeen became the first side other than Celtic or Rangers to win the title since Kilmarnock in 1964–65. During Strachan's term at the club, he would gain another title medal and add three Scottish Cup-winners' medals, a League Cup medal and those European Cup-Winners' Cup and European Super Cup winner's medals to his personal trophy cabinet. Strachan admitted that Ferguson employed a similar motivation at United as they battled to end Liverpool's domination as he had used years earlier at Aberdeen to overhaul the Old Firm, telling his Dons men, 'Get at their f***in' throats!'

Of course, the two men had their fallings out. Indeed, it was at Aberdeen in 1981 that Ferguson's reported habit of throwing teacups first began to surface in a dispute with Strachan as the Dons fell 2–0 behind in Romania against Arges Pitesti – opponents they had beaten 3–0 at Pittodrie in the first leg of their UEFA Cup tie. Ferguson had told Strachan and Peter Weir to stay on the wings so that the team kept its shape, but Strachan continually roamed inside. Ferguson, just as regularly, was up yelling from the dug-out area on the side of the pitch for Strachan to do what he had asked. Just before half-time, sick of his constant moaning, Strachan is said to have snarled at his manager, 'Eff off and shut your face.'

In his autobiography, Ferguson explained what had followed:

> In the dressing-room, I set about Gordon in a manner
> that could fairly be described as blunt. The wee man
> was, however, in one of his nippy-sweetie moods,
> full of caustic comments. What he regarded as smart
> ripostes struck me as meaningless meanderings and
> I swung a hand in anger at a huge tea urn standing
> nearby.

In later years, Strachan would state that he did not like this side of Ferguson, although he did concede it helped to build his own mental strength – having coped with and survived Fergie's outbursts, he could cope with anything. But in his later days on the pitch he preferred playing for Ron Atkinson and Howard Wilkinson, men with 'a less dictatorial and controlling' style. All these elements of character building would, of course, go into the mix that would form Strachan the manager himself.

Despite their disagreements, Strachan is the first to concede that Ferguson is the undoubted managerial genius of the modern era. He is also swift to acknowledge the debt he owes him, saying: 'Until his arrival at Aberdeen, my career was going nowhere.' Strachan also notes that at Pittodrie the big man developed 'an excellent schoolboy and youth system', that essential skill of Ferguson's that would be a major attraction for United when they came knocking in 1986. The Old Trafford board were keen to return to the principles of the Busby era after two decades of spending which had led to the obvious decline in top-class youngsters emerging from the ranks.

Strachan admits that sometimes Ferguson's confrontational approach had more amusing angles. For instance, when Aberdeen lost 5–0 on aggregate to Liverpool in the 1980–81 European Cup campaign, Ferguson was seething on the coach back from Anfield. Strachan tells of how the manager threatened to fine anyone who laughed £10 – and how, like a kid, he kept looking around from his seat at the front of the bus to try to catch out any offenders behind him.

At the end of his Aberdeen career, Strachan had made 293 appearances and scored 90 goals. It had looked as though he might move to Cologne in Germany: uncertain of where he would end up after his contract had expired, he had signed a provisional agreement to join them. Luckily, they did not stand in his way when United moved in for him. Strachan is honest enough to admit that money was a key factor in his decision to leave Pittodrie: at Aberdeen, he was on a basic of £12,000 a year; at Cologne, he would have earned a starting rate of £64,000 and United were offering £70,000.

The relationship between Strachan and Ferguson was at a low when the player asked to leave Pittodrie, though it improved when it became apparent he would be moving to Old Trafford. Strachan says that Ferguson used his move as an opportunity to have a look around United and meet the top players – he even joined him at his contract signing.

Again, there would be an amusing spin-off. Strachan asked Ferguson and his wife to be his guests at United's celebration dinner after winning the 1985 FA Cup against Everton. United's South African-born keeper Gary Bailey, believing his teammate was with his parents, made a point of coming over to them all and introducing himself. He then said to Ferguson, 'Nice to meet you, Mr Strachan.'

Strachan would be effusive in his praise of Ferguson when United supremo Martin Edwards asked him about the Aberdeen boss, and the pair would team up again when Ferguson replaced Atkinson in November 1986. But by now Strachan was no longer prepared to be 'hit with the big stick': he had enjoyed the Atkinson era at United and the way Big Ron had 'treated him as an adult rather than a child'. He would later say of his manager, 'I love big Ron. He is an absolute gem of a guy.' He remains convinced that his first 18 months at the club were the best football he played in his career.

He would also reveal how the man differed from Ferguson: he had a sunbed in his office and one day, when Strachan sneaked a look into his briefcase, he found no notes on tactics or football . . . just a can of hairspray and a bottle of aftershave.

Atkinson had bought him in August 1984 for £600,000 as part of his plan to make United an entertaining side, as well as a winning one. As we have noted, he would succeed to an extent, turning United into a successful cup team at domestic level but failing to take them up that extra notch in the league. But with players like Strachan, Bryan Robson, Norman Whiteside and Paul McGrath, he certainly put the smile back on the faces of United fans after the dull days of Dave Sexton.

When Ferguson took over, Strachan lasted for just three seasons. The wee man admits his confidence suffered. Ferguson himself would say of Strachan:

> There was little evidence of the zest and cocky assurance that characterised his play in Scotland. Verbally, he was as assertive as ever . . . but in matches, he appeared diminished by living in the shadow of Robson, Whiteside and McGrath.

When Ferguson tried to sign Trevor Steven from Everton, Strachan knew the writing was on the wall. In March 1989, at the age of 32, he moved to Leeds. He had made 160 appearances for the Red Devils, scoring 33 goals. Again, money was a motivation – Leeds doubled his Old Trafford salary. Many pundits viewed his decision as 'his retirement option'. They could not have been more wrong. Confounding those who had written him off as a has-been, he exhibited another powerful motivation.

Mirroring Johnny Giles's route from Old Trafford to Elland Road, Strachan moved in 1989 to a Leeds mired in Second Division mediocrity. And just as Giles would go on to become a key man in Don Revie's legendary side, so Strachan would play an important role as Howard Wilkinson's team moved from the second tier to become league champions.

The Scot captained Leeds to the Division Two title in 1990 and two years later, at the age of 35, led them to that Division One championship in its last year before the inception of the Premier League. He had already been voted Scottish Footballer of the Year in 1980, and in 1992 he won the English equivalent, thus becoming the only man to pick up the honour on both sides of the border. The £300,000 that Howard Wilkinson had paid for his services certainly turned out to be a bargain.

In March 1995, Strachan moved to Coventry City to renew his relationship with his favourite manager, working as player-coach under the club's new boss, Ron Atkinson. Strachan was not a regular first-team player at Highfield Road, but he helped coach the club's players to escape relegation from the Premiership in 1995–96.

As a player, he also did his bit for Scotland, making fifty appearances and scoring five goals. He won his first cap against Northern Ireland in 1980 and appeared in two World Cups, in 1982 and 1986, winning his final cap against Finland in 1992.

Strachan started out on his managerial journey in November 1986, when Atkinson moved upstairs at Highfield Road to become director of football. He finally retired as a player at the end of that season, making his last appearance at the age of 40, at the time a record in the Premiership.

Strachan was successful in preserving the Sky Blues' top-division record, having remained there since 1967, until the 2000–2001 season, when the club finally dropped into the Championship. He was sacked at the start of the next campaign.

Within six weeks, he was back in the game, having signed up as the new manager of another outfit of perennial Premiership strugglers, Southampton. The south coast club had moved into a new stadium, St Mary's, and could not afford to go down. Strachan turned their fortunes around, lifting them from the bottom of the table: that first season they finished a credible 11th in the Premiership. Relieved of the burden of firefighting at the bottom and with a chairman who backed him with hard funds, Strachan finally showed what he was about as a manager. Always a man with a sharp tactical nous, Strachan took the Saints to a new level – one they had not reached since 1976, when they had beaten Manchester United 1–0 at Wembley to lift the FA Cup.

In 2002–03, they finished eighth under Strachan and reached the FA Cup final, where they lost 1–0 to Arsenal. As Arsenal had already qualified for the Champions League, Southampton took their place in the 2003–04 UEFA Cup. It was a brilliant achievement at a club of traditional underachievers.

Yet by the following March Strachan, typical of the man's uncanny ability to do the unexpected, was gone. He had announced earlier that season that he would not be renewing his contract – then he decided to leave earlier, so he could spend more time with his family.

Just as Gordon Strachan was on the brink of proving himself as an exceptional football manager, he parachuted out of the game. It was something you could easily have understood when times were tough at Coventry; it was not so easy to fathom given the success story at St Mary's.

He would spend the next 12 months with his family and guesting as a pundit on TV football shows. After savouring the high times at Saints, it would take a big deal to lure Strachan back into football management. He certainly had no plans for any Houdini-style campaigns at the likes of Coventry.

But again . . . cometh the hour, cometh the club, and they don't come much bigger than Celtic. Ironically, as Strachan had quit the game to spend more time with his wife, so his chance to re-emerge would be on the back of another man quitting the game to spend more time with his wife.

On 25 May 2005, Celtic announced that Martin O'Neill was resigning as manager to care for wife Geraldine, who was suffering with lymphoma. On 1 June 2005, his replacement walked into Celtic Park: Gordon Strachan, much to the surprise of many of the club's loyal fans. Manfred Lurker, writing for the online arm of the Celtic fanzine, *Not the View*, summed up the sense of shock:

> Apart from achieving an extraordinary level of success [at Aberdeen], his relationship with the Celtic fans was almost as bad as the one he had with Alex Ferguson. The very sight of him could reduce some habitués of the Jungle to apoplectic rage. Understandable enough; Aberdeen would regularly beat us (occasionally humiliate us) and Strachan would invariably be one of our tormentors in chief.

Martin O'Neill had been embraced full-heartedly by the fans; his passion and commitment and love of the club shone through. He was one of them. Strachan was an outsider who would have to work – and work damned hard – to gain their affection. His antics while playing for Aberdeen had certainly not been forgotten and the same supporters were hardly enamoured with his record as a manager. His appointment had not been greeted with sighs of joy and welcoming open arms; more often with resigned grimaces. 'Here we go again, another chapter in the bloody messes that the board love to conjure up every few years.'

In his autobiography, Strachan succinctly summed up his problem as this:

> I have lost count of the number of times I have heard it said that I am not a true 'Celtic man'... I was not born in Glasgow, did not support Celtic as a boy and I would have been the last person that any Celtic

follower would have thought of approaching for an autograph when I played for Aberdeen.

And then there was the incident back in 1980 when Strachan was attacked by a Celtic fan while playing for Aberdeen at Parkhead. He has since laughed it off, saying: 'I think the guy got fined £100, and they had a whip-round in the pub and he made £200.' But he must surely have felt some trepidation at joining the club, given the clearly combustible opposition to him as typified by that blast from the past.

The Celtic fans' worst fears over his appointment appeared well grounded when the new manager's tenure at Parkhead got off to the worst possible start, with Celtic losing 5–0 to Artmedia Bratislava in the first leg of their Champions League second-round qualifying tie. Strachan declared it was 'the worst night of my footballing life'. Three days later, his team could only draw 4–4 with Motherwell in their first SPL match under his control. The pundits were discussing whether he would last the month, never mind until the traditional stay of execution till Christmas.

Yet after beating Artmedia 4–0 in the home leg, Strachan and Celtic would eventually embark on a run in the league in which they would drop just four points over the next fourteen games. From being almost as unpopular as David Murray, Strachan won the CIS Cup, the SPL title and the Scottish Football Writers' Manager of the Year award in his first campaign. And that championship was secured with a seventeen-point advantage – and with six matches to spare: a remarkable turnaround for an apparently condemned man.

Strachan admitted that the job was as big as he expected; in fact, it was bigger. He professed himself amazed at the level of support, and the energy of the fans and all those concerned with Celtic FC: 'Manchester United are the biggest club in Britain, if not the world, but when I played for United I never really sensed the sort of overwhelming commitment to them that I have seen from those who attach themselves to Celtic.'

He is proud of his signings that first season – the pick of them, he says, were Shunsuke Nakamura and Maciej 'Magic' Zurawski – and the way he evolved the team's play, refining the direct style much loved by O'Neill to a slightly more cautious, patient approach redolent of Chelsea.

That change of style has not pleased everyone. Some of the Celtic fans I interviewed told me of their discontent that Strachan had made the team boring to watch. One fan told me he and some others even stayed on the coach playing cards and having a laugh at some away fixtures rather than watching the game. It had all become too predictable: they still loved Celtic and proved it by following them everywhere, they just wished the team played with more creativity. There was also the argument that domestic football in Scotland had become a bore, that it was likewise too predictable. They said they wished Celtic could join the English Premiership. These feelings had led to a sometimes muted atmosphere at matches. Yet joining the Premiership remains an unlikely scenario given the (understandable) reluctance of a couple of struggling teams to give up their places for Celtic and Rangers to prosper at their expense.

In the 2006–07 season, Strachan's Celtic would again win honours and advance further in the Champions League than they had done before. On 22 April 2007, Strachan guided Celtic to their 41st league championship, and his second in succession. He also won the inaugural Scottish PFA Manager of the Year award.

On Saturday, 26 May, Jean-Joël Perrier Doumbé grabbed an 84th-minute winner to clinch a 34th Scottish Cup – and the double – for Celtic against Dunfermline at Hampden. The 1–0 win brought Strachan his fourth trophy in two years – a fine achievement. The match was also memorable in that Neil

Lennon was captaining Celtic for the last time before leaving the club after almost seven years' service.

But still some fans voiced fears about the future under Strachan. It reminded me of the situation at Chelsea under Jose Mourinho. The Portuguese had brought unprecedented success to Stamford Bridge, yet many within the club – and some fans – believed it had been at the expense of entertainment. In this regard, I can sympathise with those Celtic fans who remain unconvinced that Gordon is a true Celt, in the sense that, as at Manchester United, it is not enough just to win, you have to win with style – with entertaining, attacking football; with fantasy football.

On one occasion in the 2006–07 season, Strachan's team certainly played fantasy football. Ironically, it would be when they beat Manchester United 1–0 at Celtic Park in a Group game in the Champions League.

Ferguson's side had won the first leg 3–2 on a memorable night in Manchester. Jan Vennegoor of Hesselink, another of Strachan's good buys, had put Celtic ahead with a low shot after 21 minutes, but Louis Saha grabbed a fine brace to see United home. United had brushed Celtic aside 3–0 in a pre-season friendly at Celtic Park the previous July, but this match – the first competitive fixture between the clubs since the Coronation Cup match of 1953 – saw a much more equal battle.

In the second leg United played like big-heads, as if they only had to turn up and show off a few ball skills to win. United's indulgence, I felt, was best summed up by the performance of Louis Saha (known as 'Balsa Boy' by the Stretford End because of his habit of collapsing too easily with a plethora of injuries). He was guilty of a terrible miss when he appeared to assume he was offside and later would punt a penalty kick straight at Artur Boruc.

United's arrogant strollers were put in their place, Celtic chalking up a superb victory. And the man who claimed it certainly had magic in his feet. I knew the remarkable Shunsuke Nakamura's free-kick would bulge the back of the net before he even stroked it home so majestically from 25 yards out. It was the same back in David Beckham's heyday at United. You just knew.

The 1–0 win put the Bhoys through to the final 16 of the Champions League for the first time since the competition had been re-formatted in 1993. Celtic would go on to lose in the knockouts against AC Milan, missing out on a place in the quarter-finals, but they had shown their progress under Strachan by beating United, who would also fall to the skills of Kaka in the semi-finals.

The *Manchester Evening News* had summed up the European spectacle of the first leg of the United-Celtic match in this way: 'To ignore the contribution of Celtic and their magnificent supporters to a truly memorable evening would be a supreme injustice, as the United Kingdom's two best supported sides delivered a tie for the rest of Europe to envy.'

Indeed it was – a match to grace any theatre of dreams and a fine advert for football. Yet it was also a match Celtic lost. I suppose it means you can't always have it both ways. For those Hoops fans who complain about the quality of the feast served up under Strachan, there are others who point to the fact that when Celtic play in his image, they don't lose. Or if they do, it is only by the slightest of margins (as in Milan).

Maybe Strachan deserves a pat on the back for what he has achieved with only a fraction of the spending power of Ferguson at Old Trafford. He is keeping the club in with the European big boys on a virtual shoestring of a budget by comparison. While Ferguson was splashing out the best part of £50 million on Hargreaves, Anderson and Nani, Strachan was bringing in Aussie Scott McDonald for £700,000 on a three-year deal from Motherwell and Hibs midfielder Scott Brown for a fee of around £4 million – a record between Scottish clubs but small fry compared with Ferguson's spending spree. Only time will tell, but given Strachan's shrewd previous incursions in the market (apart from the obvious case of the disappointing Thomas Gravesen), the two new boys could well prove fine additions to a developing squad of talented young players.

My feeling in the close season of 2007–08 was that United and Celtic were both in capable hands with Ferguson and Strachan at the respective helms. In the case of Strachan, it is worth asking this: who could replace him if he left? And how would they better his first two seasons' haul and those advances in the Champions League? Strachan, for all his initial lack of emotional compatibility and credibility at Parkhead, could be precisely the man to take the club further, precisely because of these factors, as he has no nostalgic ties to stop him from making hard decisions. He is an outsider who can become an insider through his achievements. And already, as the new campaign commences, there are encouraging signs that the wee man is beginning to feel a genuine pride in Celtic FC and that there is a debt to be paid.

When it was suggested that he might leave Parkhead for Manchester City, Gordon dismissed the gossip, saying, 'I love what I'm doing and working for this club.' I believe Strachan will bring a new era of stability and prosperity to Parkhead . . . if he is allowed to get on with the job.

And maybe, one day, when he feels part of the furniture and truly accepted, we'll hear him reciprocate the affection by humming the tune to that old Rod Stewart classic about Celtic and United . . .

ANORAK SECTION

ALL-TIME CELTIC MANAGERS
Willie Maley, 1897–40
Jimmy McStay, 1940–45
Jimmy McGrory, 1945–65
Jock Stein, 1965–78
Billy McNeill, 1978–83
David Hay, 1983–87
Billy McNeill, 1987–91
Liam Brady, 1991–93
Lou Macari, 1993–94
Tommy Burns, 1994–97
Wim Jansen, 1997–98
Jozef Venglos, 1998–99
John Barnes, 1999–2000
Kenny Dalglish, 2000 (previously serving as director of football)
Martin O'Neill, 2000–05
Gordon Strachan, 2005–present

ALL-TIME NEWTON HEATH/MANCHESTER UNITED MANAGERS
A.H. Albut 1892–1900
James West 1900–03
J. Ernest Mangnall 1903–12
John Bentley 1912–14
John Robson 1914–21
John Chapman 1921–6
Clarence Hilditch 1926–27
Herbert Bamlett 1927–31
Walter Crickmer 1931–32, 1937–45

Scott Duncan 1932–37
Sir Matt Busby 1945–69, 1970–71
Wilf McGuinness 1969–70
Frank O'Farrell 1971–72
Tommy Docherty 1972–77
Dave Sexton 1977–81
Ron Atkinson 1981–86
Sir Alex Ferguson 1986–present

TESTIMONIAL MATCHES, CELTIC V. MAN UTD

Bobby Charlton – Old Trafford, 1972
Bobby Lennox – Celtic Park, 1976
Jimmy Johnstone – Celtic Park, 1976
Danny McGrain – Celtic Park, 1980
Lou Macari – Old Trafford, 1984
Roy Aitken – Celtic Park, 1987
Brian McClair – Old Trafford, 1987
Bryan Robson – Old Trafford, 1990
Mark Hughes – Old Trafford, 1994
Paul McStay – Celtic Park, 1995
Tom Boyd – Celtic Park, 2001
Ryan Giggs – Old Trafford, 2001
Roy Keane – Old Trafford, 2006

TRIBUTE MATCHES, CELTIC V. MAN UTD

Lisbon 25th anniversary – Celtic Park, 1992

CELTIC FC HONOURS

EUROPEAN CUP

Winners: 1967
Finalists: 1970

UEFA CUP

Finalists: 2003

SCOTTISH LEAGUE

Winners: (41 times) 1893, 1894, 1896, 1898, 1905, 1906, 1907, 1908, 1909, 1910, 1914, 1915, 1916, 1917, 1919, 1922, 1926, 1936, 1938, 1954, 1966, 1967, 1968, 1969, 1970, 1971, 1972, 1973, 1974, 1977, 1979, 1981, 1982, 1986, 1988, 1998, 2001, 2002, 2004, 2006, 2007

CELTIC UNITED

SCOTTISH CUP

Winners: (34 times) 1892, 1899, 1900, 1904, 1907, 1908, 1911, 1912, 1914, 1923, 1925, 1927, 1931, 1933, 1937, 1951, 1954, 1965, 1967, 1969, 1971, 1972, 1974, 1975, 1977, 1980, 1985, 1988, 1989, 1995, 2001, 2004, 2005, 2007

SCOTTISH LEAGUE CUP

Winners: (13 times) 1957, 1958, 1966, 1967, 1968, 1969, 1970, 1975, 1983, 1998, 2000, 2001, 2006

OTHER HONOURS

Glasgow Cup: (29 times) 1891, 1892, 1895, 1896, 1905, 1906, 1907, 1908, 1910, 1916, 1917, 1920, 1921, 1927, 1928, 1929, 1931, 1939, 1941, 1949, 1956, 1962, 1964, 1965, 1967, 1968, 1970, 1975*, 1982 (*1975 shared with Rangers after 2–2 draw)
Glasgow International Exhibition Cup: 1902
Scottish League Commemorative Shield: 1905, 1910
Coronation Cup: 1953

MANCHESTER UNITED FC HONOURS

EUROPEAN CUP

Winners: 1968, 1999

EUROPEAN CUP-WINNERS' CUP

Winners: 1991

EUROPEAN SUPER CUP

Winners: 1991

INTERCONTINENTAL CUP

Winners: 1999

FA PREMIER LEAGUE

Winners: (nine times) 1993, 1994, 1996, 1997, 1999, 2000, 2001, 2003, 2007

LEAGUE DIVISION ONE

Winners: (seven times) 1908, 1911, 1952, 1956, 1957, 1965, 1967

FA CUP

Winners: (record 11 wins) 1909, 1948, 1963, 1977, 1983, 1985, 1990, 1994, 1996, 1999, 2004

LEAGUE CUP

Winners: 1992, 2006

SELECT BIBLIOGRAPHY

Blundell, Justin *Back from the Brink* (Empire Publications, 2006)

Campbell, Tom (ed.) *Ten Days that Shook Celtic* (Fort Publishing, 2005)

Campbell, Tom and Pat Woods *Dreams, And Songs to Sing* (Mainstream Publishing, 2000)

Docherty, Tommy *The Doc: Hallowed Be Thy Game* (Headline, 2006)

Dunphy, Eamon *A Strange Kind of Glory* (Mandarin, 1994)

Ferguson, Alex *Managing My Life* (Coronet, 2000)

Gemmell, Tommy *Lion Heart* (Virgin, 2005)

Inglis, Simon *Soccer in the Dock: A History of British Football Scandals, 1900 to 1965* (Willow Books, 1985)

Larsson, Henrik *A Season in Paradise* (BBC Books, 2001)

Law, Denis and Pat Crerand *United: The Legendary Years* (Virgin Publishing, 1997)

MacBride, Eugene *Talking with Celtic* (Breedon Books, 2001)

Macpherson, Archie *Jock Stein: The Definitive Biography* (Highdown, 2005)

McClair, Brian *Odd Man Out: A Player's Diary* (Manchester United Books, 1998)

McColl, Graham *The Head Bhoys* (Mainstream, 2003)

McColl, Graham and George Sheridan *The Essential History of Celtic* (Headline, 2002)

McNeill, Billy *Hail Caesar: Billy McNeill – The Autobiography* (Headline, 2004)

Matthews, Tony and John Russell *The Complete Encyclopedia of Manchester United FC* (Britespot Publishing, 2002)

Meek, David *Legends of United: The Heroes of the Busby Era* (Orion Books, 2006)

Potter, David W. *Jimmy Delaney: The Stuff of Legend* (Breedon Books, 2006)

Potter, David W. *Willie Maley: The Man Who Made Celtic* (Tempus Publishing, 2003)

Shury, Alan and Brian Landamore *The Definitive Newton Heath FC* (Soccerdata, 2002)

Strachan, Gordon *My Life in Football* (Time Warner Books, 2006)

Taylor, Daniel *Deep into the Wood* (Parrs Wood Press, 2005)

Worrall, Frank *Red Man Walking* (Mainstream, 2006)

The following websites also proved helpful: RedCafe.net, unitedonline.co.uk, manutdtalk.com, manureds.co.uk, stateofthegame.co.uk (extracts from Tom Brogan), ntvcelticfanzine.com. Also informative was Douglas Alexander's interview with Henrik Larsson published in 2003 in the *Sunday Times*.